LITERATURE AND SCIENCE, 1660–1834

Volume 1

LITERATURE AND SCIENCE, 1660–1834

Volume 1

Science as Polite Culture

Edited by Cheryce Kramer,
Trea Martyn, Michael Newton

With a General Introduction by
Judith Hawley

LONDON
PICKERING & CHATTO
2003

Published by Pickering & Chatto (Publishers) Limited
21 Bloomsbury Way, London, WC1A 2TH

2252 Ridge Road, Brookfield, Vermont 05036, USA

www.pickeringchatto.com

BRITISH LIBRARY CATALOGUING IN PUBLICATION DATA

Literature and Science, 1660–1834
1. Science 2. Science – Early works to 1800 3. Science – Literary collections 4. Science in literature
I. Hawley, Judith
820.8'0356

ISBN 1851967370

LIBRARY OF CONGRESS CATALOGING-IN-PUBLICATION DATA

Literature and science, 1660–1834/ Judith Hawley, general editor.
    p. cm.
Includes indexes.
Contents: v.1. Science as polite culture / edited by Cheryce Kramer, Trea Martyn and Michael Newton – v. 2. Science of body and mind / edited by Clark Lawlor and Akihito Suzuki – v. 3. Earthly powers / edited by Richard Hamblyn – v. 4. Flora / edited by Charlotte Grant.
    ISBN 1-85196-737-0 (alk. Paper)
1. English literature-History and criticism-Theory, etc. 2. Literature and science-History-Sources. 3. Science-History-sources. 4. English literature. I. Hawley, Judith.

PR21. L595 2002
820'.9'356-dc21   2001059122

Typeset by P&C

Printed and bound in Great Britain by
Cromwell Press, Trowbridge

CONTENTS OF THE EDITION

CONTENTS

ACKNOWLEDGEMENTS

The editors wish to thank Judith Hawley for being a patient and generous editor; Sarah Brown and all the team at Pickering & Chatto for keeping us at it and for bearing with us.

Michael Newton would like to thank Richard Hamblyn, Professor René Weis and Tim Longley.

Judith Hawley wishes to thank Patricia Fara for the advice she has offered at every stage of work on this edition.

FOR ROY PORTER

1946–2002

he 'wrote, an' please your worships, against the spleen'
Laurence Sterne, *Tristram Shandy*

NOTE ON COPY-TEXTS

The following texts are reproduced in facsimile.

In order to fit texts comfortably onto the pages of this edition, certain liberties have been taken with the format of the originals: occasionally right-hand pages have become left-hand pages (and vice-versa) and text from consecutive pages has been fitted onto a single page.

Endnotes in this edition refer to Pickering & Chatto page and line numbers.

For permission to reproduce the texts included in this edition, we could like to thank Cambridge University Library and the British Library.

GENERAL INTRODUCTION

Oh, most magnificent and noble Nature!
Have I not worshipped thee with such a love
As never mortal man before displayed?
Adored thee in thy majesty of visible creation,
And searched into thy hidden and mysterious ways
As Poet, as Philosopher, as Sage?[1]

The poet, philosopher and sage who is here ennobling himself while glorifying nature is the natural philosopher and pioneering chemist, Humphry Davy. That combination of roles might surprise those used to thinking of the poet and the natural philosopher – or scientist – at odds with each other, especially during the Romantic era. More familiar might be Blake's scathing attack on 'Bacon & Newton, sheath'd in dismal steel', whose 'terrors hang / Like iron scourges over Albion', or Keats's poignant lament that [natural] philosophy

will clip an Angel's wings
Conquer all mysteries by rule and line,
Empty the haunted air, and gnomed mine –
Unweave a rainbow, as it erewhile made
The tender-person'd Lamia melt into a shade.[2]

The example of Davy stands over against this idea that science engineers the industrial enslavement of man and the disenchantment of nature. Himself a lover of nature and a friend of such nature-loving poets as Robert Southey and Samuel Taylor Coleridge, Davy's work as a chemist was animated by Romantic concepts of genius and organic unity. So intimate was he with Coleridge, that he proof-read the second edition of Wordsworth and Coleridge's *Lyrical Ballads* (1800), the famous Preface of which contains Wordsworth's claim that: 'The knowledge both of the Poet and the Man of science is

---

1 John Davy (ed.), *Fragmentary Remains, Literary and Scientific, of Sir Humphry Davy* (London, 1858), p. 14. For more on Davy, see the selection below, and Christopher Lawrence, 'The Power and the Glory: Humphry Davy and Romanticism', in Andrew Cunningham and Nicholas Jardine (eds), *Romanticism and the Sciences* (Cambridge, Cambridge University Press, 1990), pp. 213–27.

2 William Blake, *Jerusalem*, Chapter 1, ll. 6–20; John Keats, *Lamia*, ll. 234–8, both excerpted in John Heath Stubbs and Phillips Salman (eds), *Poems of Science* (Harmondsworth, Penguin Books, 1984), pp. 165, 198.

pleasure'.[1] Davy, although highly individual, also exemplifies the possibility of combining these roles in the long eighteenth century.

Understanding the interrelatedness of literature and science has moved a long way from the model of mutual antagonism sketched by C. P. Snow.[2] So great have been the changes in both the history of science and in literary studies that it is now more common to argue that both science and literature are aspects of a wider culture. This statement is, perhaps, nowhere more true than of the long eighteenth century, a period that is better thought of as pre-disciplinary than viewed in terms of the opposition between the two cultures of letters and science. People pursuing a wide range of interests met socially – in shared spaces such as learned societies and coffee-houses – and also in one person, in the figure of the polymath and virtuoso. In the era from Restoration to Reform, ways of understanding and representing the world were being reformulated in an exciting period of intellectual ferment and artistic experimentation. In the Royal Society, in the gentleman's library, in Grub Street and the lady's closet, the impact of natural philosophy was registered, assimilated, extended, and sometimes challenged and rebuffed.

At the same time, each of the terms of our title merits further consideration. Chosen for the convenience of the reader, they are anachronistic and possibly misleading. 'Literature' – notoriously difficult to define – was not confined in this period to the modern sense of 'creative writing'. Samuel Johnson defined it in his *Dictionary* (1755) as: 'Learning; skill in letters'. Confusingly for us, his primary definition of science was 'Knowledge'. In its modern usage, science means natural knowledge, especially that produced by particular professionals employing specialised methodologies. Yet the term 'scientist' was not coined until 1834, when it was first used by William Whewell; as late as 1882, Matthew Arnold could argue that 'science' can mean all knowledge that reaches us by books, including Euclid's *Geometry* and Newton's *Principia*.[3] So, both literature and science can suggest 'knowledge' and 'writing'. The extent to which natural philosophers saw similarities between reading texts and interpreting the world is hinted at in the commonplace idea, here expressed by the great seventeenth-century natural philosopher and apologist for the new science, Robert Boyle: 'the two great Books, of Nature and of Scripture, have the same Author'.[4] Before the emergence of specialised edu-

1 William Wordsworth, 'Preface to *Lyrical Ballads*', in Nowell C. Smith (ed.), *Wordsworth's Literary Criticism* (London, Henry Milford, 1905), p. 27.

2 C. P. Snow, *The Two Cultures and the Scientific Revolution* (Cambridge, Cambridge University Press, 1959).

3 Matthew Arnold, 'Literature and Science' (1882). It was his reply to Thomas Henry Huxley's paper, 'Science and Culture', delivered in 1880, and published the following year.

4 Robert Boyle, *The Excellency of Theology, compar'd with Natural Philosophy, (as both are Objects of Men's Study)* (London, Henry Herringman, 1674), p. 121.

cation, men of science and men of letters would also have studied the Classics; Classical allusions, the common currency of the upper classes, appear frequently in scientific treatises, as well as in literary works.

However, the fact that we use 'and' in our title suggests that literature and science are sufficiently different to need yoking together. 'Doing' science, and 'doing' literature, however similar the themes they treat, are different sorts of activities. Science is a set of practices, and not just another form of writing. Indeed, Wordsworth, having identified the common ground between 'the Poet and the Man of science', goes on to assert the differences between their attitudes to knowledge. The copula, as George Levine has pointed out, 'cloaks many different sorts of relationships'.[1] We could think in terms of correspondence, influence, analogy, opposition, response to shared subjects. The relationship between science and literature was negotiated at every level. The nature of language, and of the language most appropriate to science, were subjects keenly debated by such figures as Thomas Sprat, John Wilkins and Jonathan Swift, while literary tropes such as metaphor and analogy were used as expressive and interpretative tools in science. Boyle defended his 'frequent use of Similitudes, or Comparisons' with reference to their explanatory force, but also because of their role in reasoning and discovery: 'Apposite Comparisons … are not always bare Pictures and Resemblances, but a kind of Arguments; being oftentimes, if I may so call them, Analogous Instances, which do declare the Nature, or Way of operating, of the Thing they relate to.'[2] Analogy, the most significant example of which was the Argument from Design, underpins much of the philosophising and writing of the period. Other governing ideas and methodologies similarly operated across literature and science: empiricism and realism, the mechanical universe and systems of order dominate thinking in scientific and religious treatises, realistic novels, and Augustan poetry alike. New developments in physiology underpinned the depiction of characters in sentimental fiction and informed the development of sensibility in the culture at large. Moreover, major scientific figures had a widespread cultural impact, while writers addressed changes in natural knowledge. Authors such as Samuel Johnson and Oliver Goldsmith, whom we think of as literary men, actively engaged with contemporary scientific issues and contributed to the writing of science. At the same time, science employed literary forms didactically to address popular audiences, including women and

---

1 George Levine, 'One Culture: Science and Literature', in George Levine and Alan Rauch (eds), *One Culture: Essays in Science and Literature* (Madison, University of Wisconsin Press, 1987), pp. 6–7. See also Ludmilla Jordanova's Introduction to *Languages of Nature: Critical Essays of Science and Literature*, ed. Jordanova (London, Free Association Books, 1986), esp. pp. 15–17, 34–5.

2 Robert Boyle, Preface, *The Christian Virtuoso* (London, John Taylor and John Wyat, 1690), n. pag.

children (for example, John Desaguliers, Francesco Algarotti, Benjamin Martin, Erasmus Darwin, Charlotte Smith, and Bernard Fontenelle wrote highly literary popularisations). Furthermore, travel writing, combining as it did elegance of style, intellectual curiosity, and accuracy of report, is a genre which is innately interdisciplinary.

While these responses were often creative and positive, there were numerous opponents to the implicit and explicit tendency and values of natural philosophy, from the often scurrilous satires of the Scriblerians to the visionary metaphysics of William Blake. Some of the relationships were paradoxical: Charlotte Smith, correcting Shakespeare's identification of a flower, complained that 'poets have never been botanists', at the same time as proving in her scholarly poem that she was both poet and botanist.[1] As well as recognising the shared territory, we should acknowledge what Gillian Beer calls 'the transformations undergone when ideas enter other genres or different reading groups, the destabilizing of knowledge once it escapes from the initial group of co-workers, its tendency to mean more and other than could have been foreseen'.[2]

This anthology aims to go beyond the idea that a pre-existing body of science 'influenced' creative writers, or that creative writers applied their imaginations to the uncreative works of scientists. We are not just interested in literary appropriations of scientific ideas, but other, broader relationships. The interconnections between what we now call science and literature are many and various, and this introduction can only indicate a few of the paths that this anthology would allow readers to trace. The selection and arrangement of the texts is experimental: it is hoped that the juxtapositions will prompt new discoveries and set off fresh chains of associations.

The texts included here are, with a few exceptions, rare texts which are difficult to find outside of the major research libraries. Well-known literary works will not be included because of their easy availability, and because we are keen that the voice of science should be heard. The medical and scientific texts, sometimes aimed at a specialised audience, sometimes at a popular one, are interesting as writing in their own right, as well as significant for the light they shed on a wider culture. Further reading, including literary parallels, are indicated in the editorial material.

The first issue of this series comprises the following volumes: *Science as Polite Culture*, *Sciences of Body and Mind*, *Earthly Powers*, and *Flora*. The second contains: *Fauna*, *Astronomy*, *Natural Philosophy* and *Chemistry*. The

---

1 Charlotte Smith, 'Beachy Head', in Stuart Curran (ed.), *The Poems of Charlotte Smith* (Oxford, Oxford University Press, 1993), p. 242.

2 Gillian Beer, 'Forging the Missing Link: Interdisciplinary Stories', in *Open Fields: Science in Cultural Encounters* (Oxford, Clarendon Press, 1996), p. 115.

organisation of the material into themed volumes is partly pragmatic, and partly provocative. We cannot hope to give full coverage of the field, nor, lest we misrepresent the cultural landscape of the time, did we want to restructure the field of natural knowledge in the eighteenth century in terms of modern disciplines. Given the rapid pace of intellectual change in the eighteenth century, it would be false to try to fix a disciplinary pattern on it. Rather, we have tried to strike a balance between reflecting the map of knowledge of the past, and anticipating the needs and interests of modern readers.

I   Science as Polite Culture

This volume demonstrates how natural knowledge was absorbed into and played a part in the emergence of polite culture. It opens with an excerpt from Sprat's *History of the Royal Society*, a text which exemplifies the assumption that science and letters were not at odds, an assumption which paradoxically coexisted with an awareness that gentlemen needed to be persuaded that natural knowledge and mechanical philosophy were not just the province of 'rude mechanicals'. Hero worship was one of the ways in which the new science was rendered polite. The exemplary figure of Newton dominated eighteenth-century science and is represented here in eulogies and biographies. As a whole, the volume traces an arc from Sprat's proselytising through Algarotti's packaging of Newton for women, to Priestley's radical experiments, through to Whewell's 1834 paper which coined the term 'scientist', a coinage which Michael Newton describes as 'the moment of self-consciousness in which the subjectivity of the natural philosopher finds its own linguistic identity' (p. 373). Thus, this volume traces the way science moved from the realm of the polite to the grip of the professional, from the miscellaneous curiosity of the amateur to the disciplinarity of the specialist.

II   Sciences of Body and Mind

The application of mechanical philosophy to the workings of the mind and body raised issues of the definitions of the self and of science, questioning the boundaries of both. The volume reports on what Clark Lawlor calls the 'literary-medical dialogue' (p. xviii) concerning materialism and vitalism, and demonstrates how new medical regimes attempted to regulate the life of the individual and of the body politic. Pain and suffering, the influence of ill health on personality, the 'disease' of love, and the growth of the mind are all treated by both doctors and writers. Texts by Cheyne and Trotter, for example, examine the nervous system and anatomise relations between physical and social refinement. Such texts participate in the wider culture of sensibility which gave rise to the sentimental novel. This volume also includes poems on doctors and on diseases (by Cowley and Finch), and accounts of the workings of both body and soul which were taken up by writers such as Pope, Sterne, and the Romantic poets.

III Earthly Powers

From Athanasius Kircher's descriptions of his encounters with 'the fabled courts of Vulcan to William Scoresby junior's awed accounts of the ice fields of the high Arctic', as Richard Hamblyn points out (p. xviii), this volume illustrates the period's developing engagement with the then nascent sciences of the earth. All the four of the ancient elements – earth, air, fire, and water – are covered by the chosen extracts which, taken together, form a narrative of the emergence of a series of allied intellectual disciplines such as geology, meteorology, and hydrology. As with all the volumes, the organisation is broadly chronological, with the work of both pioneers and popularisers represented. Richard Hamblyn argues that the very breadth of the appeal of study of earthly powers 'lead at times to conflicts of interpretation, in which divergent ways of viewing and understanding the natural world and its processes ended up in direct competition.' (p. xi) This competition produced vivid writing of lasting value.

IV Flora

Human dependence on the plant world for food, medicines, and materials has made botany a central concern and have produced texts such as floral emblem books and practical herbals. The Georgic and farming textbooks were both vital to gentlemanly culture. With the widespread introduction of the Linnaean system of classification and the introduction of foreign plants, botanising became a national pastime from the mid-eighteenth century, one considered particularly suitable to women and children. Erasmus Darwin's encyclopaedic poem, *The Botanic Garden*, a generous selection of which is included in this volume, was one of the most important vehicles for the transmission of and reflection on the significance of the new botany. But his anthropomorphic fantasies on the 'Loves of the Plants', heavily indebted, as Charlotte Grant argues, to Alexander Pope, heightened anxiety about the sexual nature of Linnaeus's system. The erotic connotations of exotic plants and sexual scientists were also exploited and satirised in floridly pornographic works by Thomas Stretser and James Perry. The volume closes with Charlotte Smith's botanical 'conversations' for children, published shortly before professional botanists were to urge that women and children – 'Flora's daughters' – should be considered in merely symbolic relationship with flowers rather than as rational students of nature.

We are not attempting a comprehensive survey, but rather aiming to suggest possible routes through the field. It would have been possible for us to choose a different selection of texts, or to organise our material in other ways. We could, for example, have included a volume on technology, although this would have been problematic since historians of science often ally it to the Industrial Revolution which is treated as a branch of economic history. Alternatively, we could have presented volumes on a number of themes and genres such as: satire and celebrations of science and scientists, science fictions, the ancients–moderns debate, the argument from design and so on. It is hoped that the present arrangement will provide a useful way of thinking about literary and scientific relations, while leaving open the possibility for alternative approaches. By using the index, readers can track themes across the volumes and study such issues as method, religion, gender, imagination, and identity. Moreover, the headnotes draw attention to the fascinating individuals and complex networks involved in the interface of literature and science – many of which merit further study.

It is also hoped that the experience of reading these volumes could be like attending a vast colloquium, or eavesdropping at one of the many gatherings where natural knowledge was produced and disseminated in the long eighteenth century. Perhaps we can counterbalance Keats's dismay at the unweaving of the rainbow, and recapture the excitement expressed in James Thomson's exclamation about Newton's theories of light:

> Did ever poet image aught so fair,
> Dreaming in whispering groves by the hoarse brook?
> Or prophet, to whose raptures heaven descends?
> Even now the setting sun and shifting clouds,
> Seen, Greenwich from thy lovely heights, declare
> How just, how beauteous the refractive law.
> ('To the Memory of Sir Isaac Newton' (1727), ll. 119–24.)

Judith Hawley

INTRODUCTION

> I cannot countenance the traditional belief which postulates a natural dichotomy between the objectivity of the scientist and the subjectivity of the writer ...[1]
>
> Roland Barthes, *Mythologies*

Preview

This anthology of facsimile texts presents an overview of the popular literature on science from the founding of the Royal Society in London to William
Whewell's coining of the word 'scientist' in 1834. As a whole the volume
demonstrates that popular reception of scientific knowledge has relied equally
on faith, persuasion and comprehension. An interesting feature of the broad
range of polemical strategies on display in these historical documents is that
they continue to be operative in contemporary popularisations of scientific
knowledge. We are the heirs of the experimental tradition as expounded by
the authors in the volume.[2] But the texts themselves can be elusive to a modern reader. Here the authors themselves can provide some guidance. As
Charles Babbage (1791–1871) points out in *Reflections on the Decline of Science
in England* (1830): 'An object is frequently not seen, from not knowing how to
see it, rather than from any defect in the organ of vision.'[3] The same can be
said of reading: a text is frequently not understood, from not knowing how to
understand it, rather than from any defect in the organ of comprehension.

What's in a Rubric?

There is a conceptual rift between the title of this volume and its contents in
that these texts have never before appeared under the rubric of science as
polite culture. A history book on English natural philosophy in the age of
Newton and Priestley, of which there are many fine examples in the social
studies of science, would mediate this rift by situating the argument,

---

1 Roland Barthes, *Mythologies*, trans. Annette Lavers (New York, Hill and Wang,
1972), p. 12 (quotation from preface to the 1957 edn).

2 Steven Shapin and Simon Schaffer, *Leviathan and the Air-pump: Hobbes, Boyle,
and the Experimental Life* (Princeton, NJ, Princeton University Press, 1985).

3 Babbage, p. 210.

marshalling the evidence and streamlining its methodology.[1] Even studies accentuating heterogeneity would situate the dissonance of this history in a framework of coherence. But an anthology of facsimile texts – each of which served to disseminate scientific knowledge to its respective lay audience over a 174-year period ending over one and a half centuries ago – cannot pretend to put forward a coherent authorial voice, nor a compelling master narrative. Although the collection is governed by a tight editorial policy, readers are called upon to navigate the inevitable rift between narrative purposes, past and present, on their own.

Science as Polite Culture is not about arguments. Being an anthology of excerpts, it presents only parts of whole works. Because this inevitably disrupts the compositional flow of the original, the coherence of argument can have little claim on the reader's attention. *Science as Polite Culture* is not about authors either. Although each author is introduced in headnotes preceding the selections, in short biographies that greatly enhance the expressive depth of the excerpts, these character portraits are suggestive rather than exhaustive. The authors do not constitute a tight network of collaborators; some were associates and friends, others merely refer to each other's work in print. By and large, they were self-appointed champions for the scientific experiment and the moral virtues it was held to epitomise. The excerpts assembled in this volume show them proselytising for a new set of doctrines about nature and a new regimen for the production of empirical knowledge about nature. Their motives are many and varied, their moralised vision of the scientific experiment multiple and sometimes at cross-purposes.

Science as Polite Culture is not even framed in terms of a clear and definite historicity. When polite culture was polite culture, science was natural philosophy; and now that science is modern science, polite culture has pretty much ceased to exist. Whereas the key dates, 1660 and 1834, locate the texts as cultural artifacts, they should not be misconstrued as definitive guides to our thinking about the texts. The notion of science as polite culture places us within a variable historical continuum, one that invokes two distinct spheres of human activity: the doing of science and the manifestation of civic ritual. It designates a set of themes whose urgency relates as much to the present as to the past.

Since the series is entitled *Literature and Science*, why not call this volume *Science 'and' Polite Culture*? Why *Science 'as' Polite Culture*? What's in the connective? 'As' alludes to the structure of the historical phenomenon that the phrase denotes; it implies a historical causality. The title leaves interpretative

---

1 Jan Golinski, *Science as Public Culture: Chemistry and Enlightenment in Britain, 1760–1820* (Cambridge, Cambridge University Press, 1992); Jenny Uglow, *The Lunar Men: The Friends Who Made the Future* (London, Faber and Faber, 2002).

leeway by abbreviating numerous possible perspectives – *Science as 'the Epit-ome of' Polite Culture, Science as 'a Modality of' Polite Culture, Science as 'a Function of' Polite Culture* and so on. This cryptic connective invites readers to reconsider their assumptions about the larger historical picture which may involve areas of structural equivalence between science and polite culture, or may consist of local interactions. Primarily, 'as' serves as a reminder that our conception of the overall phenomenon at issue in this volume will influence, inevitably, our reading of the individual texts.

The archival materials in the collection have a peculiar literary quality. Like the novels and stories featured in the Literary Parallels listing, these didactic accounts on the ways of nature and natural philosophers can fruit-fully be read as stories. This entails attending not merely to the scientific knowledge they purport to convey but also, and especially, to their narrative qualities. Written for sensibilities far removed from our own, some texts may appear dated. But what we perceive to be stylistic quirkiness was also deliber-ate in some cases. In the preface to his poem on the *Newtonian System of the World* (1728), John Theophilus Desaguliers (1683–1744) pleads 'that the Truth of the Philosophy may excuse the Badness of the Poetry'.[1] His balance of priorities is revealed by the relative length of footnotes to poetry; the poem forms the body of a text whose bulk is in the explanatory footnotes, where sci-entific concepts are elaborated in plain and concise prose.

Given that these are the very kinds of texts that first introduced the dichotomy between science and literature into our stockpile of assumptions, endowing it with that compelling aura of naturalness it enjoys to this today, such a reading *ipso facto* challenges the terms of the dichotomy. Even Whewell (1794–1866), a relative latecomer to the process of scientific legiti-mation documented here, invites readers to question the dichotomy itself. With a perceptual acuity peculiar to the carefully trained observer, he identi-fies a polemical technique used to popularise the scientific experiment. The trick is in his opinion to elide reality and illusion, merge what *is* and what *seems to be*, fuse the objective and subjective content of experience:

> The office of language is to produce a picture in the mind; and it may easily happen in this instance, as it happens in the pictures of some of our un-Pindaric artists, that we are struck by the profound thought and unity dis-played in the colouring, while there is hardly a single object outlined with any tolerable fidelity and distinctness.[2]

On Whewell's account popular understandings of science are based on a delusion akin to an optical illusion. The process of presenting the laws of

---

1 Desaguliers, p. 6.
2 Whewell, p. 55.

nature purely as matters of fact, as opposed to matters of interpretation, is misleading. Polemical language, be it about scientific truths or political verities, compels consent. Popular science enthrals.

Lamentable? Not in all respects. Science enthrals because it appeals to the imaginative faculty of both practitioners and spectators. Imagination, the driving force behind both science and literature, does not recognise or adhere to dichotomies; correct imaginings and false imaginings only part ways with the benefit of hindsight. The visionary prescience of Fontenelle's *Conversations With A Lady On The Plurality of Worlds* (1719) is a case in point:

> I'll lay a Wager … that one of these Days there may be a Communication between the Earth and the Moon. … Did the Americans believe there would ever be any between them and Europe, till it came to pass? … The Art of Flying is but newly invented; it will improve by degrees, and in time grow perfect, then we may fly as far as the moon.[1]

Fontenelle's wager turned out to be correct, but it could just as well have been wrong. In reading these texts it is useful to treat imaginative and empirical ways of knowing as two modes of a single creative process – even if, as Whewell observes with a note of regret, most natural philosophers of his day, swayed perhaps by their own polemics, had ceased to do so:

> Formerly, the 'learned' embraced in their wide grasp all the branches of the tree of knowledge … But these days are past; the students of books and of things are estranged from each other in habit and feeling.[2]

From Whewell's perspective, the task at hand – reading archival documents – would seem to designate us as 'students of books'. But many of us are in habit and feeling the 'students of things'. Reading the texts in this anthology as stories can mitigate against the worst effects of entrenched estrangement.

This volume aims to prompt an experience, rather than to impart a message. It is, in effect, a sampling of historical voices made audible through the medium of print. It works through selective proximity and evocative juxtaposition. The rubric, science as polite culture can be said to function as a filter in the sense that it regulates fidelities of tone and enables contemporary readers to discern nuances of inflection they might otherwise fail to hear. It establishes a connection between bygone sensibilities and current perceptions and collapses thereby a second dichotomy, closely related to the first, between the experience of a historical actor and that of a contemporary reader.

---

1 Fontenelle, pp. 60–1.
2 Whewell, p. 59.

Smells and Bells

Science as Polite Culture sets the stage for, and presents the modalities of communication accompanying the rise of English experimental philosophy in the long eighteenth century.[1] Specifically, this volume seeks to exemplify the cultural milieu of the scientific experiment where 'Men of the first rank and talent, – the literary and the scientific, the practical and the theoretical, bluestockings and women of fashion, the old and the young, all crowded – eagerly crowded the lecture-room.'[2] At issue is not only the curiosity of identifying the laws of nature by means of the scientific experiment but equally the curiosity of witnessing the effect of such experiments when performed before an audience. The stakes were high. Thomas Sprat (1635–1713) expressed a sentiment widely shared by his colleagues when he uttered with such pathos in *The History of the Royal Society* (1667):

> This, I hope, most men will acknowledg ... that in all past and present times ... there can never be shewn, so great a Number of Contemporaries, in so narrow a space of the World, that lov'd truth so zealously; sought it so constantly; and upon whose labours, mankind might so freely rely.[3]

The cultural milieu at issue is not directly on display in the excerpts collected in this volume; mostly these are not eyewitness accounts of scientific soirees. Rather, the cultural milieu is reflected, implicitly, in the discursive strategies informing the texts, strategies that facilitated what an English society called the 'Diffusion of Useful Knowledge' from private laboratories and royal societies or practitioners to the remote households of the Empire.[4] The volume charts the making popular of the enterprise as a whole by means of polemical techniques which extended in print the histrionic appeal of the experimental lecture with its 'bells and smells' and rhetorical embellishments.

Ironically these strategies of popularisation, while consolidating the authority of the experiment in public opinion, also agitated against the professed aim of natural philosophy 'to separate the knowledge of *Nature*, from the colours of *Rhetorick*, the devices of *Fancy*, or the delightful deceit of *Fables*'.[5] Sprat praised natural philosophy for producing minds 'invincibly arm'd against all the inchantments of Enthusiasm'.[6] Yet both in the lecture

---

1 Roy Porter, *Enlightenment: Britain and the Creation of the Modern World* (London, Allen Lane, 2000).

2 Paris, p. 90.

3 Sprat, p. 70.

4 Alan Rauch, *Useful Knowledge: Morality and 'The March of Intellect' in the Victorian Novel* (Durham, NC, Duke University Press, 2001).

5 Sprat, p. 62.

6 Ibid., p. 53.

room and the popularising literature, it was precisely fancy, fable and enthusiasm that came to the fore. How to strike an appropriate balance between these conflicting demands was a matter of much contest and debate amongst the philosophers themselves. Humphry Davy (1778–1829), one of the most widely-revered lecturers of his day, was chastised variously for adopting a style 'too florid and imaginative for communicating the plain lessons of truth', for describing the 'objects of Natural History by inappropriate imagery', and for employing 'violent conceits' which 'frequently usurped the place of philosophical definitions.'[1] As the new discipline of experimental philosophy was struggling to assert the supremacy of its investigative methods in public estimation, its spiritual integrity was put dangerously at risk. Too much display of the marvellous and fantastic would seriously jeopardise the cognitive faculties of practitioners and their audiences. Joseph Priestley (1733–1804), a premier virtuoso of the experimental lecture circuit in his day, maintained that striking the right balance between dazzle and detail required extraordinary discipline. The mind, he says, must disregard all 'Pleasantness or Gainfulness of the Experiment' because these are 'like sweet singing Syrens' who 'seduce their Followers out of their right way to their utter Destruction'.[2]

This volume traces the complex politics of denial by which the natural sciences were popularised and the norms of society transformed. Disavowal of the literary imagination and reliance upon literary forms of persuasion went hand in hand in the scientific re-fitting of polite culture. The global transformation of science and society was propelled by, and associated with, myriad vectors of social, cultural and economic change. The main features of this transformation, as put forward in Steven Shapin's *A Social History of Truth*, can be summarized as follows: (1) the scientific experiment became the privileged means of establishing incontrovertible matters of fact; (2) the natural philosopher, a gentleman 'free and unconfin'd'[3] whose personal virtue vouchsafed the veracity of his empirical observations, became a professional man of science; (3) experimental techniques were propagated as the bearers of an ennobling moral influence conducive to the supremacy of truth in the adjudication between conflicting knowledge claims; 4) the order of nature, as well as the routines for investigating that order, were used to promote social and political institutions founded upon the incontrovertible self-evidence of the matter of fact.[4]

From the perspective of the historical actors, however, it was not the pattern of social transformation that captured the imagination. It was the

---

1 Paris, p. 92.

2 Hooke, p. 20.

3 Sprat, p. 67.

4 Steven Shapin, *A Social History of Truth: Civility and Science in Seventeenth-century England* (Chicago, University of Chicago Press, 1994).

visceral immediacy of the public lecture and the private experiment. This immediacy was echoed in the popular literature too, where allusions to bodies, minds and sexual union abound.

Astute Bodies and Fragile Minds

Both the practitioners and the popularisers of natural philosophy enlisted sensuality in their endeavours to educate. So, for example, these authors frequently portray themselves as more fully engaged in their subject than any philosophers before them. They thematise the fullness of their engagement as being something quite new, peculiar and special. According to them, natural philosophy is a mode of enquiry which, to borrow a recurring image, engages equally the mind and the hand. Indeed Sprat attributes the increase in knowledge deemed possible by means of this new discipline to its 'settling an inviolable correspondence between the hand, and the brain.'[1] Priestley commends natural philosophy as a most agreeable subject because it mixes 'something of action with speculation' and gives 'some employment to the hands and the arms, as well as the head'.[2] Unlike other speculative systems in which the mind, which stands for abstract thinking, was merely assisted by the actions of the hand, which stands for thinking through doing and perceiving, this was a realm where the hand and mind became equal partners in the process of philosophical investigation. The practical skills of observation, instrument use and experimental design were commensurate with the powers of abstraction, analysis and representation. As a result, many of these authors cast themselves as fully invested sentient beings committing body and soul to the study of nature.

Research conducted at such a high level of personal engagement was physically taxing for anyone who pursued it in earnest. The demands of the hand, far more than those of the mind, intensified the rigours of natural philosophy. Priestley was presumably expressing a more widely shared sentiment when he noted:

> I can truly say … that single sections in this work have cost me more than whole volumes of the other; so great is the difference between writing from the head only, and writing, as it may be called, from the hands.[3]

Thinking through the hand, instead of only the mind, had the advantage of bringing the process of investigation close to the materiality of natural phenomena. Routines of precision, the tacit knowledge of timing and know-how,

---

1 Sprat, p. 62.
2 Priestley, *The History of Electricity*, p. xii.
3 Ibid., 'Experiments and Observations', p. vi.

and the sheer physical thrill of inspiration were all aspects of reason understood as handicraft. Yet body knowledge was closely associated with sensuality and could, if not tightly monitored, become a dangerous ruling passion. Indeed Priestley warns that the temptations of electrical experimentation are greater even than those of the flesh:

> Lastly, let it be remembered, that a taste for science, pleasing, and even honourable as it is, is not one of the highest passions of our nature, that the pleasures it furnishes are even but one degree above those of sense, and therefore that temperance is requisite in all scientifical pursuits.[1]

If the flesh was weak, the spirit was weaker still. Psychology had to be taken into account to the extent that mental deviance might compromise sound observation and hence the validity of experimental findings. In 'The Present State of Natural Philosophy' (1705), Robert Hooke (1635–1705) notes that human understanding is 'very prone to run into the affirmative way of judging' and, therefore, also 'very apt to be seduc'd in pronouncing positively for this or that Opinion.'[2] He maintains that the intellect is too weak an instrument to be trusted without the assistance of 'some Method or Engine' and gives instructive hints for a 'Philosophical Algebra, or an Art of directing the Mind in the search after Philosophical Truths'.[3]

A further destabilising moment in the partnership of hand and mind was the sheer diversity of minds. Mental idiosyncrasy introduced a wild card into the replicability of scientific investigations in that it would have the effect of causing different philosophers to perceive the same experiment in different terms. Specificities in mental functioning could generate vast differences in the perceived implications of an experimental finding. Mental difference was attributed in part to the effect of personality. So, for instance, Babbage explores 'the curiously different structure' of the minds of Wollaston and Davy:

> In associating with Wollaston, you perceived that the predominant principle was to avoid error; in the society of Davy, you saw that it was the desire to see and make known truth. Wollaston never could have been a poet; Davy might have been a great one.[4]

But mental difference was also attributed to the influence of culture, geography and climate. In his *Conversations With A Lady*, Fontenelle observes that we would be unlikely to find human beings living on the moon, or if we did they would be hard to recognize as such, because differences in culture

---

1 Priestley, *The History of Electricity*, p. xxv.

2 Hooke, p. 6.

3 Ibid., pp. 6–7.

4 Babbage, p. 203.

and race are directly proportional to the geographical distance separating the regional territories between populations. The example motivating this observation is telling:

> I do not believe there are Men in the Moon: for do but observe how much the Face of Nature is chang'd between this and China; other Visages, Shapes, Manners, nay almost other Principles of Reason; and therefore between us and the Moon the Alteration must be much more considerable.[1]

According to Fontenelle, cultural difference manifests itself not only in the physical attributes of race and behaviour but also, and most importantly, in the very structure of reasoning. If cultural specificity is revealed in the configuration of cognition, then the universality of reason is constrained, at least to some extent, by cultural factors. The same experiment performed in England and China might result in very different conclusions being drawn not because of a feature intrinsic to the experiment but due to cultural factors alone.

Another influence on the distinctiveness of mind at least as potent as personality and culture was gender. For these authors, men and women were fundamentally different creatures and the differences between them were most apparent in the distinctive structure of their minds. As Whewell succinctly comments: 'Notwithstanding all the dreams of theorists, there is a sex in minds.' He then proceeds to elaborate the sexual attributes of mind. His portrayal of the female intellect, which he deems to be innately superior to the male intellect, sounds surprisingly flattering. He casts the *weaker* sex as possessing the *stronger* mental capacities:

> One of the characteristics of the female intellect is a clearness of perception ... with them, action is the result of feeling; thought, of seeing; their practical emotions do not wait for instruction from speculation; their reasoning is undisturbed by the prospect of its practical consequences. ... The heart goes on with its own concerns, asking no counsel of the head and, in return, the working of the head (if it does work) is not impeded by its having to solve questions of casuistry for the heart.[2]

Whewell's portrayal of feminine reason is, of course, informed by operative stereotypes prevalent at the time. Women were perceived to be more confined to their bodies than men, more subject to the laws of nature in the workings of their physical and spiritual make-up. Trapped in their bodies, 'asking no counsel of the head' as the quotation states, they were liable to act on whim and first impulse. With respect to natural philosophy such proclivities were

---

1 Fontenelle, p. 55.
2 Whewell, p. 65.

beneficial; women were body-bound and hence compelled to think through their hands.

We must be careful, however, not to overestimate the emancipatory thrust of Whewell's thinking. This excerpt is taken from 'Review of Mrs Somerville's *On the Connexion of the Physical Sciences*' (1834). He is paying his respects to a female colleague and his writing displays the conventional deference that 'gentlemen' owed 'ladies' – he is helping her out of a carriage, as it were. But his complimentary remarks are not as far-fetched as they might have sounded to some male colleagues of whom Whewell says they belong to 'that gender which plumes itself upon the exclusive possession of exact science'. Given the special status accorded to sensual knowledge and physical ways of exploring the natural world, women's proximity to nature could be construed as a competitive advantage. Whewell's favourable comments on feminine intelligence draw on the high estimation in which natural philosophers held sense perception in general. The prevalent stereotypes about women here played out to their advantage, for a change.

The problem with men, as Whewell puts it, is that their mentalities are too far removed from nature and they must expend much energy in trying to bring their sensual lives in accord with reason. Their predicament is that, unlike women, they are not able to think through their bodies. Their hands, in other words, are further removed from their minds than are women's. At this point in the text Whewell translates the image of the hand and mind into the more internalised image of the mind and the heart. But the crucial role of sensuality, of feelings, of the truths of the body and the body's ways of knowing, are centrally at issue in characterising the difference between the male and female mind. Whewell summarises the limitations of the male intellect in the following words:

> In men, on the other hand, practical instincts and theoretical views are perpetually disturbing and perplexing each other. Action must be conformable to rule; theory must be capable of application to action. The heart and the head are in perpetual negotiation, trying in vain to bring about a treaty of alliance, offensive and defensive. The end of this is, as in many similar cases, inextricable confusion – an endless seesaw of demand and evasion. ... He does not know whether his opinion is founded on feeling or on reasoning, on words or on things.[1]

The conclusion he draws from positing gender differences in cognitive make-up sound surprisingly emancipated and modern. Women, he concedes, do not generally have the benefit of a sound education, but should they once acquire

---

1 Ibid., p. 65.

the advantage of learning, the relative strengths in their mental formation would shine forth:

> It follows, that when women are philosophers, they are likely to be lucid ones; that when they extend the range of their speculative views, there will be a peculiar illumination thrown over the prospect. If they attain to the merit of being profound, they will add to this the great excellence of being also clear.[1]

Even though women rarely excelled as practitioners in their own right, it is worth remembering that in many cases the wives of natural philosophers were working in close association with their husbands.[2]

The Seductions of Science

The excerpts in this volume mix promises of fame and riches with ample sexual innuendo – sex could sell science. Both Fontenelle and Francesco Algarotti (1712–64) employ heavy-handed flirtatious banter in their instructive dialogues on the laws of nature. For instance, Fontenelle has his Countess insinuate that the movements of the planets resemble a great galactic mating dance:

> The Moon hath a kind of trembling, which causeth a little Corner of her Face to be sometimes hid from us ... but then, upon my word, she attributes that trembling to us, and fancies that we have in the Heavens the Motion of a Pendulum, which vibrates to and fro.[3]

This suggestive image does not expound a sexual theory of the universe. Ambiguous repartee is merely a linguistic device to interest Fontenelle's readers in the text and the natural phenomena described therein. Nevertheless it is striking that licentious metaphors should be used to frame a scientific theory, Newtonian planetary motion to be precise, which was itself risqué in that it crossed conceptual boundaries and threatened to overthrow existing religious taboos. The outré dimension of illicit practices, be they sexual or philosophical, is invoked by allusion to transgressive desire. In *Sir Isaac Newton's Philosophy Explained* (1739), a text closely modelled on the example of Fontenelle's dialogue, Algarotti spells out even more explicitly the difficulties seekers of truth might have to face in withstanding the endearments of philosophy:

---

1 Ibid., p. 65.

2 Paul White, 'Science at Home', in *Thomas Huxley: Making the 'Man of Science'* (New York, Cambridge University Press, 2002), Chapter 1.

3 Fontenelle, p. 40.

> The Marchioness insisted upon seeing my Newtonian Picture as she called it. I begged she would at least have Patience till Evening, telling her that the Night had always been the Time consecrated to philosophical Affairs; and that the most polite Philosopher in France had made use of it in a Circumstance resembling mine and made no Scruple of entertaining a fine Lady with philosophical Discourses in a Wood at Mid-night.[1]

The point of Algarotti's protestations is not *whether* he and the Marchioness will consummate their philosophical passion, but *when*. Can she control herself until evening, 'the Time consecrated to philosophical Affairs', or will she insist upon a quickie before tea? The reader is not left in suspense. Although Algarotti pleads 'Incapacity and many other Excuses, which are made use of on the like Occasions', the Marchioness demands immediate satisfaction. For what she has in mind, the day is 'certainly more proper than the Night'. They promply proceed to solve the Romantic conundrum of light and colours from a Newtonian perspective and employ, as it readily appears, the condoned tools of philosophical investigation: hands (four) and minds (two).

But the seductive potential of science far exceeds its mere instrumentalisation as an *ars erotica*. Many naturalists construed the forces of nature as being riddled with a sexual dynamic of their own.[2] Studies of plants and animals were intrinsically sexualised due to the procreative force governing all organic life forms. Philosophers went further, however, and also interpreted the physical laws of nature as governed by a profound and abstracted sexual principle. In his poem on 'Nature' excerpted from *Introduction to the Philosophy of Newton* (1738), Voltaire (1694–1778) orchestrates the movements of earth, sea and air as a sexual tumult comparable to the act of coitus. Dedicated to his 'Immortal Emily', the verse equates human and non-human forms of bed sports. In his words:

> The Sea too hears him. With stupendious Dance
> I see the humid Element advance!
> Tow'rds Heav'n it rises; Heav'n attracts it high:
> But central Pow'r, more potent, as more nigh,
> Each Effort stops: The Sea recoils; it roars;
> Sinks in its Bed, and rolls against the Shores[3]

Elsewhere the authors in this collection extend the erotic potential of scientific language to the activity of natural philosophy itself, that is to say to their own practices of investigation. Casting the object of study as an object of

---

1 Algarotti, pp. 16–17.

2 Londa Schiebinger, *Nature's Body: Gender in the Making of Modern Science* (Boston, MA, Beacon, 1993).

3 Voltaire, p. vi.

desire, nature is anthropomorphised, the female sexual partner to a male philosopher, and experimental science equated with the love they make.[1] At times transfixed by mutual longing, at others locked in passionate embrace, the amorous encounters could be wild and frenzied, or calm and deliberate. The imagery pervading these texts runs the gamut. Philosophy has its peculiar foreplay – 'His learned Hand unfold the glitt'ring Robe, That clothes yon lucid, animated Globe'[2] – but also its methods of taking far greater liberties: 'Philosophy unleavens, Lifts up the Veil, and open'd are the Heavens.'[3]

Figuring nature as woman exposes an author's views on nature and women in general. In his *Poem addressed to the Young Ladies who Attended Mr Booth's Lectures*, Jones claims that nature was seen to strike every register of female demeanour from demure coyness to abandoned wantonness; she

> ... turns her Face aside,
> And mocks th' enquiring Sages learned Pride,
> Here less reserved she shows her plainer Course
> In mutual Contest of Elastic force[4]

And Jones does not limit himself to just one indelicate observation; his poem revels in saucy iambic pentameters. Booth is described as a young man who gazes upon his beloved with 'raptur'd Eye' wishing to 'enjoy th' ecstatic Blaze'. Nature, the object of his desire, signals her assent with a provocative, come-hitherish gesture: 'See! Like a Seraph, how she smiles and burns.'[5] So, allegedly, nature yearned to have her secrets penetrated by the philosophers. Now consider that the lecture room was full of women. What did they make of Jones's raucous rendering?

Personifying nature as a sexually-aggressive female might have appealed to an audience of men by inviting them to assume the posture of the probing philosopher. But much of this literature is directed at female readers. They are being invited to identify with the part of nature and to conjure in their minds the image of a receptive female eager for intimate connection with a young man. Why should mute, stolid nature be cast in such animated terms? Why is she attributed the agency of encouraging the fumbling advances of a philosopher? These authors must have felt that such identification would make female listeners more receptive to the findings of naturalists, and the facts of

---

1 Ludmilla Jordanova, 'Nature Unveiling Before Science', in *Sexual Visions. Images of Gender in Science and medicine between the Eighteenth and Twentieth Centuries*, (Madison, University of Wisconsin Press, 1989), Chapter 5.

2 Ibid., p. v.

3 Voltaire, p. v.

4 Jones, p. 4.

5 Ibid., p. 5.

nature too. Brawn will bring enlightenment appears to have been the motto. And indeed why not? If human nature is a part of nature and governed by the same principles, then talking dirty is another expression of natural law. Sexual attraction and the laws of gravity, Jones rhapsodises, are but two manifestations of a single force: 'Mysterious Energy! stupendous Themes!'[1] Small wonder women were discouraged from receiving this kind of education.

Storyalign

As science has prospered, polite culture has withered. We live in an era of cultural production dominated by popular rather than polite culture. Popularisation, as it is understood today, means to establish mass appeal of a subject or a product, not merely to enhance its appeal in the eyes of a privileged few. A box office hit is measured not in terms of a movie's critical acclaim but the numbers it grosses in ticket sales. Our entertainment industries make few stipulations regarding attention or demeanour amongst members of the target audience. Polite culture, by contrast, made enormous demands on individuals to primp, posture and parleyvoo.

The inverse trajectories of science and polite culture are not an historical coincidence. Scientific innovation has been a contributing factor in the evolutionary triumph of the popular over the polite. In asking ourselves, what was polite about science as practised in the eighteenth century, we are simultaneously also asking a corollary question, namely what is popular about science as practised today. Together these questions invite us to think about how, when and why polite science became popular science.

Given the reigning hegemony of scientific protocols in the Western world, interest in the scientific process, in any of its aspects, requires no justification. Popular demand for books on the history of science has burgeoned. An enduring faith in the abiding naturalness of natural knowledge, a faith whose origin was contemporaneous with the documents in this anthology, long rendered the question of the history of the production of that knowledge irrelevant, a non-question; the 'objectivity of the scientist' admitted to no history. But popular attitudes changed once the enabling enthusiasms – stoked by scientific, technological and medical innovation relentlessly buffeting the collective consciousness of laypersons – yielded to deep-seated anxiety about the emergent conditions of life in the scientific world order. Today 'science' can be used as a term of opprobrium and its high-priests, the 'scientists', are seen by some to be puppets of entrenched commercial and political interests. At a time when public faith in scientific institutions is waning, it is not surprising that the very category of 'the natural', as established in the wake of the

---

1 Ibid., p. 6.

experiment's ascendant authority, is subjected to critical scrutiny. Reconsideration of the historical origins of scientific objectivity leads inevitably to an examination of the epistemological foundations of objectivity itself.[1]

When Isaac Newton (1733–1804) and his colleagues at the Royal Society dominated the scene, the scientific experiment was an entrenched feature of English high society. Air-pumps, galvanic piles and pendulum experiments were the stuff of refined soirees amongst privileged members of society. They were to be consumed, like truffles and oranges, as the tokens of a luxurious existence.[2] Table-top experiments conducted in the private laboratory of a country manor could be transported with relative ease into the more public settings where they were performed for a lay audience. This bears little resemblance to circumstances in the natural sciences today – the era of big science.[3] Only specialist institutions, maintained by highly-skilled teams of experts who work in collaboration with each other internationally, can hope to conduct significant experimental research at the cutting-edge of scientific discovery. The outlay of resources involved would exceed the possibilities of all but a few tycoons, and even these philanthropists of science can scarcely hope to make a substantial contribution to the advancement of knowledge. Leading scientists must excel as science managers and as creative problem solvers; they are responsible for everything from experimental design and testing schedules to budgetary control and employee benefits. Big science is not amenable to the individual heroism of pioneering natural philosophers. Robert Hooke (1635–1703) compares natural philosophy to Columbus's voyage of discovery, and Priestley pronounces electrical experimentation to be a field where 'raw adventurers have made themselves as considerable ... as the greatest philosophers'.[4] Such ambitions are bound to be disappointed by contemporary science labour.

Whereas the promise of individual glory is greatly diminished – and the predominance of individual pop icons like Einstein and Dawkins is no exception to this rule – other attributes of science work have been remarkably constant. A process of fragmentation, propelled by the constant drive towards scientific specialisation, has not abated since Whewell remarked on it in 1834:

> The tendency of the sciences has long been an increasing proclivity to separation and dismemberment. ... The mathematician turns away from the

---

1 Peter Galison and Lorraine Daston, *Images of Objectivity* (in preparation).

2 Related issues discussed in Mario Biagioli, *Galileo, Courtier: The Practice of Science in the Culture of Absolutism* (Chicago, University of Chicago Press, 1993).

3 Peter Galison and Bruce Hevly, *Big Science: the Growth of Large-scale Research* (Stanford, CA, Stanford University Press, 1992).

4 Priestley, *The History of Electricity*, p. xiii.

chemist; the chemist from the naturalist; the mathematician, left to himself, divides himself into a pure mathematician and a mixed mathematician, who soon part company; the chemist is perhaps a chemist of electro-chemistry; if so, he leaves common chemical analysis to others; between the mathematician and the chemist is to be interpolated a 'physicien' (we have no English name for *him*), who studies heat, moisture and the like. And thus science, even mere physical science, loses all traces of unity.[1]

But this very process of fragmentation is a function of the expansive growth and success that the natural sciences have enjoyed. In agreeing on rules for reliably establishing matters of fact, the natural philosophers under consideration in this anthology also opened the gateway to diversification. The scientific method with its experimental modes of enquiry created a common denominator around which specialist areas of investigation could proliferate and flourish.

To the extent that the old spirit of polite discovery still persists, it is in primary education, where the electrical and magnetic experiments performed in classrooms full of students continue to evoke some of the mystique of those elegant drawing rooms. Some of the experiments have hardly changed since they were first performed. Although schoolteachers have adapted the style of their presentation to the pedagogical needs at hand, wonderment over the revealed mysteries of nature prevails and can be enlisted for noble purpose, namely to inspire young minds with a fascination for science. This fascination ensures that, as taxpayers, these same young minds will endorse government investment in scientific research and development, especially basic research as opposed to applied research. It also draws youngsters into the fold of science worship so that a new generation of scientists will step into the shoes of the current one. A further purpose, still advanced in our schools, is to rehearse and propagate the moral values associated with proper scientific method. Even students who reject high school physics, chemistry and biology learn to revere the knowledge base these disciplines continue to generate and the routines of scientific methodology – falsifiability, replicability and transparency – which they all share.

In contrast to science, polite culture in the eighteenth-century sense has been marginalised to the point of obscurity. Its curtsies and crinolines, familiar mainly through the mediations of period drama, are now objects of idle curiosity. Baroque elaborations of manners and graces have given way to a ubiquitous, at times obdurate, rule of the casual.[2] A behavioural apparatus,

---

1 Whewell, p. 59.

2 Related issues discussed in Thomas Frank, *The Conquest of Cool: Business Culture, Counterculture, and the Rise of Hip Consumerism* (Chicago, University of Chicago Press, 1997).

minutely articulated, for the formal demarcation of social distinction has been supplanted by the random guesswork of detecting a person's upbringing or station from the cues of mass-consumptive uniformity.[1] As concerns decorum, forms of conviviality, courtship rituals and dress codes: almost any situation we encounter can be treated as 'dress-down Tuesday' or 'casual Friday'. A prime exception to this trend is to be found in the realm of lobbying and high-end corporate entertainment, echelons where performative power continues to be displayed with gusto and consequence. What has happened to that vast potential of human energy formerly directed towards cultivating the art of role-playing in public settings?[2] And how does one even address the question when the very definition of what qualifies as a public setting has radically shifted?

Much contemporary scholarship has argued that in the course of the modern period, located somewhere between the Enlightenment and the present, public enactment of social identity has given way to the psychological experience of 'being me'. In this modern approach to the assertion of identity, distinction and distinctiveness are radically internalised and expressed primarily through a special sense of 'me-ness', with little reference to where me might be placed on the social spectrum. At least that is the theory. The same politics of denial evident in the promotion of science as a whole are replicated in the self-positing logic of authentic self-hood. Moreover, the exponential growth of the self-empowerment industry suggests that unreconstructed me-ness is both perpetuating and itself fuelled by a haunting identity vacuum for which the science of psychology can provide only temporary relief.

The audiences to whom these texts were originally addressed were intimately familiar with the bearing of the drawing room. Today's reader is not. Instead of trying to picture a specific historical site of polite science, it is perhaps more productive to imagine a generic, amorphous space in which leisured sociability takes place whenever and wherever human beings assemble for purposes of play (that form of play which carries influence beyond the immediate circle of participants by helping to establish, maintain and continually readjust power relations in society at large). Try to imagine the varied loci in which the gregarious jousting of adults take place and what these loci may have in common. Although the games played are culturally and historically specific – premised variously on virtue, honour, wealth and celebrity – their functional role in organising the social sphere is relatively constant. Even the virtual world is subject to their ongoing influence as attested to by the appearance of the webzine 'salon.com' in the early days of the internet

---

1 Richard Sennett, *The Fall of Public Man* (New York, Knopf, 1977).

2 Norbert Elias, *The Civilizing Process: the History of Manners and State Formation and Civilization* (Oxford, Blackwell, 1994).

and those specific rules of conduct for the digital generation falling under the general heading of 'netiquette'. Furtive ogling around a dinner table has been replaced by excited googling of information on a business card. Virtual propagation hinges on chatrooms and online dating.

When sterilised intimacies of television and digital communication timeshare with the old-fashioned nearness of the face-to-face interface, reliance on primitive determinants of social trust such as odour, gesture and instinct must be diminished. Subjectivity, that is to say heightened awareness of the qualitative uniqueness of experience, is little cultivated or exercised outside the liberal arts courses of universities; 'me's' special 'me-ness' is deemed sufficient to vouchsafe personality. Subjectivity is not considered a personal attribute on a par with physical fitness, academic learning, and emotional maturity. The notion that subjective reality should be developed through interpretative exchange between sensualised subjects, like a spiritual drill exercise, no longer computes. The short attention span is symptomatic of our lack of stamina for interpretation. More comfortable consuming our messages than producing them, the messages we produce bear a striking resemblance to those previously consumed.

The drawing room has moved closer to the bedroom. Since the invention of the pill, sexuality has taken its place amongst the other biological drives. The arcane social machinery on display in these texts, and formerly in place for organising contact and communication between the sexes, is no longer required. 'Hi' establishes contact; communication, or what passes for the same, takes place without the buffer of form. The notion of 'casual sex' indicates that the down-scaling of the drawing room has been closely tracked by a parallel development in the physical expressions of intimacy. Indeed, with advances in endocrinology the libido has become a switch to be turned on and off at will by means of appropriate medication. Thanks to science we have been able to dispense almost entirely with the former inefficiencies of romantically-charged courtship.

The arrival of the computer in the corporate world forced dress codes to be relaxed as the new technology brought in its wake technicians, collectively known as computer geeks, who steadfastly refused to cut their hair, don a tie and wear a suit. Like so many Trojan horses, this indispensable class of sartorial non-conformists transplanted the casualness of manners now common in the world of science into their new environments. This small example is emblematic of the much broader process by which scientific innovation has effected cultural transformation.

Conclusion

Popularisation is still central to the promotion of scientific interests. But today science is popularised not to bring it to public attention but to maintain its mass appeal. Yet the very process of popularisation – appealing as it does to an imaginative faculty which 'in order to understand has to be pleased' (Algarotti) – continues to undermine the epistemological foundations of the undertaking as a whole. This inherent contradiction, between scientific values and the strategies of popularisation, alerts us to a politics of denial evident in both the excerpts and the public reception of scientific knowledge. Dichotomies abound where denial operates: in science, in popularising literature, in ourselves. Our examination of the historical origins of the dichotomy between science and literature, between objective and subjective registers of experience, involves questioning another dichotomy pertinent to these texts, and closely related to the first, that between past history and present reality.

The historical authors featured in this volume relied on 'the office of language' to conjure an image of science in the mind of the reader. Contemporary strategies of popularisation would favour a visual medium. These can be more compelling and also more illusory. Images of science enthral, more than ever. We too will conclude with an image whose internal composition evokes the interpretative framework sketched in this introduction. The image draws on the world of fashion, specifically eighteenth-century courtly women's fashion in France. Several of the authors collected in this anthology make explicit reference to the role of fashion in public demonstrations of the scientific experiment. Davy was accused of succumbing to the temptations of fashionable society. Algarotti, by contrast, casts the influence of fashion in favourable terms. Pointing out that scientific knowledge can 'serve to polish and adorn Society',[1] he argues that the refinements of experimental practice require as much care and attention to detail as the finest ladies' garments:

> How much Pains and Study are necessary to frame a right Philosophy! It requires no less Art and Labour, than to make those fine Silks which you Ladies are adorned with.[2]

Indeed Algarotti suggests that the inner life is subject to fashions of its own. He commends himself for having spotted the latest cognitive trends in philosophy and for bringing 'into Italy a new Mode of cultivating the Mind, rather than the present momentary Fashion of adjusting their Head-dress and placing their Curls'.[3]

---

1 Algarotti, p. xvi.
2 Ibid., p. 23.
3 Ibid., pp. xiii–xiv.

The problem with the fashions of the inner life is that they are most troublesome to display. How might a lady show herself to be *au courant* with speculations *a la mode*? Marie Antoinette's infamous hair creations come to mind. She is said to have placed entire scenes of French pastoral life in and amongst the mountain of curls balanced on top of her head. Had her reign lasted, she might have paid similar homage to the honourable gentlemen of the *Académie de Sciences* in Paris. Certainly her stylists could have created a splendid hair-do staging, in the manner of a nativity scene, a lecture hall with public performance of an experiment in progress, little figurines of the convening philosophers and stray bits of technology upheld by hairpins and nets.

One can only imagine the impact her entrance might have had on the worthy gentlemen of the Academy. Behold and be bold: the excerpts in this volume can assist in picturing this make-believe event – a mere caricature of the decorative essence of experimental natural philosophy – and its many untold historical equivalents in real life.

Cheryce Kramer

SPRAT:

The History of the Royal Society

Thomas Sprat, *The History of the Royal Society of London for the Improving of Natural Knowledge* (London: J. Martyn, 1667). pp. 52–62, 67–71.

As the official history of an institution, Thomas Sprat's *History of the Royal Society* is unusual in having been published just seven years after the founding of the Society itself. It was still early days for the Society although Sprat presented it as 'now so well establish'd'. In his prefatory ode, Abraham Cowley alluded to the fact the Society was still in its infancy: 'None e're but Hercules and you could be/ At five years Age worthy a History' ('To the Royal Society', ll. 171–2). Cowley took 1662 as the Society's inaugural year, when it received its royal charter. With his flattering comparison of the Royal Society to Hercules, Cowley represented natural philosophers as heroes, a rhetorical strategy adopted by later popularizers of the new science.

Although 1667 might have appeared early for an official history of the institution, Sprat had begun his work in 1663, with plans for publication that year which were deferred. The correspondence of distinguished members of the Society between 1663 and 1664 gives an indication of the genesis of the *History*. On 24 November 1664, the Society's first secretary Henry Oldenburg wrote to Robert Boyle to inform him that 'Mr. Sprat intends to begin next week to print the History of our Institution, which hath been perused by lord Brouncker, Sir R. Moray, Dr. Wilkins, Mr. Evelyn, and others' (Thomas Birch (ed.), *The Works of the Honourable Robert Boyle*, 6 vols (London, 1772), Vol. 6, p. 180). Lord Brouncker was the first president of the Society, John Evelyn and Sir Robert Moray were distinguished founder members, and John Wilkins, Master of Wadham College, Oxford, was Sprat's patron and had proposed his election to the Society in 1663. Sprat was then twenty-eight years old and no scientist but rather a versifier and man of letters. Some of the earliest meetings of the 'invisible college' (Birch, *Works of the Hon. Robert Boyle*, Vol. 1, p. xxxiv), which preceded the Royal Society, had been held in Wilkins's rooms, attended by future founder members Christopher Wren, Dr Ralph Bathurst and Seth Ward. Sprat's *History* was the collaborative work of the most influential members the Society, exemplifying the Baconian ideal of co-operation embraced by the Society.

Printing of the *History* seems to have started towards the end of 1664 but was not completed because of the catastrophes of the next two years: the outbreak of plague in 1665 and the Great Fire of 1666. In the interim Sprat published his *Observations on Monsieur de Sorbier's Voyage into England* (1665), which defended the activities of the Royal Society in a witty critique of a French portrait of English manners. It was dedicated to Wren, whom Sprat would celebrate in the *History* as the model natural philosopher.

Sprat's *History* set the agenda for the new science. The primacy of experiment, the importance of utility and the potential for achievement of modern philosophy were keynotes in this programme. Sprat expressed extraordinary expectations. Since the Royal Society had been founded in 'the wonderful pacifick year, 1660 [...] when our Country was freed from confusion, and slavery: So it may, in its progress, redeem the minds of Men, from obscurity, uncertainty, and bondage'. The *History* is, as Michael Hunter observes, 'as much a confession of faith as a factual record' (Michael Hunter, *Science and Society in Restoration England* (Cambridge: Cambridge University Press, 1981), p. 29).

By 1663, the Society had already attracted hostile criticism which the Fellows sought to defuse by means of the *History*. In the event it provoked further controversy. The difficulty of defining the identity of the new man of science dogged the Society's efforts to establish good relations with the public, especially the merchant community. Although Sprat enthused about the comprehensive nature of the membership, the Society resembled a gentleman's club: the gentleman, 'free, and unconfin'd', was the model for the natural philosopher.

As a public relations exercise, the *History* was not as successful as more practical books published by means of the Society's imprimatur, the two most important being Evelyn's *Sylva, or A Discourse of Forest-trees, and the Propagation of Timber* (1664) and Robert Hooke's impressively illustrated *Micrographia* (1665). Yet Sprat's *History* identified the single issue that would shape the ideology of science over the next century and would unite scientists. What really mattered was the power to manipulate nature and so to 'obtain a Dominion over Things'.

THE
HISTORY
OF THE
ROYAL SOCIETY.

The SECOND PART.

Hus I am, at length, arriv'd at the second Part of my Method, The *Narration* it self. This I shall divide into three Periods of Time, according to the several Degrees of the *preparation*, *growth*, and *compleat Constitution* of the *Royal Society*.

The First shall consist of the *first occasions* of this Model, and the *Men*, who first devis'd to put it in execution: and shall end, where they began to make it a form'd, and *Regular Assembly*.

The Second shall trace out their *first attempts*, till they receiv'd the publick assistance of *Royal Authority*.

The Third shall deliver, what they *have done*, since they were made a *Royal Corporation*.

It may seem perhaps, that in passing through the first of these, I go too far back, and treat of things, that may appear to be of too private, and Domestick concernment, to be spoken in this publick way. But if this *Enterprise*, which is now so well establish'd, shall be hereafter advantageous to Mankind (as I make no scruple to foretel, that it will)

it

it is but juſt, that future times ſhould hear the *names*, of its firſt *Promoters* : That they may be able to render particular thanks to them, who firſt conceiv'd it in their minds, and practis'd ſome little draught of it long ago. And beſides, I never yet ſaw an Hiſtorian that was cleer from all Affections: that, it may be, were not ſo much to be call'd *Integrity*, as a ſtoical *inſenſibility* : Nor can I, more then others, reſiſt my inclinations, which ſtrongly force me to mention that, which will be for the honor of that place, where I receiv'd a great part of my Education. It was therefore, ſome ſpace after the end of the Civil Wars at *Oxford*, in *Dr. Wilkins* his Lodgings, in *Wadham College*, which was then the place of Reſort for Vertuous, and Learned Men, that the firſt meetings were made, which laid the foundation of all this that follow'd. The *Univerſity* had, at that time, many Members of its own, who had begun a *free way* of reaſoning ; and was alſo frequented by ſome *Gentlemen*, of Philoſophical Minds, whom the misfortunes of the Kingdom, and the ſecurity and eaſe of a retirement amongſt Gown-men, had drawn thither.

Sect. II.
The Meet-
ings at Ox-
ford.

Their firſt purpoſe was no more, then onely the ſatisfaction of breathing a freer air, and of converſing in quiet one with another, without being ingag'd in the paſſions, and madneſs of that diſmal Age. And from the Inſtitution of that *Aſſembly*, it had been enough, if no other advantage had come, but this: That by this means there was a race of yong Men provided, againſt the next Age, whoſe minds receiving from them, their firſt Impreſſions of *ſober* and *generous knowledge*, were invincibly arm'd againſt all the inchantments of *Enthuſiaſm*. But what is more, I may venture

venture to affirm, that it was in good meaſure, by the influence, which theſe Gentlemen had over the reſt, that the *Univerſity* it ſelf, or at leaſt, any part of its Diſcipline, and Order, was ſav'd from ruine. And from hence we may conclude, that the ſame Men have now no intention, of ſweeping away all the honor of Antiquity in this their new Deſign: ſeeing they imploy'd ſo much of their labor, and prudence, in preſerving that *moſt venerable Seat* of antient Learning, when their ſhrinking from its defence, would have been the ſpeedieſt way to have deſtroy'd it. For the Truth of this, I dare appeal to all unintereſſed men, who knew the Temper of that place ; and eſpecially to thoſe who were my own contemporaries there: of whom I can name very many, whom the happy reſtoration of the Kingdom's peace, found as well inclin'd, to ſerve their *Prince*, and the *Church*, as if they had been bred up in the moſt proſperous condition of their Country. This was undoubtedly ſo. Nor indeed could it be otherwiſe: for ſuch *ſpiritual Frenſies*, which did then bear Rule, can never ſtand long, before a cleer, and a *deep skill* in *Nature*. It is almoſt impoſſible, that they, who converſe much with the ſubtilty of *things*, ſhould be deluded by ſuch *thick deceits*. There is but one better charm in the world, then *Real Philoſophy*, to allay the impulſes of the *falſe ſpirit*: and that is, the bleſſed preſence, and aſſiſtance of the *True*.

Nor were the good effects of this converſation, onely confin'd to *Oxford*: But they have made themſelves known in their printed Works, both in our own, and in the learned Language: which have much conduc'd to the Fame of our Nation *abroad*, and to the ſpreading of profitable Light, *at home*. This I
truſt

truſt, will be univerſally acknowledg'd, when I ſhall
have nam'd the Men.   The principal, and moſt con-
ſtant of them, were Doctor *Seth Ward*, the preſent
Lord Biſhop of *Exeter*, Mr. *Boyl*, Dr. *Wilkins*, Sir
William Petty, Mr. *Mathew Wren*, Dr. *Wallis*, Dr. *God-
dard*, Dr. *Willis*, Dr. *Bathurſt*, Dr. *Chriſtopher Wren*,
Mr. *Rook:* beſides ſeveral others, who joyn'd themſelves to them, upon occaſions. Now I have produc'd
their Names, I am a little at a ſtand, how to deal with
them.   For, if I ſhould ſay what they deſerve; I fear
it would be intepreted flatt'ry, inſteed of juſtice.
And yet I have now lying in my ſight, the example
of an *Elegant Book*, which I have profeſs'd to admire:
whoſe Author ſticks not, to make large Panegyricks,
on the Members of that *Aſſembly*, whoſe *Relation* he
Writes.   But this Preſident is not to be follow'd by
a *yong Man*; who ought to be more jealous of publick cenſure, and is not enough confirm'd in the good
liking of the world; to think, that he has ſuch a
weighty, and difficult work, as the making of Characters, committed to him.   I will therefore paſs by
their praiſes in ſilence; though I believe, that what I
might ſay of them, would be generally confeſs'd:
and that if any ingenuous man, who knows them, or
their writings, ſhould contradict me, he would alſo
go neer to gainſay himſelf, and to retract the ap-
plauſes, which he had ſometime, or other, beſtow'd
upon them.
   For ſuch a candid, and unpaſſionate company, as
that was, and for ſuch a gloomy ſeaſon, what could
have been a fitter Subject to pitch upon, then *Natural Philoſophy?* To have been always toſſing about
ſome *Theological queſtion*, would have been, to have
made that their private diverſion, the exceſs of
                                                    which

which they themselves diflik'd in the publick.: To have been eternally mufing on *Civil bufinefs*, and the diftreffes of their Country, was too melancholy a reflexion: It was *Nature* alone, which could pleafantly entertain them, in that eftate. The contemplation of that, draws our minds off from paft, or prefent misfortunes, and makes them conquerers over things, in the greateft publick unhappinefs: while the confideration of *Men*, and *humane affairs*, may affect us, with a thoufand various difquiets; *that* never feparates us into mortal Factions; *that* gives us room to differ, without animofity; and permits us, to raife contrary imaginations upon it, without any danger of a *Civil War*.

Their *meetings* were as frequent, as their affairs permitted: their proceedings rather by action, then difcourfe; cheifly attending fome particular Trials, in *Chymiftry*, or *Mechanicks*: they had no Rules nor Method fix'd: their intention was more, to communicate to each other, their difcoveries, which they could make in fo narrow a compafs, than an united, conftant, or regular inquifition. And me thinks, their conftitution did bear fome refemblance, to the *Academy* lately begun at *Paris*: where they have at laft turn'd their thoughts, from *Words*, to experimental *Philofophy*, and perhaps in imitation of the *Royal Society*. Their manner likewife, is to affemble in a private houfe, to reafon freely upon the works of Nature; to pafs Conjectures, and propofe Problems, on any Mathematical, or Philofophical Matter, which comes in their way. And this is an Omen, on which I will build fome hope, that as they agree with us in what was done at *Oxford*, fo they will go on farther, and come by the fame degrees, to erect

another

another *Royal Society* in *France*. I promise for these Gentlemen here (so well I know the generosity of their Design) that they will be most ready to accept their assistance. To them, and to all the Learned World besides, they call for aid. No difference of *Country*, *Interest*, or profession of *Religion*, will make them backward from taking, or affording help in this enterprize. And indeed all *Europe* at this time, have two general Wars, which they ought in honor to make: The one a *holy*, the other a *Philosophical*: The one against the common Enemy of *Christendom*, the other also against powerful, and barbarous Foes, that have not been fully subdu'd almost these six thousand years, *Ignorance*, and *False Opinions*. Against these, it becomes us, to go forth in one common expedition: All civil Nations joyning their *Armies* against the one, and their *Reason* against the other; without any petty contentions, about privileges, or precedence.

Sect. III.
Their first meetings at London.

Thus they continued without any great Intermissions, till about the year 1658. But then being call'd away to several parts of the Nation, and the greatest number of them coming to *London*, they usually met at *Gresham* College, at the *Wednesdays*, and *Thursdays* Lectures of Dr. *Wren*, and Mr. *Rook*: where there joyn'd with them several eminent persons of their common acquaintance: The Lord *Viscount Brouncker*, the now Lord *Brereton*, Sir *Paul Neil*, Mr. *John Evelyn*, Mr. *Henshaw*, Mr. *Slingsby*, Dr. *Timothy Clark*, Dr. *Ent*, Mr. *Ball*, Mr. *Hill*, Dr. *Crone*: and divers other Gentlemen, whose inclinations lay the same way. This Custom was observ'd once, if not twice a week, in Term time; till they were scat-

H   t'red

t'red by the miferable diftractions of that Fatal year; till the continuance of their meetings there might have made them run the hazard of the fate of *Archimedes* : For then the place of their meeting was made a *Quarter* for *Soldiers*. But, (to make haft through thofe dreadful revolutions, which cannot be beheld upon Paper, without horror ; unlefs we remember, that they had this one happy effect, to open mens eies to look out for the true Remedy) upon this follow'd the *King's* Return ; and that, wrought by fuch an admirable chain of events, that if we either regard the *eafinefs*, or *fpeed*, or *bleffed iffue* of the Work ; it feems of it felf to contain variety, and pleafure enough, to make recompence, for the whole Twenty years Melancholy, that had gone before. This I leave to another kind of Hiftory to be defcrib'd. It fhall fuffice my purpofe, that Philofophy had its fhare, in the benefits of that glorious Action : For the *Royal Society* had its beginning in the wonderful pacifick year, 1660. So that, if any conjectures of good Fortune, from extraordinary *Nativities*, hold true ; we may prefage all happinefs to this undertaking. And I fhall here joyn my folemn wifhes, that as it began in that time, when our Country was freed from confufion, and flavery : So it may, in its progrefs, redeem the minds of Men, from obfcurity, uncertainty, and bondage.

Thefe Gentlemen therefore, finding the hearts of their Countrymen inlarg'd by their Joys, and fitted for any noble Propofition : and meeting with the concurrence of many Worthy Men, who, to their immortal Honor, had follow'd the King in his banifhment, Mr. *Erskins*, Sir *Robert Moray*, Sir *Gilbert Talbot*,

Sect. IV. The beginning of the Royal Society.

bot, &c. began now to imagine. some greater thing; and to bring out experimental knowledge, from the *retreats*, in which it had long hid it self, to take its part in the *Triumphs* of that universal Jubilee. And indeed Philosophy did very well deserve that Reward: having been always Loyal in the worst of times: For though the Kings enemies had gain'd all other advantages; though they had all the Garrisons, and Fleets, and Ammunitions, and Treasures, and Armies on their side: yet they could never, by all their Victories, bring over the Reason of Men to their Party.

While they were thus ord'ring their platform; there came forth a Treatise, which very much hasten'd its contrivance: and that was a Proposal by Master *Cowley*, of erecting a Philosophical College. The intent of it was, that in some place neer *London*, there should liberal Salaries be bestow'd, on a competent number of Learned Men, to whom should be committed the operations of Natural Experiments. This Model was every way practicable : unless perhaps, in two things, he did more consult the generosity of his own mind, than of other mens: the one was the *largeness of the Revenue*, with which he would have his College at first indow'd : the other, that he impos'd on his Operators, a Second task of great pains, the *Education of youth*.

The last of these is indeed a matter of great weight: The Reformation of which ought to be seriously examin'd by prudent Men. For it is an undeniable Truth, which is commonly said; that there would be need of fewer Laws, and less force to govern Men, if their Minds were rightly inform'd, and set strait, while they were yong, and pliable. But

H 2   perhaps

perhaps this labor is not fo proper, for Experimenters to undergo: For it would not only devour too much of their Time: but it would go neer, to make them a little more *magifterial* in Philofophy, then became them; by being long accuftom'd to command the opinions, and direct the manners, of their Scholars. And as to the other particular, the large eftate, which he requir'd to the maintenance of his College: It is evident, that it is fo difficult a thing, to draw men in to be willing to divert an antient Revenue, which had long run in another ftream, or to contribute out of their own purfes, to the fupporting of any new Defign, while it fhews nothing but promifes, and hopes: that, in fuch cafes, it were (it may be) more advifable, to begin upon a fmall ftock, and fo to rife by degrees; then to profefs great things at firft, and to exact too much benevolence, all in one lump together. However, it was not the excellent Author's fault, that he thought better of the Age, then it did deferve. His purpofe in it was like himfelf, full of honor, and goodnefs: moft of the other particulars of his draught, the *Royal Society* is now putting in practice.

I come now to the Second Period of my Narration; wherein I promis'd, to give an account of what they did, till they were publickly own'd, incourag'd, and confirm'd by Royal Favor. And I truft, that I fhall here produce many things, which will prove their attempts to be worthy of all Mens incouragement: though what was perform'd in this interval, may be rather ftyl'd the *Temporary Scaffold* about the building, then the *Frame it felf*. But in my entrance upon this Part, being come to the top of the Hill, I begin to tremble, and to apprehend the greatnefs of

my

my Subject. For I perceive that I have led my Readers Minds on, by fo long, and fo confident a Speech, to expect fome wonderful Model, which fhall far exceed all the former, that I have acknowledg'd to have been imperfect. Now, though this were really fo, as I believe it is ; yet I queftion, how it will look, after it has been disfigur'd by my unskilful hands. But the danger of this ought to have deterr'd me in the beginning. It is now too late to look back ; and I can only apply my felf to that *good Nature*, which a *Great Man* has obferv'd to be fo peculiar to our *Nation*, that there is fcarce an expreffion to fignifie it, in any other Language. To this I muft flye for fuccor, and moft affectionately intreat my Countrymen, that they would interpret my failings to be onely errors of obedience to fome, whofe commands, or defires, I could not refift : and that they would take the meafure of the *Royal Society*, not fo much from my lame defcription of it ; as from the honor, and reputation, of many of thofe Men, of whom it is compos'd.

Sect. V.
A model of their whole defign.

I will here, in the firft place, contract into few Words, the whole *fumme* of their *Refolutions* ; which I fhall often have occafion, to touch upon in *parcels*. Their purpofe is, in fhort, to make faithful *Records*, of all the Works of *Nature*, or *Art*, which can come within their reach : that fo the prefent Age, and pofterity, may be able to put a mark on the Errors, which have been ftrengthned by long prefcription : to reftore the Truths, that have lain neglected : to pufh on thofe, which are already known, to more various ufes : and to make the way more paffable, to what remains unreveal'd. This is the compafs of their
Defign.

Defign. And to accomplifh this, they have indeavor'd, to feparate the knowledge of *Nature*, from the colours of *Rhetorick*, the devices of *Fancy*, or the delightful deceit of *Fables*. They have labor'd to inlarge it, from being confin'd to the cuftody of a few; or from fervitude to private interefts. They have ftriven to preferve it from being over-prefs'd by a confus'd heap of vain, and ufelefs particulars; or from being ftraitned and bounded too much up by General Doctrines. They have try'd, to put-it into a condition of perpetual increafing; by fettling an inviolable correfpondence between the hand, and the brain. They have ftudi'd, to make it, not onely an Enterprife of one feafon, or of fome lucky opportunity; but a bufinefs of time; a fteddy, a lafting, a popular, an uninterrupted Work. They have attempted, to free it from the Artifice, and Humors, and Paffions of Sects; tô render it an Inftrument, whereby Mankind may obtain a Dominion over *Things*, and not onely over one anothers *Judgements*. And laftly, they have begun to eftablifh thefe Reformations in Philofophy, not fo much, by any folemnity of Laws, or oftentation of Ceremonies, as by folid Practice, and examples: not, by a glorious pomp of Words; but by the filent, effectual, and unanfwerable Arguments of real Productions.

This will more fully appear, by what I am to fay on thefe four particulars, which fhall make up this part of my Relation, the *Qualifications* of their *Members:* the *manner* of their *Inquiry:* their *weekly Affemblies:* and their *way* of *Regiftring.*

Sect. VII. But, though the *Society* entertains very many men
It consists of *particular Professions*; yet the farr greater Number
chiefly of are *Gentlemen*, free, and unconfin'd. By the help of
Gentlemen. this, there was hopefull Provision made against *two
corruptions* of Learning, which have been long complain'd of, but never remov'd : The *one*, that *Knowledge* still degenerates to consult *present profit* too soon;
the *other*, that *Philosophers* have bin always *Masters*, &
Scholars; some imposing, & all the other submitting;
and not as equal observers without dependence.
　　　The first of these may be call'd, the *marrying of Arts
The advan-* too soon*; and putting them to generation, before
tages of this. they come to be of Age; and has been the cause of
　　　　　　　　　　　　I 2　　　　　　　　much

much inconvenience. It weakens their ſtrength; It makes an unhappy diſproportion in their increaſe; while not the *beſt*, but the *moſt gainfull* of them floriſh: But above all, it diminiſhes that very profit for which men ſtrive. It buſies them about poſſeſſing ſome petty prize; while Nature it ſelf, with all its mighty Treaſures, ſlips from them: and ſo they are ſerv'd like ſome fooliſh Guards; who, while they were earneſt in picking up ſome ſmall Money, that the Priſoner drop'd out of his Pocket, let the Priſoner himſelf eſcape, from whom they might have got a great randſom. This is eaſily declam'd againſt, but moſt difficult to be hindred. If any caution will ſerve, it muſt be this; to commit the Work to the care of ſuch men, who, by the freedom of their education the plenty of their eſtates, and the uſual generoſity of Noble Bloud, may be well ſuppo'd to be moſt averſe from ſuch ſordid conſiderations.

The ſecond Error, wich is hereby endeavour'd to be remedied, is, that the Seats of Knowledg, have been for the moſt part heretofore, not *Laboratories*, as they ought to be; but onely *Scholes*, where ſome have *taught*, and all the reſt *ſubſcrib'd*. The conſequences of this are very miſchievous. For firſt, as many *Learners* as there are, ſo many hands, and brains may ſtill be reckon'd upon, as uſeleſs. It being onely the *Maſter's* part, to examine, and obſerve; and the Diſciples, to ſubmit with ſilence, to what they conclude. But beſides this, the very inequality of the Titles of *Teachers*, and *Scholars*, does very much ſuppreſs, and tame mens Spirits; which though it ſhould be proper for Diſcipline and Education; yet is by no means conſiſtent with a free Philoſophical Conſultation. It is undoubtedly true; that ſcarce any man's
                                                                    mind,

mind, is so capable of *thinking strongly*, in the presence of one, whom he *fears* and *reverences*; as he is, when that restraint is taken off. And this is to be found, not only in these weightier matters; but also (to give a lighter instance) in the Arts of *Discourse*, & *raillery* themselves. For we have often seen men of bold tempers, that have over-aw'd and govern'd the Wit of most Companies; to have been disturb'd, and dumb, & bashful as children, when some other man has been near, who us'd to out-talk them. Such a kind of natural soveraignty there is, in some mens minds over others: which must needs be farr greater, when it is advanc'd by long use, & the venerable name of a *Master*. I shall only mention one prejudice more, & that is this; That from this onely teaching, and learning, there does not onely follow a continuance, but an increase of the yoak upon our Reasons. For those who take their opinions from others Rules, are commonly stricter Imposers upon their Scholars, than their own Authors were on them, or than the first Inventors of things themselves are upon others. Whatever the cause of this be; whether the first men are made meek, and gentle, by their long search, and by better understanding all the difficulties of Knowledg; while those that learn afterwards, onely hastily catching things in small *Systems*, are soon satisfy'd, before they have broken their pride, & so become more imperious: or, whether it arises from hence, that the same *meanness of Soul*, which made them bound their thoughts by others Precepts, makes them also *insolent* to their inferiors; as we always find *cowards* the most *cruel*: or whatever other cause may be alleg'd; the observation is certain, that the *successors* are usually more positive, and Tyrannical, than the *beginners* of Sects.

If

If then there can be any cure devis'd for this ; it muſt be no other, than to form an *Aſſembly* at one time, whoſe privileges ſhall be the ſame ; whoſe gain ſhall be in common ; whoſe *Members* were not brought up at the feet of each other. But after all, even this cannot be free from prevarication in all future Ages. So apt are ſome to diſtruſt, and others to confide too much in themſelves : ſo much ſweetneſs there is, in leading parties : ſo much pride, in following a Facti-on : ſuch various artifices there are, to enſnare mens *Paſſions*, and ſoon after their *Underſtandings*. All theſe hazards, and many more, are to be ſuppos'd ; which it *is* impoſſible, for mortal Wit, wholly to fore-ſee, much leſs to avoid. But yet we have leſs ground of jealouſie from this Inſtitution, than any other, not only, becauſe they only deal in matters of *Fact*, which are not ſo eaſily perverted ; but alſo upon ſecurity of the Inclinations of the greateſt part of the *Members* of the *Society* it ſelf. This, I hope, moſt men will ac-knowledg, and I will take the permiſſion, to ſay in general of them, that in all *paſt* and *preſent* times, I am confident, there can never be ſhewn, ſo great a Number of *Contemporaries*, in ſo narrow a ſpace of the World, that lov'd truth ſo zealouſly ; ſought it ſo conſtantly ; and upon whoſe labours, mankind might ſo freely rely. This I ſpeak, not out of Bravery to *Foreiners* (before whoſe eyes, I believe this negli-gent Diſcourſe will never appear) but to the learned Men of this *Nation*, who are better Judges of what I ſay. And this too, I dare affirm, in an *Age*, wherein I expect to be condemn'd of falſhood, or partiality, for this Character, which I have given. For ſo it happens, that we are now arriv'd at that exceſſive cenſuring humor, that he who takes upon him to commend any
thing,

thing, though never so worthy, will raise to himself farr more Enemies than Friends. And indeed this *sowrness* of *Criticism*, which now bears all down before it, is very injurious to the honour of our Countrey. For by despising men, for not being absolutely excellent; we keep them from being so : while *admonitions*, join'd with *praises*; and *reproofs*, with *directions*; would quickly bring all things to a higher perfection. But the rudeness of such *Criticks*, I do not so much regard;as the objections of soberer men, who have a real good will to the promotion of this design,and yet may be a little dissatisfy'd in this place. For here especially they may doubt of two things. The first,whether the *Royal Society*,being so numerous as it is, will not in short time be diverted from its primitive purpose;seeing there wil be scarce enough men of Philosophical temper always found, to fill it up ; and then others will crowd in, who have not the same bent of mind ; and so the whole business will insensibly be made,rather a matter of noise and pomp,than of real benefit ? The second, Whether their number being so large, will not afright private men, from imparting many profitable secrets to them ; left they should thereby become common, and so they be depriv'd of the gain, which else they might be sure of, if they kept them to themselvs.

HOOKE:

'The Present State of Natural Philosophy'

Robert Hooke, 'The Present State of Natural Philosophy' in *The Posthumous Works of Robert Hooke* (London: R. Waller, 1705), pp. 3–7, 19–21.

This is one of Hooke's papers left, after his death, to Richard Waller, Fellow of the Royal Society. Waller published it in a volume of miscellaneous papers prefaced by a biography celebrating Hooke as 'one of the greatest Promoters of Experimental Natural Knowledge', but also describing his character as 'Melancholy, Mistrustful and Jealous' (Richard Waller (ed.), *The Posthumous Works of Robert Hooke* (London 1705), p. i, p. xxvii). The other manuscripts in Waller's edition consist of lectures and presentations given to the Royal Society on a diverse range of topics: light, comets, earthquakes, navigation and astronomy.

Hooke's first salaried position at the Royal Society was a lectureship set up in 1664, from which he earned 50*l.* a year. The following year he was given rooms at Gresham College and earned an extra 30*l.* a year as Curator of Experiments. His duties included looking after the library and cataloguing the repository. 'The Present State of Natural Philosophy', written about 1668, stemmed partly from Hooke's duties as cataloguer and possibly originated as lectures. It may also have been work-in-progress relating to Hooke's plans to write a discourse on 'the manner of compiling a Natural and Artificial History' (Robert Hooke, *Micrographia* (London, 1665), Preface).

Hooke was a professional in a world of gentlemanly amateurs. Early in his career, he was employed by Wren as an architect and surveyor. Afterwards he became technical assistant to Boyle in his Oxford laboratory. Together they developed the famous air-pump. The Fellows of the Royal Society soon saw its public relations potential and arranged Hooke's release from Boyle's employment so that he could perform demonstrations for the King and foreign dignitaries. Steven Shapin has pointed out how, in the Preface to his *Micrographia*, Hooke 'tellingly placed himself in a condition riven with social tension and ambiguity', identifying himself as 'a master of technicians and technician of masters' (Steven Shapin, 'Who was Robert Hooke?' in Michael Hunter and Simon Schaffer (eds), *Robert Hooke. New Studies* (Woodbridge: Boydell Press, 1989), p. 264). John Aubrey called him 'the greatest

Mechanick this day in the World' (Oliver Lawson Dick (ed.), *Aubrey's 'Brief Lives'*, 3rd edn (London: Secker and Warburg, 1958), p. 165). Nevertheless his professionalism precluded him from the category of natural philosopher as defined and exemplified by Robert Boyle. In his *Christian Virtuoso* (1690), Boyle would describe his ideal experimental philosopher as nobly above all interest in material rewards. In the second extract below, Hooke seems to acknowledge his exclusion from his own criteria for a natural philosopher: 'Besides, there is much of Expence requisite, which every one cannot so well bear, that may perhaps be otherwise fit for this Employment'.

What is remarkable about Hooke's list of 'requisites' is his representation of the natural philosopher as an explorer. This is one of the first examples of what Larry Stewart calls the 'myth of the scientist as a man of adventure' (Larry Stewart, *The Rise of Public Science* (Cambridge: Cambridge University Press, 1992), p. xvi). Hooke compares his ideal natural philosopher to the greatest explorer, Columbus, describing philosophical enquiry as a voyage of discovery. In line with the Royal Society's gentlemanly ethic, Hooke's comparison dwells on method rather than rewards. Like Columbus, the natural philosopher needs a good 'Design' which he should carry out in a heroic manner, despite all obstacles. Hooke's use of analogy and narrative links him with Sprat in his attempts to broaden the appeal of the new science.

One of Sprat's more extreme claims in his *History* was that 'the True Natural Philosophy' should chiefly be intended for the use of 'Mechanicks, and Artificers' (Thomas Sprat, *The History of the Royal Society* (London, 1667), p. 117). In the second extract below, Hooke's presentation of nature as mechanical develops ideas from *Micrographia*, with its description of 'that greater machine the pristine vegetable' (Hooke, *Micrographia*, p. 134). In both works, the secret 'Operations of Nature' are compared to the motions of a watch. As part of his quest to discover longitude, Hooke developed the spring-balance watch. This invention led to an acrimonious dispute over priority with Dutch scientist Christian Huygens, which resulted in Hooke's increasing secretiveness, contrary to Baconian principles of openness. Hooke's rifts with Huygens, Oldenburg, Newton and Hevelius might have appeared ungentlemanly. Yet the Society relied on practical men like Hooke, without whom the discoveries of the new science could not have been transmitted to the wider public.

FIRST GENERAL.

The Present State of Natural Philosophy, and wherein it is deficient.

THE Business of Philosophy is to find out a perfect Knowledge *First General* of the Nature and Proprieties of Bodies, and of the Causes of Natural Productions, and this Knowledge is not barely acquir'd for it self, but in order to the inabling a Man to understand how by the joyning of fit Agents to Patients according to the Orders, Laws, Times and Methods of Nature, he may be able to produce and bring to pass such Effects, as may very much conduce to his well being in this World, both for *satisfying his Desires*, and the relieving of his *Necessities*: And for advancing his State above the common Condition of Men, and make him able to excel them as much, almost, as they do Brutes or Ideots.

Now though there have been many Men, in divers Ages of the World, which *The Present* seem to have had some confus'd and imperfect Conception of this Idea of the *State of Na-* Business of Philosophy, and accordingly seem to have had some Aims and De-*tural Philoso-* signs towards the attaining of their propos'd end; yet having not a right Un-*phy* derstanding of the chief end, and failing much more in the Knowledge of the Means, or the manner of making use of them, they have generally left Philosophical Knowledge almost in the Condition they found it. Without making any considerable Increase or Addition to it. Whence this kind of Knowledge has been very little promoted ever since the very first times we have had any History of it: And though it has always made a fair shew of flourishing, yet upon Examination, it has been found to yield Leaves instead of sound Fruit, to be a Knowledge very confus'd and imperfect, and very insignificant as to the inabling a Man to practise or operate by it.

This seems to have proceeded from divers Causes, as

First, from the Unskilfulness of the Inventors and Founders of it, who seem to have many ways contributed thereto.

1. First in that they had not a true idea of the Design and thing it self, their *The Reasons of* Aims were low and mean, and reacht but at small things, such as the giving the *the Deficiency* Explication of things in hard words, which might serve to amuse their Auditors, *of Natural Phi-* and to raise some Esteem of themselves amongst them, scarce ever thinking, *losophy.* I. *from the* much less indeavouring to find out the true Nature and Proprieties of Bodies; *first Inventors* what the inward Texture and Constitution of them is, and what the Internal *3 Ways.* Motions, Powers and Energies are, and how they may be made use of for producing such Changes and Transformations of Bodies from one thing to another as is desired.

2. Next in that they were as ignorant of the true *means* of attaining it, as they were of the Knowledge of the End. Some esteem indeed we find them to have had of *Natural History*, and some Imagination they had that it was conducive to Natural Knowledge, but what History was requisite, they neither had, or indeed so much as knew, for what we find in *Aristotle*, *Pliny*, and others called by that Name is so uncertain and superficial, taking notice only of some slight and obvious things, and those so unaccurately, as makes them signify but little; but as for the more subtile Examinations of Natural Bodies, by Dissections, Experiments, or Mechanical Tryals, we find them not to mention them as needful, much less to have practised them. Nor can I perceive that they had any Affection or Industry for Experiments, much less for such as ought to be vigorously prosecuted with Care and Judgment: Nor do they seem to have had that Strictness and Accurateness as is requisite in setting down or registring those things which their Writings contain, but good and indifferent

and

and ftark naught àre without Diftinction mixt together, true and probable and falfe are all alike dignified, nor are they fo accurate in their Defcriptions, even of not common things that they help us with; but a great part of them we find to be a needlefs infifting upon the outward Shape and Figure, or Beauty, and the like, or elfe of fome Magical and Superftitious Effects Producible by it feeming to aim at creating Pleafure, and Divertifement or Admiration and Wonder, and not of fuch a Knowledge of Bodies as might tend to Practice.

3. *Thirdly*, In that, as they knew not the means, fo neither did they the *manner* of making ufe of them, in which Particular we may find them to be much more to feek than in knowing what Materials were requifite. Their Method herein indeed was moft prepofterous and very pernicious, for firft we find them much inclin'd to a Belief of implanted Notions, at leaft in their Practice, though fome of them affirm, *Nihil effe in intellectu quod non fuit prius in fenfu,* yet upon the whole, we may find that in their manner of proceeding they did quite otherwife. From a very few uncertain Hiftories they ufually rais'd the moft general Deductions, and from them though never fo imperfect, would needs prefcribe Laws to the Univerfe and Nature it felf. In this they were very fupercilious, and very angry to be contradicted, and maintained their Opinions more becaufe they had afferted them, than becaufe they were true, they ftudied more to gain Applaufe and make themfelves admired, or the Head of fome Sect, or the Author of fome ftrange Opinion, or the Oppofer of fome one already famous Doctrine, or the like, than to perfect their Knowledge, or to difcern the Secrets of Nature, or advance the active Power of Man over the Creatures. Nor was this all; but we may find them even to wreft thofe few Experiments and Obfervations they had read, or collected, and to endeavour rather to adapt them to their Hypothefis, than to regulate their Thoughts by them, efteeming their own Underftandings to be the Mine of all Science, and that by pertinacious ruminating, they could thence produce the true Image and Picture of the Univerfe.

II. *From the Sectators from feveral Caufes.* Nor was this the only ill Fortune of true Science, but there is fomewhat more behind. A Second Reafon therefore why Philofophy has not increafed is to be afcribed to the Sectators of thefe Theories, who at beft have not improv'd it to a nearer Approach to Truth, but have rather made it worfe than better, and more obfcure by Interpretation. The Reafon of which feems to be from thefe Particulars.

1.　　From their manner of Inftitution, being bred up with a Prejudice againft the fearch of Truth elfewhere, than in Books thereby chained up by the imbib'd Principles and Dictates of their Teachers, and their Minds habituated to a loathing of any thing that offered it felf as a Novelty or new Difcovery, and upon that account whether true or falfe rejected. This proceeded partly in the 2d. Place.

2.　　From an Imagination they have that Arts are already come to their higheft pitch of Perfection, and that therefore 'tis in vain to endeavour to find out that by the moft difficult way, which might be obtained more eafily and fully out of Books.
　　This Averfion alfo to Inquiries and New Difcoveries proceeded partly alfo in the 3d. Place.

3.　　From a too great Reverence and Efteem for the Writings of the Ancients, as fuppofing thofe to be the greateft Men for Wifdom and Knowledge, and thofe Ages wherein they liv'd to be the elder Times of the World; and therefore they accounted it a great piece of Folly, and a kind of Impiety to contradict, or endeavour to be wifer than their Fore-fathers.
　　Hence proceeded a *Fourth* Impediment, namely,

4.　　From their following the fame Way and Method in illuftrating or endeavouring to underftand their Writings, that the Authors themfelves did in compofing them: And therefore 'tis not to be expected that Water fhould rife higher than the Fountain Head from whence it came; or that greater and more notable Effects fhould be produced by any other than an extraordinary Method. For the Logick or way of Ratiocination they have made ufe of, hath been rather an Hindrance than a Furtherance. For neither is the way of *Syllogifing* as it ought nor

nor are their firſt *Notions* ſtated aright, and conſequently their Axioms and Concluſions cannot be better than the Grounds and Principles from which they were rais'd ; ſo that it does not only not promote real Knowledge, but is inju-rious to it, by begetting an Opinion of Science where there is no ſuch thing.

5*ly*, From their miſtaken Aim or Scope, which is an indeavour by Nice Diſtin-ctions to wreſt over all the Obſervations they chance to ſtumble upon, and make them correſpondent with their already believ'd *Theory* ; inſtead of an in-deavour to rectify and regulate thoſe ſo receiv'd Theories by thoſe Intimations, which careful and accurate Obſervations would afford.

6*ly*, Such as have a little varied from the receiv'd Opinions, the Alteration has been rather for the bringing in ſome one New Hypotheſis or Opinion of their own inſtead of the Old, and not for the renewing or Amending the whole.

7*ly*, And ſome that have indeavoured to make uſe of Arguments rais'd from the Experiments, and Obſervations, have been ſo confounded with them, for want of a Method of proceeding ; that it has been to little purpoſe, ſave the putting of Men upon new Tryals, whereby perhaps ſome uſeful Experiment has been light on, and thereby ſome latent Error in the former Theories detected. For neither having a true Idea of making Obſervations and Experiments, nor a con-venient way of ordering, nor a right Method of uſing them, the greater num-ber of them they have, the more are they confounded ; for 'tis not the Multi-tude of Experiments nor the Excellency of them, nor is it indeed the ſubtile and curious Ratiocinations of an accompliſht Mind, nor the Endeavours of a Multitude of ſuch joyned together, that will be able to do any great matter in this Deſign ; for ſuch Endeavours do at beſt but raiſe new Probabilities, and conſequently augment Diſputes on the one hand, and new Tryals on the other, and all to as little purpoſe as 'twould be to attempt to find ſome extreamly difficult Geometrical Problem by the Ruler and Compaſs, without the Know-ledge or Help of Geometrical Algebra.

For where the Examination and Compariſon of ſo great a Number of Parti-culars is requiſite, and where the Proceſs is long, and the Informations but thinly ſcatter'd, and thoſe alſo in the Dark, 'tis not to be expected from the moſt ſubtile Wit, that the whole Operation ſhould be only performed by the Strength of its Memory, and the Activity of its Ratiocination, though each of them in the greateſt pitch of Perfection ; much leſs can it be hoped from Endeavours, that want either of theſe Accompliſhments. And how uſual 'tis for one of theſe to be defective where the other prevails, may be ſufficiently evident from the al-moſt Proverbial Saying, that good Wits have ill Memories. Some things indeed have been by lucky Inquirers light on by chance, but thoſe ſo few and ſeldom, that 'twas not abſurd in *Pythagoras* to offer up a *Hecatomb* for a ſingle Invention in Geometry. I do not here with the Scepticks affirm, that nothing is or can be known, my Deſign is quite another thing ; their end only in deny-ing any thing to be knowable, ſeems to be Diſpute, and tends to Ignorance and Lazineſs, mine on the other ſide ſuppoſes all things as poſſible to be known, and accordingly ſtudies and conſiders of the Means that ſeem to tend to that end, and rouſes up the deceiv'd Faculties to ſeek a Means of recovering themſelves out of their Thraldom, and of improving, rectifying and inlarging their Powers. They affirm poſitively nothing can be known any way, I only that many more things may be diſcover'd by this Method I here propound, than are already known.

Nor is the State of Philoſophy as yet very much improved by our Modern Writers, who have endeavour'd to illuſtrate or piece up the old, by adding ſome Placits of their own : There are yet many Impediments to be removed, and many Helps to be ſupplied before any very great Increaſe in Knowledge is to be expected. It may be queſtioned whether piecing or mending will ſerve the turn, or whether there muſt not be a new Foundation laid on the Informa-tions of our Senſes, and more ſtrictly examined and ſurveyed by accurate and judicious Experiments and Obſervations. That which hath had the Cultivation of many Hundreds of Years, and by divers very acute Men in all Ages, and yet as to the Inquiry after the Cauſes of Natural Efficients, has made ſo little, if any Progreſs at all, cannot with any Probability be imagined to afford a Me-thod ſufficient for this Inquiry. I do not here altogether reject *Logick*, or the

III. Philoſophy hitherto not much improved by the Mo-derns, and the Reaſons why.

C   way

way of Ratiocination already known; as a thing of no ufe. It has its peculiar Excellencies and Ufes, in ordinary Difcourfe and Converfation: And affords fome Helps to fome kinds of Invention, efpecially of Arguments, as well
as to the Memory, by its Method: It affords copious Matter for Difputes as
well for, as againft the Truth, and teaches how to folve, as well as how to
make a fallacious Affertion. It fhews how the Modes of fpeaking and arguing may be reduced to certain Rules, and how each compleat Sentence may be
trifected into its conftituent Parts, and how thofe may be various ways fhuffl'd
and chang'd, and likewife on occafion alfo how each of thefe bigger may be divided into three lefs. But as to the Inquiry into Natural Operations, what are
the Kinds of fecret and fubtile Actors, and what the abftrufe and hidden Inftruments and Engines there made ufe of, may be; It feems not, to me, as yet at
all adapted and wholly deficient. For 'tis not to be expected from the Accom-
plifhments the Creator has endowed Man withal, that he fhould be able to
leap, from a few particular Informations of his Senfes, and thofe very fuperficial at beft, and for the moft part fallacious, to the general Knowledge of
Univerfals or abftracted Natures, and thence be able, as out of an inexhauftable
Fountain, to draw out a perfect Knowledge of all Particulars, to deduce the
Caufes of all Effects and Actions from this or that Axiome or Sentence, and as
it were intuitively, to know what Nature does or is capable of effecting: And
after what manner and Method fhe works; and yet that Method fuppofes little
lefs: Man's Memory feems very fhallow and infirm, and fo is very prone to
forget many Circumftances, befides it cannot fo well propound all it does remember, to be examin'd at once by the Judgment; but prefers fome things firft
in order, before others, and fome things with more Vehemence and greater concern, and accordingly the Underftanding is more apt to be fway'd to this or
that hand, according as it is more affected or preft by this or that Inftance,
and is very liable to overfee fome confiderable Paffages, or to neglect them;
and thence very apt to be feduc'd, in pronouncing pofitively for this or that
Opinion, efpecially being very prone to run into the affirmative way of judging,
and wanting Patience to follow and profecute the negative way of Inquiry, by
Rejection of Difagreeing Natures.

Farther, a great Caufe why Philofophy has not formerly or of late increafed,
is becaufe the greateft part of Learned Men have applied themfelves to other
Studies, Divinity, Law, Phyfick, &c. as being thofe ftanding Profeffions whereby Men of the moft liberal and ingenuous Education and Spirit might provide
for themfelves, and promote their Fortune in the World: Taking only a tran-
fient View of Natural Philofophy, in their Paffage to other things, thinking it
fufficient to be able to talk of it in the Phrafe of the School. Nor is it only fo
now, but it has been fo almoft in all Ages, fo that for about two Thoufand
Years, of which we have fome account in Hiftory, there is not above one quarter of that fpace wherein Men have been Philofophically given, and among
fuch as have been fo, feveral of them have been fo far disjoined by Time, Language, and Climate, by manner of Education, Manners, Opinions, and divers
other Prejudices, that it could not be expected it fhould make any confiderable
Progrefs: For either becaufe it feemed to promife little, Men for the moft part
have neglected it, or in thofe fhort fpaces of time in which it was fomewhat
more minded and look'd after, what from the want of Dowry belonging to
other liberal Profeffions, what from the Contefts of feveral Theorifts, and the
Defect of applying of it to fuch things as might be ufeful to Humane Life;
Men have been either difcouraged from the Study, or tired out in it.

Some other Courfe therefore muft be taken to promote the Search of Knowledge. Some other kind of Art for Inquiry than what hath been hitherto made
ufe of, muft be difcover'd; the Intellect is not to be fuffer'd to act without its
Helps, but is continually to be affifted by fome Method or Engine, which fhall
be as a Guide to regulate its Actions, fo as that it fhall not be able to act amifs:
Of this Engine, no Man except the incomparable *Verulam*, hath had any
Thoughts, and he indeed hath promoted it to a very good pitch; but there is
yet fomewhat more to be added, which he feem'd to want time to compleat.
By this, as by that Art of *Algebra* in Geometry, 'twill be very eafy to proceed in any Natural Inquiry, regularly and certainly: And indeed it may not
improperly

improperly be call'd a Philofophical Algebra, or an Art of directing the Mind in the fearch after Philofophical Truths, for as 'tis very hard for the moft acute Wit to find out any difficult Problem in Geometry, without the help of *Algebra* to direct and regulate the Acts of the Reafon in the Procefs from the Queftion to the *quæfitum*, and altogether as eafy for the meaneft Capacity acting by that Method to compleat and perfect it, fo will it be in the Inquiry after Natural Knowledge.

The greateft and moft accomplifht Wits for thefe many Ages have labour'd and fweat in thefe Inquiries, and yet they have not been able to bring forth any greater Effects than Probabilities: Whereas I cannot doubt but that if this Art be well profecuted and made ufe of, an ordinary Capacity with Induftry, will be able to do very much more than has yet been done, and to fhew that even Phyfical and Natural Enquiries as well as Mathematical and Geometrical, will be capable alfo of Demonftration; fo that henceforward the bufinefs of Invention will not be fo much the Effect of acute Wit, as of a ferious and induftrious Profecution : And therefore, I hope as I fhall not feem to detract from the Parts and Excellency of the Ancients, but rather to admire and magnify their Wit and Induftry that they were able to proceed fo far as they did, without the Help of this Method, fo I hope I fhall not be look'd on as vain or boafting, or extolling of the prefent Abilities of this Age, if by the Profecution of this Method I expect and affert a much greater Proficiency. And this Art we owe firft and chiefly to that excellent Perfon I now mention'd, who was able to overcome all the Difficulties of Prejudice, with which Mens Minds are ufually befet, and to confider and weigh the Nature of things fo far, as not only to difcover the Impediments of Learning, but to contrive a Method how to free the Mind from them ; and likewife to fortify and inrich it with fuch a Method, as fhall be a conftant Guide and Affiftant to regulate all its Motions, fo that by the ufe of it, it may be able to go through with its Undertaking, and as with an Engine to perform incomparably much more than 'tis poffible to do without that Affiftance.

This Similitude therefore hints unto us the whole Method of making a Philosophical History, according to which, I shall enumerate the several things neceffary to this Design, and according to my Ability, endeavour to explain each
Particular in such Order, and so far forth as to me seems most natural and con-
sonant to my present Purpose. But first I shall premise some of the Accomplishments requisite for a Natural Historian.

§ I. *Of the*
Requisites in
a Natural Hi-
storian.
There seem therefore these Requisites to accomplish one, that intends to
prosecute or do any thing considerable in this Work, without which the Collections may very much fail of the desirable Excellency in this or that Particular, though perhaps as to the kind they may contain many good things.

The First is, That he ought to be very well skill'd in those several kinds of
Philosophy already known, to understand their several Hypotheses, Supposi-
tions, Collections, Observations, &c. their various ways of Ratiocinations and
Proceedings, the several Failings and Defects both in their way of Raising, and
in their way of managing their several Theories: For by this Means the Mind
will be somewhat more ready at guessing at the Solution of many Phenomena
almost at first Sight, and thereby be much more prompt at making Queries, and
at tracing the Subtilty of Nature, and in discovering and searching into the true
Reason of things ; and though perhaps none of those Methods of Philosophy
he has been accustomed to, may any way direct him in the Contrivance of this
New Fabrick, yet 'tis with the Exercises of the Mind as with the Operations of
the Body ; one that has been bred up, and well skill'd in any Trade, shall go
much more readily and handily about it, and make a much better piece of Work
of a quite new Design in that Trade, than one that has not been at all us'd to
such kind of Operations; there must be a time to bring and fix the Mind to a
Regard and Heedfulness of this kind of Contemplation, and a time also to ac-
custom it to Meditation and Contrivance, and a time to acquaint it with ratio-
nating from material Observations before it can go about such a Design dexte-
rously. Besides this also, the Mind will, by being acquainted with various Conjectures and Solutions of things, be much sooner and better freed from Prejudice ; for by discovering experimentally the Errors in this or that Hypothesis,
'twill be much easier taken off from adhering to any, and so enjoy a greater
Freedom of perceiving and 'imbracing Truth from what occasion soever it be
offered.

· Next, As he ought to be knowing in Hypotheses, so ought he also to be very well furnished with those things, which will most assist the Mind in making,
examining, and ratiocinating from Experiments. And these are chiefly two,
Mathematicks and Mechanicks ; the one somewhat more speculative, the other
more practical : The one qualifying the Mind with a most exact Idea and Pattern of Ratiocination, Demonstration, Invention, and Detection : The other ac-
quainting and instructing it with the Processes of Action, and Operation. He
ought first of all, and chiefly to be very well skill'd in Geometry and Arithmetick, the more demonstrative Parts, and Algebra the more inventive Part of it :
And this not only, as it furnishes the Mind as it were with Numbers, Weights,
and Measures to inquire into, examine and prove all things ; but as it also instructs and accustoms the Mind to a more strict way of Reasoning, to a more
nice and exact way of examining, and to a much more accurate way of inquiring into the Nature of things: The other more Physical Parts of Mathematicks are
also very useful in their kind ; shewing a Way and Method of applying the former to Physical Uses and Inquiries. Mechanicks also being partly Physical, and
partly Mathematical, do bring the Mind more closely to the Business it designs,
and shews it a Pattern of Demonstration, in Physical Operations, manifests the
possible Ways, how Powers may act in the moving resisting Bodies : Gives a
Scheme of the Laws and Rules of Motion, and as it were enters the Mind into
a Method of accurate and demonstrative Inquiry and Examination of Physical
Operations. For though the Operations of Nature are more secret and abstruse ;
and

and hid from our difcerning, or difcovering of them, than thofe more grofs and obvious ones of Engines, yet it feems moft probable, by the Effects and Circumftances ; that moft of them may be as capable of Demonftration and Reduction to a certain Rule, as the Operations of Mechanicks or Art. And from thofe, which are yet fomewhat more fpeculative, he ought to proceed to acquaint himfelf with others more complicated Mechanical Operations : Such as Chymical, and the Phyfical, yea even divers Mechanical Operations in many other Trades : For by thefe Ways, he will be better acquainted and enabled how to deal with Nature; for the procuring and getting more hidden Jewels and greateft Myfteries. But this is not yet enough, for the way to acquire thefe things certainly is not as yet fully difcovered, much lefs has it been practifed, he cannot have a Pilot to direct him certainly, to fhew the exact Courfe, and defcribe all the Turnings and Windings, and Shoalds, and many other Difficulties that are to be met withal, in this Attempt : Moft of thefe things muft be left to his own prudent and wary Management of his own Defigns.

And, as *Columbus* did in the Difcovery of the New World of *America*, he ought to contrive his Defign well ; then to procure what Helps and Affiftances he is able, laftly, thoroughly to profecute it, and not be difcouraged by the many Croffes and ill Succeffes he may at firft chance to meet with in the Attempt, and afterwards alfo in the Profecution thereof.

Thirdly, Therefore being thus well provided, he ought very thoroughly and ferioufly to confider of his Defign ; and this he fhould do firft by propofing to himfelf the end of his Inquiry ; then by confidering from the Nature of the Inquiry, what things feem moft likely to be conducive thereunto, and accordingly to fet down thofe things as *quæfita* or Requifites ; then further to confider well, and contrive by what means each of thefe Properties may be attain'd, *viz*. By what Experiments or Obfervations, what Engines, and Contrivances are neceffary, and how to be ufed : And for this end it is altogether neceffary, that he be able to defign and draw very well, thereby to be able both to exprefs his own Ideas the better to himfelf, to enable. him to examine them and ratiocinate upon them himfelf, and alfo for the better informing and inftructing of others ; for there are many things which cannot be made as plain to the Underftanding, by a large Defcription in Words, as by the Delineation of them in a quarter of a Sheet of Paper. Drawing therefore is not only neceffary in point of Invention of Mechanick Contrivances and Demonftrations, but for the Regiftring Particulars, and compiling a defirable Hiftory. Next, Having contrived his Methods of Examination, he ought to profecute them with great Diligence and Judgment, in ordering, ufing, and deducting from them.

4thly, In the Profecution of each of which, he ought to proceed with the greateft Degree of Candor and Freedom from Prejudice, not to be byaffed by this or that Opinion in making of Deductions, nor by the Pleafantnefs or Gainfulnefs of the Experiment, or any other by Confideration that does not immediately look at the prefent Difcovery he is fearching after ; for though thofe things are not to be wholly neglected, but rather mark'd by the by, and *in tranfitu*, yet the Mind is not to dwell upon them, or look otherwife after them, than as they are conducive to the prefent Inquiry, as they manifeft a Truth or difcover an Error, left like fweet finging Syrens they feduce their Followers out of their right way to their utter Deftruction. He ought alfo to proceed with the greateft Circumfpection and Diligence to find out fuch things, as are Indications of what he feeks, and from thofe to take Incouragement to profecute his Intentions, as *Columbus* did from the decreafing Depth of the Sea, the Drift of Weeds on the Surface of the Water, and the White Clouds that appear'd near the Horizon, and the like to incourage and direct him in his Courfe.

5. He ought to get what Help he can from others to affift him in this his Undertaking ; for 'tis not to be expected from the fingle Endeavours of any one Man, though the moft accomplifht, that any great Matter fhould be done, Man's Life will be well near half fpent, before he can be fit to undertake this
Work,

Work, and 'twill be a long time afterwards, before a fufficient Supellex can be gathered by his fingle Endeavours: Befides, there is much of Expence requifite, which every one cannot fo, well bear, that may perhaps be otherwife fit for this Employment; he muft therefore here alfo imitate *Columbus*, endeavour to be provided with Ships, and Men, and Money, and all thofe Affiftances he finds requifite for the thorough Profecution of this Difcovery.

6. *Laftly*, He ought, as *Columbus* did, freely and impartially to difcover what he finds; but yet with particular and more efpecial Regard to the great Promoters and Benefactors of this Defign, and what Affiftances he has receiv'd he ought candidly to acknowledge: And whatfoever he regifters, he ought to do it in the plaineft, fhorteft, and moft fignificant Defcription, the Matter is capable of, and in fuch a Method as may neither caufe Repetition of Hiftory, in more places than one, nor the Rejection of fome others, becaufe it fits not punctually to his Method : He ought likewife to own what Information any one has contributed toward the compiling of fuch a Hiftory; and to be as careful that he be not impos'd on, either by the Ignorance or Deceit of fuch as feem to be affifting.

The next thing to be confidered is, what the Subject of his Enquiry is; which I fhall endeavour to explain, by fetting down the General Scheme of the whole Matter, about which a Philofophical Hiftory is to treat.

§ II. *The Sub-ject of Philofophical Hiftory in general.* And this is not of lefs extent than the World, there is no Body or Operation in the Univerfe, at leaft if it can be any way brought to our Knowledge, that is not fome way or other to be taken notice of in this Great Work, the moft precious are here not more confiderable, nor perhaps fo much as the moft trivial and vile : Every thing is here to be taken notice of only as it is lucriferous or conducive to the Difcovery of Truth, and for a while at leaft the Lucriferoufnefs of any that occurs (anlefs for the Caufe of encouraging others in the Search) is to be omitted ; left thereby the Mind be diverted before it have gone through with its firft Undertaking. Nor though the Volumes requifite to be filled with this kind of Hiftory be many, and fo, may feem to confound the Mind with the very thought of making ufe, or examining over the Particulars therein, and much more with the thought of compiling and collecting them ; yet if we confider but the Volumes that are already writ on Subjects that have much lefs of Reality, and thofe perhaps by fome one Man, and the Volumes he has been fain to tumble and fearch over for the collecting of the Matter contain'd in them, befides the Multitude of Thoughts and Perplexities of Mind in fpinning out Niceties and ranging them, we may find the Labour and Perplexities of thefe Collections of real things, nothing comparable for Difficulty to thofe of Fiction, and Imagination ; for I have very good Reafon to believe, that the whole Mafs of Natural Hiftory, may be contain'd in much fewer words than the Writings of divers fingle Authors : And the Method of ufing them will be much more eafy, and the Labour of interpreting or underftanding them, if done aright, will be almoft as eafy as to unravel a Bottom when you begin at the right end. The Method of diftributing the Matter of Philofophical Hiftory, both for making Heads of Inquiry, and confequently alfo of regiftring them, need not be very nice or curious, they being in them laid up only · in Heaps as it were, as in a Granary or Store-Houfe ; from thence afterwards to be tranfcribed, fitted, ordered and rang'd, and Tabled, as I fhall afterward explain to be made fit for Ufe; for (as I inftanced before) a fufficient Store of found and good Materials, ought to be collected before the Work of Superftructure can be begun.

We will divide the whole Bufinefs of Philofophical Hiftory into thefe particular Heads of Inquiry, in which we have not fo much proceeded according to the Nature of the things themfelves, as according to their Appearance or Refpect to us : For though the Earth, in Comparifon of the Heavens, be as it were a Point, yet in Relation to its Nearnefs and Senfiblenefs to us, it becomes much more confiderable, and the Confideration of it and its Parts will take up the greateft Part of this Hiftory. We will divide the Subject of Philofophical Hiftory into two Parts ; to wit, into things Natural and things Artificial.

Le Bovier de Fontenelle:

Conversations with a Lady, on the Plurality of Worlds

Bernard le Bovier de Fontenelle, 'The Second Evening: That The Moon Is Inhabited', *Conversations with a Lady, on the Plurality of Worlds*, 4th edition, trans. J. Glanvill (London: 1719), pp. 34–65.

Bernard le Bovier de Fontenelle was a man of letters, the nephew of Pierre Corneille. In his comedy *La Comète* (1681), about the comet of 1680, he first showed his interest in making science the subject of a literary work. He employed the dialogue form in his play, *Nouveaux Dialogues des Morts* (1683). Fontenelle's *Entretiens sur la Pluralité des Mondes* or *Conversations on the Plurality of Worlds*, a witty and elegantly-written dialogue between a philosopher and a Marquise about Copernican and Cartesian cosmology, was first published in 1686. It became a bestseller, going through four editions within three years. Fontenelle's promotion of Copernican ideas led to its being placed on the Papal index.

With the huge success of his *Entretiens*, Fontenelle became increasingly interested in science and valued his eventual appointment as Secretary to the Académie des Sciences in 1697 more highly than his earlier election to the Académie Française. He wrote a history of the Académie des Sciences and a series of 'Eloges', short biographies of recently departed famous scientists who were presented to the public as heroes. Fontenelle revised his *Entretiens* in the light of new astronomical discoveries which did not conflict with his life-long belief in Cartesian astronomy.

Fontenelle's *Entretiens* was hugely influential. Its popularity appears nonetheless surprising since Cartesianism was already perceived as old-fashioned at the time of its first publication and 1687 saw the appearance of Newton's *Principia*, disproving the existence of the Cartesian vortices which thrilled Fontenelle's lady. Fontenelle's careful targeting of a gentlemanly audience, his literary abilities and the skills of his translators won him the admiration of men of letters, in particular, Joseph Addison and Sir William Temple. By suggesting that women might read his work in the same way that they would read a novel, Fontenelle demonstrated the accessibility of the new science.

Within two years of publication there were two English translations of Fontenelle's *Entretiens*, one by the apologist for experimental philosophy John Glanvill and the other by the first professional female author Aphra Behn. The edition of 1719 was the fourth and last edition of Glanvill's translation published in England. It includes for the first time in this translation Fontenelle's sixth dialogue that he had added in 1687 and appends his *Discourse Concerning the Ancients and the Moderns* (1688).

The extract below, the second of six evening conversations, concerns the philosopher's demonstration that it is impossible to resist the truth. On the first evening he outlined the Copernican system of the universe. On the second, he discusses the possibility that there might be people on the moon, oscillating between a positive statement of belief and one of disbelief. Whereas on the first evening he led his lady from the familiar territory of literature to the unfamiliar world of science, this strategy is subverted on the second evening. The discussion of Ariosto's *Orlando Furioso* with its voyage to the moon misleads rather than enlightens. The next evening, he admits that he does not believe that the moon is inhabited and counsels her to 'reserve half of your Understanding free and disengag'd, that you may admit of the contrary Opinion, if there be any occasion' (p. 67).

Glanvill is mainly known for his polemical works on behalf of the Royal Society, in particular his *Plus Ultra*, published in 1668. Glanvill saw his translation of Fontenelle as an opportunity to promote English science, name-dropping Astronomer Royal John Flamsteed and 'all the Philosophers of Gresham'. Whereas in Fontenelle and in Behn's translation the philosopher gallantly regrets that Cartesian whirlpools or vortices are not fit objects for the lady's raptures, Glanvill's philosopher triumphs: 'you shall see the Whirlpools are worthy of these Transports' (p. 103). The impression is that Glanvill, so assiduous a proponent of the new philosophy, could not bear to see it put down, even in jest.

The Second Evening.

IN the Morning I sent to the Countess's Apartment, to know how she had rested, and whether the Motion of the Earth had not disturbed her? She answer'd, she began to be accustomed to it, and that she had slept as well as *Copernicus* himself. Soon after, there came some Neighbours to dine with her; but they went away in the Evening; so that after Supper we walk'd again into the Park, and immediately fell upon our Systems. She so well conceiv'd what I told her the Night before, that she desir'd I would proceed without any Repetition. Well, Madam, *said I,* since the Sun, which is now immoveable, hath left off being a Planet, and the Earth which turns round him, is now become one, you will not be surpriz'd when you hear that the Moon is an Earth too, and that she is inha-

inhabited as ours is. I confeſs, *said ſhe,* I have often heard talk of the World in the Moon, but I always look'd upon it as viſionary, and mere Fancy. And it may be ſo ſtill, *ſaid I;* I am in this caſe as People in a Civil War, where the uncertainty of what may happen makes em hold intelligence with the oppoſite Party: for tho I verily believe the Moon is inhabited, I live civilly with thoſe who do not believe it; and I am (as ſome honeſt Gentlemen in point of Religion) ſtill ready to embrace the prevailing Opinion: but till the Unbelievers have a more conſiderable Advantage, I am for the People in the Moon.

Suppoſe there had never been any Communication between *London* and *Greenwich,* and a Cockney who was never beyond the Walls of *London,* ſaw *Greenwich* from the top of a Pyramid, you ask him if he believes *Greenwich* is inhabited as *London* is? He preſently anſwers, No: for, *ſaith he,* I ſee People at *London,* but none at *Greenwich,* nor did I ever hear of any there. 'Tis true, you

you tell him, that from the Pyramid he cannot perceive any Inhabitants at *Greenwich*, becaufe of the Diftance ; but all that he doth difcover of *Greenwich*, very much refembleth what he fees at *London*, the Steeples, Houfes, Walls ; fo that it may very well be inhabited as *London* is : all this fignifies nothing, my Cockney ftill perfifts, *Greenwich* is not inhabited, becaufe he fees no body there. The Moon is our *Greenwich*, and every one of us as mere Cockneys as he that never was out of the Sound of *Bow-Bell*. You are too fevere, *faid fhe*, upon your Fellow-Citizens; we are not all fure fo filly as your Cockney ; fince *Greenwich* is juft as *London* is, he is a Fool, if he doth not think it inhabited : But the Moon is not at all like the Earth. Have a care of what you fay, *I reply'd* ; for if the Moon refembleth the Earth, you are under a neceffity to believe it inhabited. If it be fo, *faid fhe*, I own I cannot be difpens'd from believing it ; and you feem fo confident of it, that I fear I muft, whether I will or no. 'Tis true, the two Motions of the Earth,

(which

(which I could never imagine till now)
do a little ſtagger me as to all the reſt:
But yet how is it poſſible the Earth
ſhould enlighten as the Moon doth,
without which they cannot be alike?
If that be all, *ſaid I,* the Difference is
not great, for 'tis the Sun which is the
ſole Fountain of Light: that Quality
proceeds only from him; and if the Planets give Light to us, it is becauſe they
firſt receive it from the Sun: the Sun
ſends Light to the Moon, and ſhe reflects it back on the Earth: the Earth in
the ſame manner receives Light from
the Sun, and ſends it to the Moon; for
the Diſtance is the ſame between the
Earth and the Moon, as between the
Moon and the Earth. But is the Earth,
ſaid the Counteſs, as fit to ſend back
the Light of the Sun, as the Moon is?
You are altogether for the Moon, *ſaid
I,* ſhe is much oblig'd to you; but you
muſt know that Light is made up of
certain little Balls, which rebound from
what is ſolid, but paſs thro what admits of an entrance in a right Line, as
Air or Glaſs; ſo that that which makes
the

Moon enlighten us, is, that she is a firm and solid Body, from which the little Balls rebound; and we must deny our Senses, if we will not allow the Earth the same Solidity. In short, the Difference is how we are seated; for the Moon being at so vast a distance from us, we can only discover her to be a Body of Light, and do not perceive that she is a great Mass, altogether like the Earth: whereas, on the contrary, because we are so near the Earth, we know her to be a great Mass, but do not discover her to be a Body of Light, for want of the due distance. It is just so with us all, *said the Countess*; we are dazled with the Quality and Fortune of those who are above us; when, do but look to the bottom, and we are all alike.

Very true, *said I*; we would judge of all things, but still stand in the wrong place: we are too near to judge of our selves, and too far off to know others. So that the true way to see things as they are, is to be between the Moon and the Earth, to be purel a Spectator

Spectator of this World, and not an In-
habitant. I shall never be satisfy'd, *said
she*, for the Injustice we do the Earth,
and the too favourable Opinion we have
of the Moon, till you assure me that
the People in the Moon are as little acquainted with their Advantages as we
are with ours, and that they take our
Earth for a Planet, with out knowing
theirs is one too. Do not doubt it, *said
I*; we appear to them to perform very
regularly our Function of a Planet. 'Tis
true, they do not see us make a Circle
round them, but that is no great matter. That half of the Moon which was
turn'd towards us at the beginning of
the World, hath been turn'd towards us
ever since; the Eyes, Mouth, and Face,
which we have fancied of the Spots in
her, are still the same; and if the other
opposite half should appear to us, we
should no doubt fancy another Figure
from the different Spots that are in it:
Not but that the Moon turns upon her
self, and in the same time that she turns
round the Earth, that is in a Month;
but while she is making that turn upon
her

her felf, and that fhe fhould hide a Cheek for example, and appear fomewhat elfe to us, fhe makes a like part of her Circle round the Earth, and ftill prefents to us the fame Cheek: fo that the Moon, who in refpect of the Sun and Stars, turns round her felf; in refpect of us, doth not turn at all: they feem to her to rife and fet in the fpace of fifteen days; but for our Earth, it appears to her to be held up in the fame place of the Heavens. 'Tis true, this apparent Immobility is not very agreeable, for a Body which fhould pafs for a Planet, but it is not altogether perfect; the Moon hath a kind of trembling, which caufeth a little Corner of her Face to be fometimes hid from us, and a little Corner of the oppofite half appears; but then, upon my word, fhe attributes that trembling to us, and fancies that we have in the Heavens the Motion of a *Pendulum,* which vibrates to and fro.

I find, *faith the Countefs,* the Planets are juft like us; we caft that upon others which is in ourfelves; the Earth faith, *'Tis not I that turn, 'tis the Sun;* the

the Moon faith, *'tis not I that fhake,
'tis the Earth*; there is a great deal of
errour every where. But I would not
advife you, *faid I,* to undertake the
reforming it; you had better convince
your felf of the entire Refemblance of
the Earth and the Moon. Imagine
then thefe two great Bowls held up in
the Heavens, you know that the Sun
always enlightens the one half of a Body that is round, and the other half is
in the Shadow : there is then one half of
the Earth, and one half of the Moon,
which is enlightned by the Sun ; that
is, which hath Day, and the other half
which is Night. Obferve alfo, that as
a Ball hath lefs force after it hath been
ftruck againft a Wall, which fends it to
the other fide; fo Light is weakned
when it is reflected. This pale Light
which comes to us from the Moon, is
the very Light of the Sun ; but it cannot come to us from the Moon but by
Reflexion : it hath loft much of the force
and luftre it had when it came directly
from the Sun upon the Moon ; and that
bright Light which fhines directly upon

us

us from the Sun, and which the Earth reflects upon the Moon, is as pale and weak when it arrives there : So that the Light which appears to us in the Moon, and which enlightens our Nights, is the Parts of the Moon which have Day; and that part of the Earth which hath Day, when it is oppofite to the part of the Moon which hath Night, gives Light to it. All depends upon how the Moon and the Earth behold one another. At the beginning of the Month, we do not fee the Moon, be-caufe fhe is between the Sun and us; that half of her which hath Day, is then turned toward the Sun; and that half which hath Night, turn'd towards us, we cannot fee it then, becaufe it hath no Light upon it : but that half of the Moon which hath Night, being turned to the half of the Earth which hath Day, fees us without being per-ceiv'd; and we then appear to them juft as the Full-Moon doth to us. So that, as I may fay, the People of the Moon have then a full Earth; but the Moon being advanc'd upon her Circle

of

of a Month, comes from under the Sun, and begins to turn towards us a little corner of the half which is Light: there's the Crefcent: then thofe parts of the Moon which have Night do not fee all the half of the Earth which hath Day, and we are then in the Wayn to them.

I comprehend you very well, *faid the Countefs*; the People in the Moon have a Month quite contrary to us; when we have a full Moon, their half of the Moon which is Light is turned to our half of the Earth which is dark; they do not fee us at all, and they have then a new Earth, this is plain. But now tell me how come the Eclipfes? You may eafily guefs that, *faid I*; when it is new Moon, that fhe is between the Sun and us, and all her dark half is turned towards us who have Light, that obfcure Shadow is caft upon us; if the Moon be directly under the Sun, that Shadow hides him from us, and at the fame time obfcures a part of that half of the Earth which is Light, which was feen by that half of the Moon which was dark: here then

is

is an Eclipse of the Sun to us during
our Day, and an Eclipse of the Earth
to the Moon during her Night. When
it is full Moon, the Earth is between her
and the Sun, and all the dark half of the
Earth is turned towards all the light half
of the Moon ; the Shadow then of the
Earth casts it self towards the Moon,
and if it falls on the Moon, it obscures
that light half which we see, which hath
then Day, and hinders the Sun from
shining on it. Here then is an Eclipse
of the Moon to us during our Night,
and an Eclipse of the Sun to the Moon
during our Day : but the reason that
we have not Eclipses every time that the
Moon is between the Sun and the Earth,
or the Earth between the Sun and the
Moon, is, because these three Bodies are
not exactly placed in a right Line, and
by consequence that that should make
the Eclipse, casts its Shadow a little be-
side that which should be obscured.

I am surprized, *said the Countess,* that
there should be so little Mystery in E-
clipses, and that the whole World should
not know the cause of 'em. Nor never
will,

will, *said I*, as some People go about it. In the *East-Indies*, when the Sun and the Moon are in Eclipse, they believe a certain Devil who hath black Claws is seizing on those Planets with his Talons; and during that time the Rivers are cover'd with the Heads of *Indians*, who are up to the Neck in Water, because they esteem it a very devout Posture, to implore the Sun and the Moon to defend themselves against the Devil. In *America*, they are persuaded that the Sun and the Moon, when eclipsed, are angry; and what is it they will not do to be reconciled with them? The *Greeks*, who were so refined, did they not believe the Moon was enchanted, and that the Magicians forc'd her to descend from Heaven, and shed a dangerous Juice on the Plants? Nay, what a panick Fear were we in, above thirty Years ago, at an Eclipse of the Sun? How many People hid themselves in their Cellars; and all the Philosophers of *Gresham* could not persuade them to come out till the Eclipse was over?

Methinks,

Methinks, *said she*, 'tis scandalous for Men to be such Cowards; there ought to be a general Law of Mankind to prohibit the discoursing of Eclipses, that we might not call to mind. the Follies that have been said and done upon that Subject. Your Law then, *said I*, must abolish even the memory of all things, and forbid us to speak at all, for I know nothing in the World which is not a Monument of the Folly of Man.

But what do you think, *said she*, of the People in the Moon.; are they as a-fraid of an Eclipse as we are? It would be very Burlesque for the *Indians* there to be up to the Neck in Water ; that the *Americans* should believe the Earth angry with them; the *Greeks* fancy we were bewitched, and would destroy their Plants; in short, that we should cause the same Consternation among them, as they do here. And why not, *said I*? I do not doubt it at all; for why should the People of the Moon have more Wit than we? What right have they to affright us, and not we them? For my part, I believe that since a prodigious

gious Company of Men have been and still are such Fools to adore the Moon, there are People in the Moon that worship the Earth, and that we are upon our Knees the one to the other. But sure, *said she*, we don't pretend to send any Influences to the Moon, and to give a Crisis to her Sick; if the People have any Wit in those Parts, they will soon destroy the Honour we flatter ourselves with, and I fear we shall have the Disadvantage.

Fear it not, Madam, *said I*; do you think we are the only Fools of the Universe? Is it not consistent with Ignorance, to spread it self every where? 'Tis true, we can only guess at the Folly of the People in the Moon, but I no more doubt it, than I do the most authentick News that comes from thence. What News comes from thence, *said she*? That which the Learned bring us, *I reply'd*, who travel thither every day with their Tubes and Telescopes: they will tell you of their Discoveries there, of Lands, Seas, Lakes, high Mountains, and deep Abysses.

I

I fancy indeed, *said she*, they may difcover Mountains and Abyſſes, becauſe
of the remarkable Inequality ; but how
do they diſtinguiſh Lands and Seas ? Very eaſily, *ſaid I* ; for the Waters letting
part of the Light paſs thro them, ſend
back but a very little, ſo that they appear afar off like ſo many dark Spots ;
whereas the Lands being ſolid, reflect
the whole Light, and appear to be more
bright and ſhining : nay, they pretend
to be ſo well acquainted with the ſeveral Parts, that they have given them all
Names : one place they call *Copernicus*,
another *Archimedes*, another *Galileus* :
there is the *Caſpian-Sea*, the *Black-Lake*,
the *Porphirite Mountains* : in ſhort, they
have publiſh'd ſuch exact Deſcriptions
of the Moon, that a very Almanack-
maker will be no more to ſeek there,
than I am in *London*.

I muſt own then, *ſaid the Counteſs*,
they are very exact ; but what do they
ſay to the inſide of the Country ? I
would very fain know that. 'Tis impoſſible, *I reply'd* ; Mr. *Flamſted* himſelf
(one of the moſt Learned Aſtrono-
mers

mers of our Age) cannot inform you. You muft ask that of *Aftolfo*, who was carried into the Moon by St. *John*. I am going to tell you one of the agreeable Follies of *Ariofto*, and I am confident you will be well pleafed to hear it : I muft confefs he had better have let alone St. *John*, whofe Name is fo worthy of Refpect, but 'tis a Poetical Licence, and muft be allow'd. The Poem is dedicated to a Cardinal, and a great Pope hath honour'd it with his Approbation, which is prefix'd to feveral of the Editions : this is the Argument; *Rowland* Nephew to *Charlemain*, falls mad becaufe the fair *Angelica* prefers *Medore* before him. *Aftolfo* a Knight-Errant, finding himfelf one day in the terreftrial Paradife, which was upon the top of a very high Mountain, whereto he was carried by his flying Horfe, meets St. *John* there, who tells him, if he would have *Rowland* cured, he muft make a Voyage with him into the Moon. *Aftolfo*, who had a great mind to fee Countries, did not ftand much upon entreaty, and immediately there came a

D   fiery

fiery Chariot which carried the Apoftle and the Knight up into the Air. *Aftolfo* being no great Philofopher, was furpriz'd to find the Moon fo much bigger than it appear'd to him when he was upon the Earth ; to fee Rivers, Seas, Mountains, Cities, Forefts, nay, what would have furpriz'd me too, Nymphs hunting in thofe Forefts : but that which was moft remarkable, was a Valley where you might find any thing that was loft in our World, of what nature foever ; Crowns, Riches, Fame, and an Infinity of Hopes ; the time we fpend in play, and in fearching for the Philofopher's Stone ; the Alms we give after ourDeath, the Verfes we prefent to great Men and Princes, and the Sighs of Lovers. I know not, *faid fhe,* what became of the Sighs of Lovers in the time of *A- riofto,* but I fancy there are very few of 'em afcend to the Moon in our days. Ah, Madam, *reply'd I,* how many doth the Countefs of *D——r* fend thither every day ? Thofe that are addrefs'd to her, will make a confiderable Heap ; and I affure you the Moon keeps all

*

safe

fafe that is loft here below. Yet I
muft tell you, *Ariofto* doth but whif-
per it, tho every thing is there, even
to the Donation of *Conftantine, i. e.* the
Popes have pretended to be Mafters of
Rome and *Italy* by virtue of a Donation which the Emperor *Conftantine*
made *Sylvefter* ; and the truth is, no-
body knows what is become of it. But
what do you think is not to be found
in the Moon? Folly, all that ever
was upon the Earth is kept there ftill ;
but in lieu of it, it is not to be ima-
gin'd how many Wits (if I may fo call
'em) that are loft here, are got up into
the Moon, they are fo many Vials full
of a very fubtile Liquor, which evaporates immediately, if it be not well
ftopp'd ; and upon every one of thefe
Vials the Names are written to whom
the Wits belong : I think *Ariofto* hath
heap'd 'em upon one another a little
confufedly ; but for order fake, we
will fancy 'em plac'd upon Shelves in a
long Gallery. *Aftolfo* wonder'd to fee
feveral Vials full infcrib'd with the
Names of the moft confiderable Statef-

D 2   men,

men, Divines, Lawyers, &c. Bless
me, *said he*, is my Lord ———— and
my Lord ———— here! Sir *Tho.* Sir
Jo. nay, Doctor ————, and Father ——— too! Why in my Country we look upon 'em as Oracles, and
after all, it seems they are but little
better than mad Men, if not stark Fools.
I find now the poor Rogue was in the
right, tho he was soundly whipp'd for't,
who told the Judge, that he had seen
an Ass clothed in Scarlet; and a right
Worshipful Alderman, that he knew not
which was the greatest Brute of the
two, the Beast that bore the Fur, or
the Beast that wore it. But had I been
there, I should have told *Astolfo,* the
sawcy Knave was well enough serv'd;
for we are not to look upon the Man,
but the Place he fills: we are to reve-
vence a Magistrate when and wherefo-
ever we meet him, and to suppose his
Merit was the sole cause of his Prefer-
ment, tho we are certain it came by
Bribery or Pimping. But enough of
this; let us return to our Vials. To
confess the truth, I begin to fear, since

I

I' have entertain'd you with these Philosophical and Poetical Visions, mine
there is not very empty: however,
'tis some Consolation to me, that while
you are so attentive, you have a little
Glass full as well as your Servant: the
good Knight found his own Wits a-
mongst the rest, and with the Apostle's
leave snuffed it all up his Nose, like so
much Queen of *Hungary*'s Water ; but
Ariosto said, he did not carry it far, it
returned again to the Moon a little
after.

*—*The Love of one fair Northern Lass,*
Sent up his Wit unto the place it was.

Well, he did not forget *Orlando*'s Vial,
which was the occasion of his Voyage ;
but he was cursedly plagu'd to carry it,
for *Heroes* Wits are naturally very heavy,
and there did not want one drop of it :
in conclusion, *Ariosto*, according to his
laudable custom, addresseth himself to
his Mistress in this manner :

---

* Sir *Jo. Harrington*'s *Translation of* Orlande Furioso,
lib. 36.

Fair Mistress, who for me to Heav'n shall fly,
  To bring again from thence my wandring Wit?
Which I still lose, since from that piercing Eye,
  The Dart came forth that first my Heart did
Nor of my loss at all complain would I,　(*hit:*
  Might I but keep that which remaineth yet:
But if it still decrease, within short space,
  I doubt I shall be in Orlando's *case.*

Yet, well I wot where to recover mine,
  Tho not in Paradise, *nor* Cynthia's Sphere,
Yet doubtless in a Place no less Divine,
  In that sweet Face of yours, in that fair Hair,
That ruby Lip, *in those two starlike Eyes,*
  There is my Wit, I know it wanders there;
And with my Lips, if you would give me leave,
  I there would search, I thence would it receive.

Is not this very fine? To reason like
Ariosto, the safest way of losing our Wits
is to be in love; for you see they do not
go far from us, we may recover 'em a-
gain at our Lips; but when we lose 'em
by other means, as for example, by Phi-
losophizing, whip they are gone into
the Moon, and there is no coming at
'em again when we would. However, *said the Countess,* our Vials have
an

an honourable Station among the Philoſophers, when 'tis forty to one but Love fixeth our Wits on an Object we cannot but be aſham'd of. But to take away mine entirely, pray tell me, but tell me ſeriouſly, if you believe there are any Men in the Moon; for methinks hitherto you have not been very poſitive. For my part, *ſaid I*, I do not believe there are Men in the Moon: for do but obſerve how much the Face of Nature is chang'd between this and *China*; other Viſages, Shapes, Manners, nay almoſt other Principles of Reaſon; and therefore between us and the Moon the Alteration muſt be much more conſiderable. In the Lands that have been lately diſcovered, we can ſcarce call the Inhabitants Men; they are rather Animals of human Shape, and that too ſometimes very imperfect, almoſt without human Reaſon: he therefore that will travel to the Moon, muſt not expect to find Men there.

What ſort of People will they be then, *ſaid the Counteſs?* Troth, Madam, *ſaid I*, I know not; for put the caſe

D 4   that

that we ourselves inhabited the Moon, and were not Men, but rational Creatures, could we imagine, do you think, such fantastical People upon the Earth, as Mankind is? Is it possible we should have an Idea of so strange a Composition, a Creature of such foolish Passions, and such wise Reflections? so learned in things of no use, and so stupidly ignorant of what most concerns him; so much Concern for Liberty, and yet such great Inclinations to Servitude? so desirous of Happiness, and yet so very incapable of being so? The People in the Moon must be wise indeed to suppose all this of us. But do we not see our selves continually, and cannot so much as guess how we were made? So that we are forc'd to say the Gods, when they created us, were drunk with Nectar, and when they were sober again, could not chuse but laugh at their own handy-work. Well, well, *said the Countess*, we are safe enough then; they in the Moon know nothing of us; but I could wish we were a little better acqainted with them; for it troubles me that we should

see

see the Moon above us, and yet not know what is done there. Why, *said I*, are you not as much concern'd for that part of the Earth which is not yet discover'd? What Creatures inhabit it, and what they do there? for we and they are carried in the same Vessel: they possess the Prow, and we the Poop, and yet there is no manner of Communication between us; they do not know at one end of the Ship, who lives, or what is done a: the other end: and you would know what passeth in the Moon, which is another great Vessel, sailing in the Heavens at a vast distance from us.

Oh, *said she*; for the Earth, I reckon it all as good as discover'd, and can guess at the People, tho I never heard a word of 'em; for certainly they all resemble us very much, and we may know 'em better when we have a mind to't: they will stay where they are, and tis no more but going to see 'em; but we cannot get into the Moon if we would; so that I despair of knowing what they do there. You would

laugh

laugh at me, *said I*, if I should answer you seriously ; perhaps I may deserve it ; and yet, I fancy, I can say
a great deal to justify a ridiculous
Thought that is just now come into my
Head : nay, to use the Fool's best Argument, I'll lay a Wager I make you
own (in spite of Reason) that one of
these Days there may be a Communication between the Earth and the
Moon ; and who knows what great Advantages we may procure by it ? Do but
consider *America,* before it was discover'd by *Columbus,* how profoundly
ignorant were those People ? they knew
nothing at all of Arts and Sciences ; they
went naked, had no other Arms but
a Bow and Arrows, and did not conceive they might be carried by Animals : they look'd upon the Sea as a wide
Space, forbidden to Man ; that it was
join'd to the Heavens, and that beyond it was nothing. 'Tis true, after
having spent whole Years in making
hollow the Trunks of great Trees with
sharp Stones, they put themselves to
Sea in these Trunks, and floated from
Land

Land to Land, as the Wind and Waves drove them: But how often was their Trough overset, and they forc'd to recover it again by swimming? So that (except when they were on the Land) it might be said ·they were continually swimming: and yet had any one but told 'em of another kind of Navigation, incomparably more perfect and useful than their own; that they might easily pass over that infinite Space of Water; that they might stop in the middle of the Waves, and in some sense command the Winds, and make their˙ Vessel go fast or slow, as they pleas'd: in short, that this unpassable Ocean should be no Obstacle to their conversing with another different People; do you think they would have believed you? And yet at last that Day is come: the unheard of and most surprizing Sight appears, vast great Bodies, with white Wings, are seen to fly upon the Sea, to vomit Fire from all Parts, and to cast on their Shores an unknown People, all scaled with Iron, who dispose and govern

govern Monsters as they please, carry Thunder in their Hands, and overthrow and destroy whoever resists them. From whence came they? Who brought them over the Sea? Who gave to them the Disposal of the Fire of Heaven? Are they Gods? Are they Sons of the Sun? for certainly they are not Men. Do but consider, Madam, the Surprize of the *Americans*; there can be nothing greater: and after this, shall any one say there shall never be a Communication between the Moon and the Earth? Did the *Americans* believe there would ever be any between them and *Europe*, till it came to pass? 'Tis true, you must pass this great Space of Air and Heaven which is between the Earth and the Moon; but did not those vast Seas seem at first as impassable to the *Americans*? You rave, I think, *said she*; did you not own the *Americans* were so ignorant, that they had not the least Conception of crossing the Sea; but we who know a great deal more than they, can imagine and fancy the going

ing thro the Air, tho we are affured it is not to be done. There is fomewhat more than Fancy, *I reply'd*, when it hath been already practis'd, for feveral have found the fecret of faftening Wings, which bear them up in the Air, to move them as they pleafe, and to fly over Rivers, and from Steeple to Steeple. I cannot fay indeed they have yet made an Eagle's Flight, or that it doth not coft now and then a Leg or an Arm to one of thefe new Birds; but this may ferve to reprefent the firft Planks that were launch'd on the Water, and which were the very beginning of Navigation. There were no Veffels then thought of to fail round the World ; and yet you fee what great Ships are grown by little and little from thofe firft Planks. The Art of Flying is but newly invented ; it will improve by degrees, and in time grow perfect, then we may fly as far as the Moon. We do not yet pretend to have difcover'd all things, or that what we have difcover'd can receive no Addition ;

dition; and therefore, pray let us agree there are yet many things to be done in the Ages to come. Were you to live a thousand Ages, *said the Countess,* I can never believe you will fly, but you must endanger your Neck. I will not, *I reply'd,* be so unmannerly as to contradict a fair Lady; but tho we cannot learn the Art here, I hope you will allow they may fly better in the Moon: 'tis no great matter whether we go to them, or they come to us; we shall then be the *Americans* who knew nothing of Navigation, and yet there were very good Ships at t'other end of the World. Were it so, *said she,* the People in the Moon would have been here before now. All in good time, *said I;* the *Europeans* were not in *America,* till at the end of some thousands of Years; they were so long in improving Navigation to the point of crossing the Ocean. The People in the Moon have already made some short Voyages in the Air; they are exercising continually, and by degrees will

be

be more expert; then we shall see 'em, and God knows how we shall be surpriz'd. It is unsufferable, *said she*, you should banter me at this rate, and justify your ridiculous Fancy by such false Reasoning. I am going to demonstrate, *said I*, you reproach me very unjustly. Consider, Madam, that the World is unfolded by degrees; for the Antients were very positive, that the Torrid and Frigid Zones were not inhabitable, by reason of their excessive Heat and Cold: and in the time of the *Romans* the general Map of the World was but very little extended beyond that of their Empire; which, tho in one sense, express'd much Grandeur, in another sense, was a Sign of as great Ignorance: however, there were Men found both in very hot and in very cold Countries; so that you see the World is already encreas'd. After that it was thought that the Ocean cover'd the whole Earth, except what was then discover'd; there was no talk then of the Antipodes, not so much as

a

a thought of 'em; for who could fancy their Heels at top, and their Heads at bottom? and yet after all their fine Reasoning, the Antipodes were discover'd. Here's now another half of the World starts up, and a new Reformation of the Map: Methinks this, Madam, should restrain us; and teach us not to be so positive in our Opinions; the World will unfold it self more to us hereafter; then we shall know the People in the Moon as well as we do now the Antipodes. But all things must be done in order; the whole Earth must be first discovered; and till we are perfectly acquainted with our own Habitation, we shall never know that of our Neighbours. Without fooling, *said the Countess*, you are so very profound in this Point, that I begin to think you are in earnest, and believe what you say. Not so neither, *said I*; but I would shew you how easy it is to maintain a chimerical Notion, that may (like some Opinions in Religion) perplex a Man of Understanding, but

never

never perfuade him : there is nothing perfuades but Truth, it hath no need of all its Proofs, but enters naturally into our Underftanding; and when once we have learn'd it, we do nothing but think of it. I thank you then, *faid fhe*, for impofing on me no longer ; for I confefs your falfe reafoning difturb'd me, but now I fhall fleep very quietly, if you think fit to go home.

Desaguliers:

The Newtonian System of the World, the Best Model of Government

John Theophilus Desaguliers, *The Newtonian System of the World, the Best Model of Government: An Allegorical Poem. With a Plain and Intelligible Account of the System of the World, by Way of Annotations: With Copper Plates: To which is Added, Cambria's Complaint Against the Intercalary Day in the Leap-Year* (Westminster: Printed by A. Campbell, for J. Roberts, 1728), pp. iii–vi, preface, 1–34.

The difficulty of Newtonian physics provided a means of earning a living for John Theophilus Desaguliers, chief among the 'Swarm of Expositors' described by Samuel Johnson (Donald D. Eddy (ed.), *The Rambler*, 2 vols (New York & London: Garland Publishing, Inc., 1978), Vol. 2, p. 633). Desaguliers was exceptional in having Newton's sanction. In many ways it was an ideal arrangement since Desaguliers's readiness to answer queries matched Newton's reluctance. Desaguliers's tremendous success as a lecturer initiated the intense demand for public lectures on science in the eighteenth century. He was remarkable for his ease in addressing different audiences in different settings, whether the Fellows of the Royal Society at Gresham College, royalty at Hampton Court or the general public in coffee-houses, making few alterations in the content of lectures addressed to the Society and to the public. Like John Harris in his *Astronomical Dialogues between a Gentleman and a Lady* (1719), Desaguliers relied on analogy and eschewed mathematics as a means of explanation.

One of the greatest practical philosophers of the age, Desaguliers was also a great showman, working on the principle that 'seeing is believing'. He covered an enormous range of topics in his public lectures, from demonstrations of electricity to methods of applying mechanical principles to waterflow and ways of mechanizing warfare (note the military analogies in this poem – for example, his reference to the flight of cannonballs in his discussion of gravitation). He was fascinated by the strong men of London taverns, testing their feats of strength and exposing many a 'pretended Sampson' (Desaguliers, *A Course of Experimental Philosophy*, 2 vols (London, 1734, 1744), Vol. 1, p. 256). A further enticement was his claim that his lectures were superior to books: 'Things which otherwise would be merely speculative, being by this means rendered Objects of the Senses, and better understood in a Month or six Weeks, than in a Year's close Application to Books only' (Desaguliers, *A Course of Mechanical and Experimental Philosophy* (London, 1725), p. 2). In lectures, writings and experiments, Desaguliers aimed to please. As Stewart comments, he 'always had the air of a projector' (Stewart, *The Rise of Public Science*, p. 133).

In this poem, Desaguliers uses the Newtonian system of the universe as a way of praising the virtues of the balanced constitution. The King is a sun, governing not by fear, in the manner of Louis XIV, but by 'mutual Love'. Stewart calls it a 'peculiar poem' representing an 'attempt to curry favor with a new regime' (Stewart, *The Rise of Public Science*, p. 154). Desaguliers's hopes for political advancement derived from his earlier experience of good fortune as a result of a change of regime. A Huguenot refugee, he was elected a Fellow of the Royal Society shortly before the death of Queen Anne. He was also made Curator of Experiments and in July 1714 reproduced for the Society experiments from Newton's *Opticks*, published in 1704. In 1716 he became chaplain to James Brydges, later 1st Duke of Chandos, who sponsored his technological enterprises. In the same year he performed for George I experiments on weight and friction. In 1717 he gave lectures on experimental philosophy to George I and to the Prince of Wales and Princess Caroline.

Officially a celebration of George II's accession to the throne, the poem is also a celebration of Newtonian physics. Desaguliers professes that it is his joy at the accession that has moved him to his 'first Poetical Experiment', as he punningly puts it. More philosophical than political encomium, however, his poem follows the example set by Thomson in his 'To the Memory of Sir Isaac Newton' (1727). John Mullan has written of the perception that poetry was the best medium for expressing the wonder inspired by Newtonian philosophy: 'as if what Desaguliers's poem calls "The Newtonian System of the World" is enough to tug even a Philosopher away from prose' (John Mullan, 'Gendered Knowledge, Gendered Minds: Women and Newtonianism, 1690–1760' in Marina Benjamin (ed.), *A Question of Identity. Women, Science, and Literature* (New Brunswick, New Jersey: Rutgers University Press, 1993), p. 52).

Desaguliers makes repeated references to his ineptness as a poet, drawing attention instead to the poem's scrupulous annotation designed to give a 'plain and intelligible Account of the System of the World', the preparation of which delayed publication. It is ironical that Desaguliers's poem should have been published in the year that Pope's *Dunciad*, weighed down by pseudo-scholarly footnotes, was presented by the unwitting First Minister Robert Walpole to the new King and Queen.

THE
NEWTONIAN SYSTEM
OF THE
WORLD,
THE BEST
Model of Government:
An *Allegorical* POEM.

With a plain and intelligible Account of the
Syſtem of the World, by Way of *Annotations*:

With COPPER PLATES:

To which is added,

CAMBRIA's Complaint

Againſt the *Intercalary* Day in the Leap-Year.

By J. T. DESAGULIERS, LL. D.   Chaplain to His Grace
the Duke of CHANDOS, and F. R. S.

WESTMINSTER:
Printed by A. CAMPBELL, for J. ROBERTS in *Warwick Lane*; and
Sold by the Bookſellers of *London* and *Weſtminſter*. 1728.
(Price 1 *s*. 6 *d*.)

To the RIGHT HONOURABLE

The EARL of *ILAY*, &c, &c, &c,

MY LORD,

HO' I never made *Politicks* my Study, but always thought it my Duty rather to take Care to be obedient my felf, than to look into the Management of my Superiors; yet, among my Philofophical Enquiries, I have confider'd *Government* as a *Phænomenon*, and look'd upon that Form of it to be moft perfect, which did moft nearly refemble the Natural

A 2

tural

tural Government of our *Syftem*, according to the Laws fettled by the *All-wife* and *Almighty Archi-tect* of the Univerfe.

THOSE Philofophers who wanted Obferva-tions and Mathematicks, or wou'd not make Ufe of them, have given us fuch incoherent *Hypothefes* con-cerning Cæleftial Appearances, and the Caufes of the Motions of the heavenly Bodies; that the very worft Form of Government cannot be fo inconvenient to thofe who live under it, as the wild Notions of fuch Philofophers are fhocking to unprejudic'd Rea-fon and common Senfe.

BUT when the incomparable Sir *Ifaac Newton* gives us Facts and Demonftrations, inftead of Sup-pofitions and Conjectures, how is the Mind charm'd with the Beauty of the Syftem? What Traces of Divine Wifdom do we fee in the moft regular A-ction of univerfal *Gravity*, (or Attraction) whofe Power is diffus'd from the Sun to the very Centers of all the Planets and Comets, and acts upon the moft diftant of thofe Bodies, in as mathematical a Manner as it does upon the neareft? How

wonder-

wonderfully does it bring back the Comets from their immenfly diftant *Aphelion,* in their very long Ellipfes, by the fame Laws that it keeps the neareft Planet *Mercury* in its Orbit : The former defcribing *equal Areas in equal Times* round the Sun, as regularly as the latter, whilft Gravity always checks the Projectile Force, (whereby the Bodies tend to fly from the Sun) in Proportion to the Quantity of that Force.

THE *limited Monarchy,* whereby our Liberties, Rights, and Privileges are fo well fecured to us, as to make us happier than all the Nations round about us, feems to be a lively Image of our Syftem ; and the Happinefs that we enjoy under *His* prefent MAJESTY's Government, makes us fenfible, that *ATTRACTION* is now as univerfal in the Political, as the Philofophical World.

YOUR LORDSHIP's confummate Knowledge of the *Laws of Nature* which are eftablifh'd in the Heavens, as well as that of the *Laws of Nations,* and particularly thofe of *Great Britain,* makes the Patronage of this Poem Your undoubted Right.

YOUR

YOUR Lordſhip can beſt judge, whether the *Allegory* be juſt; and it is by Your Lordſhip's Approbation that I deſire to ſtand or fall: Only begging, that the Truth of the Philoſophy may excuſe the Badneſs of the Poetry.

INSTEAD of attempting Your Lordſhip's Character, which wou'd require an abler Pen than mine, and even then offend Your Lordſhip, by doing Juſtice to Your Merits; I ſhall only beg Leave to return my humble Thanks for the Freedom and Goodneſs with which Your Lordſhip has always receiv'd me; and tho' Your Lordſhip is pleas'd to lay aſide Your Qualiy in Condeſcenſion to me, I ſhall always be ſenſible how great an Honour is conferr'd on,

MY LORD,

Your Lordſhip's

moſt oblig'd, and

moſt humble Servant,

J. T. D.

PREFACE.

HE Univerſal Joy that fill'd all *Engliſh* Hearts at His preſent MAJESTY's Acceſſion to the Throne, had ſo ſtrong an Effect upon me, as to draw me from the ſerious and rugged Reſearches of *Philoſophy*, to the lighter and more agreeable Amuſement of *Poetry*.

THUS influenc'd, I was reſolv'd to endeavour at ſomething that might at once ſhew my Zeal and Loyalty, and at the ſame Time divert Her moſt Gracious Majeſty with my firſt Poetical Experiment, as I have had the great Honour of entertaining Her with Philoſophical ones. The following Poem was wrote laſt Summer, and intended to be publiſh'd on the Day of the *Coronation*: Bnt when I conſider'd that ſeveral Aſtronomical Terms and Alluſions wou'd want explaining to ſuch Readers as had not
been

been converfant in the Cœleftial Science, I refolv'd to add a few Notes, tho' they were not neceffary to thofe Great Perfons, for whom my Poem was chiefly defign'd. Then again, remembring that it is a common Saying, that *Philofophers are the worft of Poets*, and yet, being unwilling to fupprefs the firft Offspring of my Mufe, I enlarg'd my Annotations, and illuftrated them with Copper Plates, fo as to give a full Account of the Syftem of the World, in a plain, and intelligible Manner, together with a Confutation of thofe falfe *Hypothefes* which have fometimes obtain'd among learned Men. Thus have I *tack'd* my Poetry to Philofophy, to make it go down ; and tho' it fhou'd be thrown out by a *Majority*, I hope, by this Expedient, to gain a fufficient Number to keep it from being wafte Paper.

CAMBRIA's Complaint was written fince the Aftronomical Poem was in the Prefs.

WHEN I confider'd the *Firft of March*, as my own *Birth-Day*, I was indeed difpleas'd at the *Intercalary* Day, which puts it off once in four Years, but bore it with Patience, becaufe the *Biffextile* was fettled by Aftronomers ; but as it is *Her Sacred* MAJESTY's *Birth-Day*, and thus delay'd in the firft Year of Her Reign, I cou'd no longer bear it ; and therefore, to revenge the Affront offer'd to the ROYAL CONSORT by an intruding Day, I invok'd the Mufe to complain, in the Perfon of *Cambria*, with all the Wrath and juft Refentment, becoming the tutelar Goddefs of that Principality.

THE

THE
NEWTONIAN SYSTEM *of the* World
THE BEST
MODEL of *Government.*
AN
Allegorical POEM.

N Ancient Times, ere Bribery began
To taint the Heart of undesigning
Man,
Ere Justice yielded to be bought and
sold,
When Senators were made by Choice, not Gold,

B

Ere

5. Ere yet the Cunning were accounted Wife,

And Kings began to fee with other's Eyes;

Pythagoras his Precepts did rehearfe,

And taught the Syftem of the Univerfe;

Altho' their Obfervations then were few,

10. Juft were his Reafonings, his Conjectures true:

Men's

VERSE 8. *And taught the Syftem of the Univerfe;*

THE Syftem of the Univerfe, as taught by *Pythagoras*, *Philolaus*, and others of the Ancients, is the fame, which was fince reviv'd by *Copernicus*, allow'd by all the unprejudic'd of the Moderns, and at laft demonftrated by Sir *Ifaac Newton*. The firft Figure will give a clear Idea of it. All the Difference between the modern and ancient Syftem, is only what is added to it fince the Invention of the Telefcope, viz. *The four Satellites, or Moons of* JUPITER, *difcover'd by* Galilœo: *The Ring of* SATURN (*a thin flat Body encompaffing it without touching*) *and one of his Satellites difcover'd by* Huygens, *and the other four Satellites of that Planet, firft feen by* Caffini; *the* Phafes *of* VENUS *and* MERCURY, *like thofe of the Moon*, thefe Planets appearing *full*, when they are beyond the *Sun*, *halv'd* when at their greateft apparent Diftance (or *Elongation*) from the Sun, as at the Points P, Q; (*Fig.* 1.) and *horned*, as they pafs between the Sun and the Earth, not directly in a Line with the Centre of the Earth and Sun; becaufe, then they lofe all their Light in Refpect of us, and appear like black Spots. paffing acrofs the Sun's Face, or *Disk*, as VENUS is drawn in this Figure. *Laftly*, The Orbit of a Comet, which was firft fettled by Sir *Ifaac Newton*, who has given us a Method from three Obfervations to determine the Path of a Comet, fo as to be able to know where a Comet will pafs as long as it is vifible; how near it will go to the Sun; with what encreafing Velocity it will approach towards it; and with what decreafing Velocity it will recede from it,

after

Men's Minds he from their Prepoſſeſſions won,

Taught that the Earth a double Courſe did run,

Diurnal round it ſelf, and *Annu'al* round the Sun, }

That the brightGlobe, from hisÆtherealThrone,

With Rays diffuſive on the Planets ſhone,   } 15

And, whilſt they all revolv'd, was fix'd alone. }

What made the Planets in ſuch Order move,

He ſaid, was Harmony and mutual Love.

The Muſick of his Spheres did repreſent

That ancient Harmony of Government: 20.

B 2   When

after it has paſs'd by it. Dr. *Halley* has ſettled the whole Time of the Revolution of ſome of the Comets, ſo as to be able to foretel their Return, and to deſcribe that remaining Part of their Orbit, in which they are inviſible by Reaſon of their great Diſtance from the Sun which enlightens, and from us who ſhould ſee them.

VERSE 19. *The Muſick of his Spheres did repreſent.*

THE Harmonical Proportion, which *Pythagoras* obſerv'd to obtain in the Motion of the Heavenly Bodies, was taken to be real Muſick by the Ignorant; who fancy'd, that the Spheres (or hollow Spherical Shells, ſuppoſ'd

When Kings were not ambitious yet to gain

Other's Dominions, but their own maintain;

When, to protect, they only bore the Sway,

And Love, not Fear, taught Subjects to obey.

25. But when the Luft of Pow'r and Gold began

With Fury, to invade the Breaft of Man,

Princes grew fond of arbitrary Sway,

And to each lawlefs Paffion giving Way,

Strove not to merit Heaven, but Earth poffefs'd,

30. And crufh'd the People whom they fhould

    have blefs'd.

Aftronomy then took another Face,

Perplex'd with new and falfe *Hypothefes*.

Ufurping

pos'd to carry the Planets in them) rubbing againft one another, produc'd melodious Sounds, but that the Mufick could not be heard, by reafon of the great Diftance.

Ufurping *Ptolemy* depos'd the Sun,

And fix'd the Earth unequal to the Throne.

This *Ptolemaick Scheme*, his Scholars faw,   35.

No way agreed with the *Phœnomena* :

But

VERSE 33. *Ufurping* Ptolemy *depos'd the Sun*, &c.

Ptolemy fuppos'd the Earth to be in the Center of the World, encompafs'd with many Orbs or Spheres, one within another. The firft immediately compaffing the Earth, he called the Sphere of *Air*, the next the Sphere of *Æther*, then the Sphere of *Fire*: After followed' feven other Solid Tranfparent Shells, which were faid to carry the Planets in them, from Weft to Eaft in the following Order, *viz.* the *Moon, Mercury, Venus*, the *Sun, Mars, Jupiter*, and *Saturn*; then a Sphere called the *Primum Mobile* (or firft Mover) encompaffing all, and fuppofed to carry the whole Machine of the Univerfe round from Eaft to Weft, in 24 Hours, without difturbing the particular Motions of each Sphere. But afterwards for folving fome apparent Motions in the Heavens, not taken notice of before, the Followers of *Ptolemy* contrived three other Spheres or *Heavens*, between *Saturn*'s Heaven and the *Primum Mobile*, which he calls the Firft, Second, and Third *Chryftalline*.

The fecond Figure reprefents the Ptolemaick Syftem, *wherein we have omitted the three* Chryftallines, *and the* Spheres *of* Air, Æther *and* Fire, *to avoid Confufion.*

But yet refolv'd that Syftem fhould obtain,

Us'd all their Arts his Tenets to maintain;

A Revolution in the Earth to fhun,

40. Immenfe Velocity they gave the Sun;

Then

VERSE 37. *But yet refolv'd that Syftem fhould obtain,*
Immenfe Velocity thus gave the Sun

THE *Ptolemaick Syftem* was very well receiv'd among the Vulgar, and fuch as were not accuftom'd to confider the Difference between *apparent* and *real* Motion. If a Man, who had never feen or heard of a Ship, fhould be carried into the Cabin of a large Man of War with his Eyes blind-folded; and whilft the Ship was failing with a fteady Motion, fhould have the Bandage taken off, he would not be fenfible of his being carried along; but would imagine Rocks, Buoys, and other fixed Objects, which he paffed by, to be carried the contrary way; and, if he did not reflect, he would think the very Shores, with the Trees, and Houfes, alfo to move. So the unphilofophical part of Mankind, (who look upon the *Sun* and *Moon* to be but fmall Bodies, and the Planets and fixed Stars much fmaller, whilft they believe the Earth to be immenfly greater, and alone to deferve the Name of the *World*) cannot conceive their own Habitation to move, but look upon fuch as affert it to be ridiculoufly whimfical, or to defign to impofe upon Mankind with a Cant of hard Words, and out of the way Notions. But when *Aftronomers* found by the *Sun*'s great Diftance and apparent Magnitude, that he muft be far greater than the Earth,; then they though it, (at leaft) as reafonable to folve the Appearances of Day and Night, and of the Seafons by attributing the Motions to the Earth, One about its *Axis* in twenty four Hours to explain the firft, and another about the Sun in a Year to account for the laft. But fuch as would always have the Holy Scriptures taken in a literal Senfe (as if the *Divine Revelation*, which was given us to teach us Morality, and our Articles of Faith, had alfo been intended to inftruct us in Philofophy)

Then *Solid Orbs* with ſtrain'd Invention found,

To ſhew how *Planets* might be carry'd round.

But

loſophy*)* quoting ſeveral Paſſages to diſprove the Motion of the Earth, declared it *Hereſy* to aſſert that it moved; and therefore choſe rather to quit the greater Probability, and find Expedients to maintain the contrary Opinion. For the Objection againſt the Motion of the Earth, by Reaſon of its Weight and Bulk, vaniſhes at once when we conſider that the Sun is about ten Hundred Thouſand times bigger, and above two Hundred Thouſand times heavier; and that, to produce only the Different Seaſons, it muſt, in the Space of one Year, run through an Orbit whoſe Semidiameter is above eighty Millions of Miles long; but when Day and Night comes to be conſidered, then the Sun muſt be ſuppoſed to run through that whole Orbit in twenty four Hours, which is a Motion incredibly ſwift, being three Hundred and ſixty five times ſwifter than the Annual Motion of the Earth, or 540666 Miles in one Minute, which is 25200 Times ſwifter than a Cannon Ball: Whereas a Revolution of the Earth about its *Axis* in 24 Hours, will as clearly explain that *Phænomenon.*

THE Syſtem of *Tycho Brahe*, who ſuppoſes all the Planets except the *Earth* and *Moon* to Move round the *Sun,* and yet that the vaſt *Sun* with all of them revolving about him is carried round our little Globe of Earth, is ſo abſurd, that the bare ſight of the Scheme (*Figure* 3d) is enough to confute that Suppoſition. Neither have I made any mention of it in the POEM; becauſe we can never ſuppoſe any Thing to have happened in any Government ſo improbable, as that a Powerful *Sun* ſhould be ſo far influenced by a *Planet* as to be carried about at his Pleaſure; when at the ſame time the other great Officers move regularly in their Orbits, eſpecially when they have *Mars* amongſt them.

But when th' Obſervers, who the Heav'ns ſur-

vey'd,

Perceiv'd the *Planets* ſometimes *retrograde*,

Sometimes *directly* mov'd with *haſty Pace*,　　45.

Sometimes more *ſlow*, then *ſtopping* in their Race,

For

VERSE 44. *Perceiv'd the* Planets *ſometimes* retrograde,
Sometimes directly *mov'd with haſty Pace*,
Sometimes more ſlow, *then* ſtopping *in their Race*, &c.

THE Planets, in reality, are always direct; that is, Move according to the Order of the Signs, running through the *Conſtellations* from *Aries* to *Taurus*, and ſo on through *Gemini*, *Cancer*, &c. but by reaſon that the Obſerver is carried along with the Earth on which he ſtands, whilſt he is inſenſible of his own Motion, the *Planets* appear to him to go ſometimes *backward* a-mong the *fix'd Stars*, and ſometimes to go much *faſter*, then much *ſlow-er*, and alſo now and then to *ſtand ſtill*, (that is to keep the ſame appa-rent Diſtance in reſpect to the *fixed Stars* about them) in which different Caſes they are ſaid to be either *Direct*, *Retrograde* or *Stationary*, as may be ſeen in *Fig.* 4 and 5.

THE 4th *Figure* ſhews the apparent Irregularity of *Mars*'s Motion, which will ſerve to explain the Cauſe of thoſe Appearances in the other two ſuperior Planets, *viz. Jupiter* and *Saturn*.

BUT for the ſake of ſuch Readers as are wholly unacquainted with *Aſtronomy*, I beg leave to begin with the Explication of ſome Things neceſ-ſary to be known, before I conſider theſe *Stations* and *Retrogradations*, &c.

WHEN we look out in a clear Night, we may diſtinguiſh the *Planets* from the *fixed Stars* by their not twinkling as the *fixed Stars* do, (or what is more certain) by the *Teleſcope*, which will magnifie them, whilſt the
fix'd

For this, Expedients muſt invented be,

That, with it ſelf, their Syſtem may agree,

And keep ſome ſhew of Probability.

C   Within

---

fix'd Stars are not magnified, but rather diminiſhed by it. The Obſervations of one Night or two only ſhew us ſuch *Planets* as we then ſee together with the *fixed Stars* about them riſing in the Eaſt, getting to their greateſt Height in the South, and ſetting in the Weſt, as we ſee the *Sun* do in the Day time, and the *Moon* thoſe Nights when it ſhines.

THIS ſeems to be performed by a Motion of the whole Concave of the Heavens in 24 Hours, call'd by *Ptolemy* the Motion of the firſt Mover (*Primum Mobile*) but that Motion is only ſuch apparently; for it is the Revolution of the Earth about its own Center the contrary way, (*viz.*) from Weſt to Eaſt) in the ſame Time, which cauſes the Appearance of Riſing and Setting, in the Heavenly Bodies.

NOW when we come to take notice of the *Moon*, or any other of the *Planets* for ſeveral Nights ſucceſſively, we find that thoſe Bodies do not appear to *Riſe* and *Set* and *Move along* with the ſame *Stars*, but *creep on ſoftly* towards the Eaſt, ſo as to Riſe and Set later than the *Stars* which they accompanied before. This is called the *Proper Motion* of the *Planets*, and is owing to their revolving about the *Sun*, in Orbits that are nearly circular, which Revolution they always perform in a certain Period of Time, *viz. Mercury* in 87 Days, or near three Months ; *Venus* in 224 Days, or a little more than ſeven Months ; the *Earth* (which makes the *Sun* ſeem to move juſt in the ſame Manner) in a Year ; *Jupiter* in almoſt twelve Years, and *Saturn* in almoſt Thirty ; and the *Moon* moves about the Earth in twenty ſeven Days, and about ſeven Hours.

IF an Obſerver were removed from the Earth, to the *Center* of the *Sun*, and ſuppoſed to have the Proſpect of the Heavens from thence, he
would

Within their thicken'd Orbs new Orbs they

    made,

Each *Deferent* its *Epicycle* had,

So round the Earth the *Planets* still convey'd.

         50.

                     Wheels

would fee all the *fix'd Stars* in the fame Order, and of the fame apparent *Magnitude* as we fee them from the Earth; for though the Diftance
from us to the *Sun* is above 80 Millions of Miles, yet all that Diftance is
but is a Point when compared with the Diftance of *fix'd Stars.*

Now fuch an Obferver would lofe fight of what we call the *Diurnal
Motion*, and only behold the *Planets* fhifting their Places among the
fix'd Stars in regular Orbits, or Ovals nearly circular, which though different from one another, yet all of them have the *Sun* for their Center
(or rather, in Terms of Art, the *Sun* is in one of the two *Foci* of thofe
Orbits) and take up but a very fmall Breadth in the Heavens, which
Breadth or Belt is called the *Zodiac.*

IF a Line be fuppofed to be drawn from the Obferver's Eye, through
the Center of the *Planet*, quite to the *fix'd Stars*, the Place where that
Line terminates among the *fix'd Stars* is called *the Place of the
Planet* ----*Heliocentrick* Place, if the Obferver be fuppofed in the Center of the
and *Sun*; *Geocentrick* Place, fuppofing the Obferver in the Center of the Earth.
If the *Planets* were near the *fix'd Stars*, vaftly diftant both from the *Sun*
and the Earth, the *Heliocentrick* and *Geocentrick* Places would always be
nearly the fame; but as they are very near the *Sun*, and one another, in
comparifon of the Diftance of the *fix'd Stars* (*Saturn* the moft remote)
not being 10 times farther from the *Sun*, than the Earth) the *Heliocentrick* and *Geocentrick* Place of the *Planets* muft differ very much fometimes, and never be precifely the fame, but when the *Sun*, Earth and Planet, have their three Centers directly in a Line.

                                SINCE

Wheels within Wheels complex'd, they thus involve,

And yet Appearances but falfely folve.

C 2   Like

SINCE then, as I have already faid, the *Planets* if feen from the *Sun*,
would appear to move perfectly regular (only appearing to be largeft in
their *Perihelion*, or when neareft the *Sun*; and leaft in their *Aphelion*, or
when fartheft from it) it is plain that as we fee them from the *Earth*,
the fhifting of the Obferver's Place, as well as that of the *Planet*, muft
give their regular Motion very irregular Appearances: Accordingly *A-
ftronomers*, when they came more nicely to obferve the *proper* Motion
of the *Planets*, found that as they went Eaftwards among the *fix'd Stars*,
they mov'd fometimes fafter, and fometimes flower; that they fometimes
continued in the fame Place, (that is rofe, fet, and appeared to be carried among the fame Stars; nay, that fometimes they
moved towards the Weft among the Stars, and therefore faid that the
Planets were *Direct*, *Stationary* and *Retrograde*; whilft the *Moon* (becaufe
it does really move round the Earth) has none of thofe Appearances.

THIS gave a great Shock to thofe who believed the Earth to be fixed
in 'the Center of the World; but it is eafily accounted for, when once the
Diurnal and *Annual* Motion of the Earth are allowed.   For Example,
Let us fuppofe *Mars (Fig. 4.)* to be at *B*, and to move from Weft to Eaft, that is
from *B*, to *D*, *F*, *K*, *P*, &c. If feen from the *Sun*, *Mars* will appear a-
mong the *fix'd Stars*, to move according to the Order of the Signs, *viz.*
from ♎ to ♏, ♐, and fo on to ♑, ♒, &c. through the twelve Parts of
the *Zodiac* diftinguifhed by the faid Signs or Characters, in a very regular Manner; but the Appearances will be quite otherwife, when that
Planet is feen from the Earth.   The Earth being at *A*, and *Mars* at *B*,
Mars will appear at ♎ among the *fix'd Stars*, the *Heliocentrick* and *Geocentrick* Place being the fame, but when the Earth has moved from *A*
to *o*, as *Mars* moves flower than the Earth, he will only move from
B to

B to *D*, and (feen from the *Sun*) fhift his Place from ♎ to ♏ through the *Arc* ♎ ♏, but feen from the Earth it will appear to have gone fafter, *viz.* through the *Arc* ♎ 1 : then when the Earth is got to *E*, *Mars* will only be got to *F*, its *Heliocentric* Place being *a*, as it has defcrib'd among the *fx'd Stars* the *Arc* ♏ *a* ; but its *Geocentrick* Place is 2, and (feen from the Earth) it will appear to have moved much fafter defcribing the *Arc* 1 2.

WHILST the Earth moves from *E* to *G*, *Mars* will move from *F* to *H*, its *Heliocentrick* Motion, (which is uniform) being from *a* to *b*; but feen from the Earth, it has not appeared to move at all but has been *Stationary* in its *Geocentrick* Place 2.

As the Earth moves from *G*, through *I*, to *L*, *Mars* in his Orbit moves from *H*, through *K*, to *M*, defcribing among the *fix'd Stars* by its *Heliocentrick* Motion the *Arc b c* ; but feen from the Earth, it will appear to have defcribed the *Arc* 2 3. by a *Retrograde Motion*, or contrary to the Order of the Signs, that is from Eaft to Weft.

AND here it is to be obferved, that in this Motion, when *Mars* was at *K*, and the Earth at *I*, the *Heliocentrick* and *Geocentrick* Place was the fame, *viz.* at ♈.

As the Earth goes from *L* to *N*, and *Mars* from *M* to *O*; *Mars* (feen from the Earth) will all the while appear *Stationary* at 3, though its *Heliocentrick* Motion has been from *c* to *d*.

LASTLY, as the Earth moves from *N* to *A*, while *Mars* goes from *O* to *P*, and its *Heliocentrick* Motion is from *c* to *d*, the *Planet* (feen from the Earth) does again become direct, and feems to move from 3 to 4, and fo on.

IT will not be improper to fhew here, how the *Sun*, as it is feen from the Earth, appears to defcribe the fame Oibit, that the Earth doth really defcribe, without *Stations*, or *Retrogradations*.

WHEN the Earth is in *R* (its *Heliocentrick* Place being in ♎) the *Sun* appears to be in ♈ ; and as the Earth goes through the Points *l*, *m*, *k*, *K*, *N*, *A*, *e*, *o*, *f*, *g*, *h*, *R*, in its Orbit (its *Heliocentrick* Place moving according to the Order of the Signs) the *Sun's* Place will alfo go thro' the

the Points ♈, ♉, ♊, ♋, ♌, ♍, ♎, ♏, ♐, ♑, ♒, ♓, likewife according to the Order of the Signs, but always appearing in the Sign oppofite to that in which the Earth is.

I f it be asked how we know the *Sun* to be in fueh and fuch Signs, fince we cannot fee the *fix'd Stars* by Day; we anfwer, that, that Part of the Heavens which we fee in the South at Midnight is direƐly oppofite to that Part in which the *Sun* has appeared at Noon, as might have been perceiv'd if there had been a total Eclipfe, or we had made ufe of a long *Telefcope* in a dark Room, to fee the *Stars* that were about the *Sun*. As for Example, If an Obfeiver in the enlightened Part of the Earth at R, cannot (by reafon of the great Light of the *Sun)* fee the *Stars* of *Aries* (♈) when the *Sun* is in that *Couftellation*, the fame Obfeiver will be carried to *q* at Midnight, by half a Turn of the Earth upon its *Axis*, from whence feeing *Libra* (♎) in the South, he will judge with certainty that the *Sun* is then in *Aries* (♈) the oppofite Sign.

M e r c u r y and *Venus* the *inferior Planets*, (fo called becaufe they are nearer to the *Sun* than the Earth is) have alfo their *Stations* and *Retrogradations*, as feen fiom the Earth, which muft be explained by a different Scheme. See the 5th *Figure*, wheie the Appearances of *Mercury* are exhibited; which will ferve to explain thofe of *Venus*.

W h e n the Earth is at *A*, and *Mercury* at *a*, that *Planet* appears among the *fix'd Stars* at 1; and as the Earth moves fiom *A* to *B*, *Mercury* which moves fafter, will go in its Orbit from *a* to *b*, and appear to have mov'd among the *fix'd Stars*, from 1 to 2, according to the Oider of the Signs, or from Weft to Eaft, being then faid to be *DireƐ*.

W h i l s t the Earth moves from *B* to *C*, and *Mercury* from *b* to *c*, *Mercury* is *Stationary*, not appearing to move out of the Point 2; but as the Eaith moves from *C* to *Ð*, and *Mercury* from *c* to *d*, it appears to defcribe the *Arc* 2 ♉ among the *fix'd Stars*, by a Motion from Eaft to Weft, or contiary to the Order of the Signs, and therefore it is then *Retrograde*.

A s the Earth moves from *D* to *E*, and *Mercury* from *d* to *e*, it becomes *Stationary* at ♉. Laftly, as the Earth moves from *E* to *F*, and *Mercu cury* from *e* to *f*, *Mercury* does again become *Direct*, appearing to move in the *Arc* ♉ 3, from Weft to Eaft.

THE Defenders of the *Ptolemaick Hypothefis* were fadly put to it, to give the leaft probable Account of the *Stations* and *Retrogradations* of the *Planets*. Their Solid Tranfparent Oibs, or Chryftal Shells, by way of Expedient, they fuppofed to be much thicker than was at fiift imagined (fee *Fig.* 2d.) and within their Thicknefs placed little Circles, call'd *Epicycles*, fuppofing the *Planet* to go round in the *Epicycle*, whilft the Orb call'd a *Deferent* (or *Excentrick* becaufe the Earth was fuppofed not to be exactly in its Center) went round from Weft to Eaft, carrying round the *Epicycle*, together with the *Planet* moving in it: Only the *Sun*'s and *Moon*'s Oib had no *Epicycle*.

SUPPOSE *Mercury*'s Orb (in this 2d Scheme to move from Weft to Eaft, and that *Mercury* being in the *Epicycle* at *A* moves fafter from *A* to *B*, than the *Deferent* carries its *Epicycle*, then *Mercury* will appear *Retrograde*. Whilft a *Planet* (fee *Venus*'s Orb) moves in its *Epicycle* fiom *E* to *F*, it appears *Stationary*; but when it moves from *C* to *D*, (fee *Mars*'s Orb) it will be *Direct*, and have its greateft Velocity: And all the *Planets* muft appear fmaller in their *Apogee* (or greateft Diftance from the Earth) and biggeft in their *Perigee*, or leaft Diftance. But when the Times and Places of the *Stations* and *Retrogradations*, and the different apparent Magnitudes of the *Planets* came to be nicely obferved, the *Ptolemaicks*, to make their *Hypothefis* or Suppofition agree with the Obfeivations, were forced to enlarge fome of their *Epicycles*, fo as to make a monftrous Syftem, efpecially in regard to *Mars*, where the *Epicycle* muft be laiger than the *Deferent* in order to folve the *Phænomena*, or Appearances of that *Planet*.

THESE and other Abfurdities, made King *Alphonfus* fay to fome Aftronomers, who were explaining to him the *Ptolemaick Syftem*-----*that, if he had been* GOD, *he would have made the World, in a more plain and fimple Manner*; which he faid rather to ridicule thofe *Philofophers*, than out of any Spiiit of Prophanenefs.

Like *Peter's* Coat, the Syſtem burthen'd grew, 55.

Keeping old Faſhions, adding ſtill the new.

But when Philoſophers explor'd the Skies,

With *Galilæo's* new-invented Eyes ;

In *Mercury* and *Venus*, then were ſhewn

Phaſes like thoſe of the inconſtant *Moon* :   60.

And

VERSE 55. *Like* Peter's *Coat, the Syſtem burthen'd grew,*
Keeping old Faſhions, adding ſtill the new.

See the Story of Lord *Peter* in Dr. *S---ts* Tale of a Tub.

VERSE 58. *With* Galilæo's *new-invented Eyes.*

Teleſcopes.

VERSE 60. Phaſes *like thoſe of the inconſtant* Moon.

THE *Phaſes* of *Mercury* and *Venus*, whereby they ſeem *horned, halv'd*
and *full*, and *Mercury* and *Venus*, appearing as Spots upon the Face of
the *Sun*, as they paſs in a direct Line between the *Sun* and *Earth*, and their
never being in Oppoſition to the *Sun* (that is on the other Side of the
Earth) ſhews that thoſe Bodies do indubitably move round the *Sun*, as
has been explained in Annotation to *Verſe* the 8*th*, and ſhewn in the firſt
Figure.

And, like black Patches, croſſing *Phœbus* Face,

Theſe two inferior Globes were ſeen to paſs;

Which ſhew'd the right of *Sol* to hold the central

    Place.

Comets, (no longer *Meteors* to be fear'd,

As threatning Vengeance with their Tail or

    Beard.)   65.

By Teleſcopes, were, laſting Bodies, prov'd,

Like *Planets,* in revolving Orbits mov'd,

                                       Whoſe

VERSE 64. Comets, *no longer* Meteors *to be fear'd.*

SEE Dr. *Halley's* Verſes on Sir *Iſaac Newton's* Principia. The Third Edition.

> Jam patet, horrificis quâ ſit via flexa Cometis:
> Jam non miramur barbati Phœnomena Aſtri.

Whofe Courfe deftroyed the *Ptolemaick World*,⎤
And all the Chryftal Orbs in ruin hurl'd;   ⎟
Prov'd 'em fictitious, as in empty Space they ⎟ 70
    whirl'd.   ⎦

  So when a Minor King the Scepter Sways,

(Some Kings, alas! are Minors all their Days)

How hard's the Task, how great muft be the Pains

For envi'd Regents to direct the Reins?

While jarring Parties rend the finking State,   75.

Machines, by Art, muft bear the tott'ring Weight;

Statefmen perplex'd, with their Invention rack't,

One Day make Edicts, and the next retract;

The Coin, to Day, fhall in its Value rife,

To morrow, Money finks and Credit dies;   80.

D   One

One Year the Minds are rais'd by specious Schemes,

The next, are wak'd from all their golden Dreams:

And now th' Expedient is a Foreign War;

And now soft Peace can ne'er be bought too dear;

And now the Work is done by Plots and Panick

    Fear.   85.

  But bright *Urania*, heavenly Virgin, say,

How th' ancient Syftem made again its Way;

And, that Confiftency might be reftor'd;

The *Sun* became, once more, the central Lord;

What Praifes to *Copernicus* are due,   90.

Who gave the Motions, and the Places, true;

But what the Caufes of thofe Motions were,

He thought himfelf unable to declare.

                                   Cartefius

Cartefius after, undertook in vain,

By *Vortices*, thofe Caufes to explain;   95.

With fertile Brain contriv'd, what feem'd to be

An eafy, probable, Philofophy;

No conjuring Terms or *Geometrick* Spells;

His gentle Readers might be Beaux and Belles.

D 2   In

VERSE 94. Cartefius *after, undertook, in vain,*
By Vortices, *thofe Caufes to explain.*

Cartefius faid, that the whole *Mundane* Space was full of Matter; and that in our Syftem, the *Sun* in revolving upon its *Axis*, carried the *Cæleftial Matter* about it round in a *Whirl Pool*, or *Vortex* (*Tourbillon*) which Matter in its Motion carried all the *Planets* round the *Sun*; but that every *Planet* had at the fame time a fmall *Vortex* moving about it as it turn'd on its *Axis*, whereby it made fome of the Bodies about it fall on its Surface, and carried others round. The *Earth*, for Example, and *Jupiter* and *Saturn* (as he faid) moved their *Satellites* by their particular *Vortices*.

NOT knowing that Comets returned again or revolved in Orbits, He afferted that they were only *Planets* flying from one Syftem to another, when one great *Vortex* got ground of another; for he gave each *fix'd Star* a *Vortex* and *Planets* to go round it, believing with the reft of the Modern *Philofophers* that every *fix'd Star* is a *Sun*. But Sir *Ifaac Newton*, and other *Mathematicians* and Experimental *Philofophers* have fhewn the Motion of *Planets* in *Vortices*, to be inconfiftent with Obfervations and Appearances, and a *Plenum* in Natue to be impoffible.

In *Plato*'s School none cou'd admitted be,   100.

Unlefs inftructed in *Geometry*;

But here it might, (nay muft) afide be laid,

And Calculations that diftract the Head.

Thus got his Vogue the Phyfical Romance,

Condemn'd in *England*, but believ'd in *France*; 105.

For the bold *Britons*, who all Tyrants hate,

In Sciences as well as in the State,

Examin'd with experimental Eyes,

The *Vortices* of the *Cartefian* Skies,

Which try'd by Facts and *mathematick* Teft, 110.

Their inconfiftent Principles confefs'd,

And jarring Motions haft'ning to inactive Reft.

But

But *Newton* the unparallel'd, whose Name

No Time will wear out of the Book of Fame,

Cælestial Science has promoted more,   115.

Than all the Sages that have shone before.

Nature compell'd, his piercing Mind, obeys,

And gladly shews him all her secret Ways;

'Gainst *Mathematicks* she has no Defence,

And yields t' experimental Consequence :   120.

His

VERSE 113. *But* Newton *the unparallel'd, whose Name*
No Time will wear out of the Book of Fame,
Cælestial Science has promoted more,
Than all the Sages that have shone before.
Nature compell'd, his piercing Mind, obeys,
And gladly shews him all her secret Ways;
'Gainst Mathematicks she has no Defence,
And yields t' experimental Consequence :
His towring Genius, from its certain Cause, &c.

SEE Dr. *Halley*'s Verses before mentioned

Quæ toties animos veterum torsere sophorum
Obvia conspicimus——

Talia

His tow'ring Genius, from its certain Caufe,

Ev'ry Appearance, a *priori* draws,

And fhews th' *Almighty Architect's* unalter'd

    Laws.

  That *Sol* felf-pois'd in *Æther* does refide,

And thence exerts his Virtue far and wide;   125.

                                              Like

Talia monftrantem celebrate——
N E W T O N U M claufi referantem fcrinia veri.——
Intima panduntur victi penetralia Cæli——
——nubem pellente mathefi,
Quæ Superum penetrare domos, atque ardua cæli,
Scandere fublimis genii conceffit acumem.

    V E R S E 124. *That* Sol *felf-pois'd in* Æther *does refide,*
    And thence exerts his Virtue far and wide, &c.

  S E E Dr. *Halley's* Verfes.

Sol folio refidens ad fe jubet omnia prono
Tendere defcenfu, nec recto tramite currus
Sidereos patitur vaftum per inane moveri;
Sed rapit immotis, fe centro, fingula gyris.

Like Minifters attending e'ery Glance,

Six Worlds fweep round his Throne in Myftick
 Dance;

He turns their Motion from its devious Courfe,

And bends their Orbits by Attractive Force;

His

V ERSE 128. *He turns their Motion from its devious Courfe,*
 And bends their Orbits by Attractive, &c.

F ROM the Laws of *Attraction* (or *Gravity*) Sir *Ifaac Newton* has de-
ducted effects which are found by Obfervation; and nothing befides the
mathematical Demonftration it felf), can be a more certain Proof of that
Attraction, whofe Laws and Manner of Acting, that incomparable Philofopher has explain'd, than to find that the Motion of the *Celeftial Bodies*,
anfwer exactly to the Effects that their mutual *Attractions* muft produce.

T HUS when it had been objected by fome confiderable Men againft
Sir *Ifaac Newton*, that it would appear by the Motion of *Jupiter* and *Saturn* in their Conjunction (that is, as they pafs by one another) that *Attraction* was a mere Suppofition, *Aftronomers* obferved thofe *Planets* in
and near the laft Conjunction with fo much the more Care, and found
that they did fo affect one another, as they came near, as to difturb
each others Motion, and thereby fhew their mutual *Attraction*; which
Appearance cannot be obferved in the inferior *Planets*, in refpect to each
other, becaufe they are fo fmall, and the *Sun* fo large and fo near them,
that the Action of the *Sun* on them as He caufes them to defcribe their
Orbs, makes their Action on each other fo infenfible as to efcape Obfervation.

THIS

His Pow'r, coerc'd by Laws, ftill leaves them

free,   130.

Directs but not Deftroys, their Liberty;

Tho'

Th I s will be better underftood, by looking into the Caufe of the Motion of the *Planets* and *Comets* round the *Sun*, which will be eafily conceiv'd by any one, that will be at the Pains to read what follows with
fome Attention.

A Body once put into Motion, endeavours to continue in that State of
Motion, and would for ever go on in a right Line, never coming to Reft,
unlefs fome other Force equal to the firft, or feveral Forces (whofe joint
Actions are equal to the firft Impulfe) do, at once, or fuccefsively de-
ftroy its Motion.

A Body thus moving is faid to go on with its *projectile* Force, from
whofe rectilineal Direction, it cannot be turn'd to move in a Curve, unlefs there be fome other Force continually acting to turn it out of the right
Line, and the Moment that fuch a Force ceafes to act, the Body will fly
out of the Curve in a right Line, called a *Tangent* to that Curve.

To illuftrate this, let us fuppofe a Stone whirl'd round in a Sling before it be thrown forward; we are fenfible, by the Pull which we feel,
that the Stone is endeavouring to fly out of the Curve or Circle wherein we whirl it; and that that Force, with which it endeavours to get
loofe, is the greater, the fwifter the Stone is whirld round. Such a Force is
called *centrifugal*, and the Pull of the String which retains the Stone, is
called a *centripetal Force*.

LE T us fuppofe, for Example, that a Stone placed at the Point *A*. (*Fig.
6*.) has an Impulfe given it in the Direction *A B*, but at the fame Time
is held by the String *S A*; inftead of going to *C*, it will go to *D* in
                                                                           the

Tho' faſt and flow, yet regular they move,

(Projectile Force reſtrain'd by mutual Love,)

E   And

the Curve *A D O B*. Since the Stone is drawn from *C*, (the Place which the *projectile* Force would have carried it to) to *D*, *D C* will repreſent the *centrifugal* Force, whereby it ſtretches the String in that Direction, and the Force of the String, or *centripetal* Force, which acts in the contrary Direction *C D*, will alſo be equal to the *centrifugal* Force.

N o w let *S* repreſent the *Sun*, whoſe *Attraction* is inſtead of the Force of the String abovementioned; and *A* a *Planet*, whoſe Tendency is to move in the Line *A B*: It is evident from what has been ſaid, that if the *Attraction* of the *Sun*, which gives the *Planet* a Tendency towards *S*, be ſo proportioned to the *projectile* Force of the *Planet*, as to carry it to *D*, it will turn it ſtill out of its rectilineal Way, whereby it endeavours to fly off at *D* in the *Tangent D E*, and make it go on to *O*, and then to *B*, and ſo to *A D*, &c. ſo that it ſhall continually deſcribe the Orbit *A D O B*.

I f *A D* be an *Arc* of a Circle, of which *S* is the Center, the Curve *A D O B* will be a *Circle*, and the *Planet* will move with equal ſwiftneſs in every Part of the Orbit. But if the *Attraction* had been greater in reſpect of the *projectile* Force, ſo as to draw the *Planet* out of its rectilineal way as far as *d*, then the Curve would have been an *Ellipſe*, or *Oval*, and the *Sun* would have been in one of its *Foci* (or Centers, as the Workmen call them) and the *Planet* would have deſcribed one half of the Orbit, *(viz.* from the *Aphelion* to the *Perihelion)* with a Swiftneſs or Velocity, uniformly accelerated, and the other half of the Orbit, *(viz.* from the *Perihelion* to the *Aphelion)* with a Velocity uniformly decreaſing.

B u t this will appear very plain, by looking on the 7th *Figure*, where the *Planet* at *A*, endeavouring to move in the *Tangent Aa*, is by the Attraction of the *Sun S*, drawn to *B* inſtead of *M*, at which Point being

nearer

And reigning thus with limited Command,

He holds a lasting Scepter in his Hand.   I 35.

By

nearer the *Sun*, it is more strongly Attracted, and confequently accelerated ; but as the *centrifugal Force*, is proportionable to the Swiftnefs of the
Body carried round, the *Planet* endeavours to fly off in the *Tangent* B *b*,
its *centrifugal Force* being increafed in the fame Proportion as the *centripetal Force*, or *Attraction* of the *Sun*. The *Planet* being more attracted as it comes nearer the *Sun* at *C*, *D*, and *P*, has alfo proportionably more
centrifugal Force, arifing from its encreafed Velocity ; and continually encreafing its Endeavour to fly off in the *Tangents C c*, *D d*, and *P p*, does
thereby efcape being drawn into the *Sun*.

WHEN the *Planet* which came from *A P*, the *Aphelion*, is got to *P*,
the *Perihelion*, it moves through the Points *P*, *E*, *F*, *G*, quite to *A* with a
retarded Motion, the *centripetal* and *centrifugal Forces*, equally and gradually decreafing in the fame Manner as they encreafed before : For in
this half of the Orbit, the Direction of the *Sun*'s *attractive Force*, is contrary to (or at *obtufe Angles*, with) the Direction of the *projectile Force*,
as appears moft plainly at the Points *C*, and *F*, *S C* the Direction of
the *Sun*'s *Attraction*, making an acute Angle with the *Tangent C c*, when
the *Planet* is at *C* , but when the *Planet* is at *F*, *S F* the Direction of the
Sun's *Attraction* makes an obtufe Angle with the *Tangent Ff*, therefore the *projectile Force* in the Direction *Ff*, is lefs than it was in *E e*
and *P p*, but greater than in *G g*, or *A a*.

N. B. S *is one Focus of the Ellipfe, and Z the other.*

IT is evident, that the longer (or the more *excentrick*) the Ellipfe is,
the greater will be the Difference of Velocity. This is not very fenfible
in the *Planets*, whofe elliptick Orbits differ but little from Circles, but
yet enough to fall under Obfervation ; for it is owing to this that our
Summer is eight Days longer than our Winter ; but in Comets, which
move in very long Ellipfes, the Motion is incredibly fwift in the *Perihelion*,
and as flow proportionably in the *Aphelion* ; the Comet which appeared
in

By his Example, in their endlefs Race,

The *Primaries* lead their *Satellites*,

Who guided, not enflav'd, their Orbits run,

Attend their Chiefs, but ftill refpect the *Sun*,

Salute him as they go, and his Dominion

own.   140.

E 2   Comets,

in 1680, and 1681, defcribing in lefs than a Year, all that Part of its Orbit in which it was vifible to us; though its whole Revolution is not performed in lefs than 575 Years.

VERSE 137. *The* Primaries *lead their* Satellites,
Who guided, not enflav'd, their Orbits run,
Attend their Chiefs, but ftill refpect the Sun,
Salute him as they go, and his Dominion own.

Saturn, *Jupiter*, Mars, *the* Earth, Venus *and* Mercury, *are* called *Primaries*, or *Primary Planets*, becaufe they move round the *Sun*; but the five *Moons*, or *Planets* which move about *Saturn*, and the four which move about *Jupiter*, and the *Moon* which goes round our Earth, as they all attend their *Primaries* in their Revolution about the *Sun*, are called the *fecondary Planets*, or *Satellites*.

Now thefe *Satellites* are kept in their Orbits, by the *Attraction* of their *Primaries* and hindered from flying out in a ftreight *Line* or *Tangent*, in the fame manner as the *Primaries* are carried round the *Sun*, as has been explain'd

Comets, with fwiftnefs, far, at diftance, fly,

To feek remoter Regions in the Sky;

But tho' from *Sol*, with rapid hafte, they roll'd,

They move more flowly as they feel the Cold;

Lan-

explain'd in the laft Note. This Motion of the *Satellites* would be entirely regular, were it not for the *Sun*'s *Attraction*, which (though it is.
not near enough to hinder them from going round their *Primaries*) di-
fturbs their Motions; as is very evident in the *Moon*, which moves with
more or lefs Velocity, and whofe Orbit becomes more or lefs Convex
according to its Pofition in refpect of the *Sun*: And that feeming Irregularity of the *Moon*, is fo various and intricate that no Body could
invent any tolerable *Hypothefis* to folve it, or Numbers to exprefs it, till.
Sir *Ifaac Newton* demonftrated every Appearance and Motion of that variable *Planet* to be the Effect of the mutual Attraction of the *Sun*, *Earth*,
and *Moon*, according to the different Pofitions of thefe three Bodies. See
Dr. *Halley*'s Verfes, before Sir *Ifaac Newton*'s *Principia*.

> Difcimus hinc tandem, qua caufa argentea Phœbe,
> Paffibus haud æquis graditur, cur fubdita nulli
> Hactenus Aftronomo numerorum frœna recufet.

VERSE 141. *Comets, with fwiftnefs, far, at diftance, fly,*
To feek remoter Regions in the Sky.
But tho' from Sol, with rapid hafte, they roll'd,
They move more flowly as they feel the Cold;

Languid

Languid, forlorn, and dark, their State they

   moan,   145.

Defpairing when in their *Aphelion*:

But *Phœbus*, foften'd by their Penitence,

On them benignly fheds his Influence,

Recalls the Wanderers, who flowly move

At firft, but haften as they feel his Love: 150

                            To

Languid————————————
——————————————*in their* Aphelion.

A s Comets move from their *Perihelion* (or their neareft Place to the *Sun* in their Orbit) to the *Aphelion* (or greateft Diftance from the *Sun*,) they begin their Motion with great Celerity, but go on flower and flower till they come to the *Aphelion*, from whence their Motion continually increafes till they come back to the *Perihelion*; juft as a Cannon Ball fhot upwards, being attracted by our Earth, moves flower and flower, till it be got up to its utmoft Height, from whence it decends with an accelerated Motion. See the laft Note but one, where we have explain'd the Motion of a Comet.

To him for Mercy bend, fue, and prevail;

Then Atoms crowd to furnifh out their Tail.

By *Newton*'s help, 'tis evidently feen

Attraction governs all the World's Machine.

But now my cautious Mufe confider well   155.

How nice it is to draw the Parallel:

Nor

VERSE 151. *To him——— bend ——— prevail ;*
   Then Atoms crowd to furnifh out their Tail.

As Comets begin to come near the *Sun*, their Orbit which was almoft in a right Line, bends very quick, and as they approach the *Sun*
its great Heat makes the Comet throw out a Vapour, or Exhalation,
in great Quantity, which Vapour is always carried in a Direction oppofite to the *Sun*, and being fhin'd upon by the *Sun*, gives a View of what
is called the Comets Tail,' which Tail is of a prodigious Length, juft after the Comet had paffed the *Sun*, if the Comet went very near it ; as
happen'd to the Comet feen in 1680, and 1681, which paffed fo very near
the *Sun*'s Surface as to receive a Degree of Heat 2000 times greater than
our culinary Fires (or Iron when it is red hot) and to throw out a
Tail as long as the Diftance from the *Earth* to the *Sun*, which is above
80 Millions of Miles.

As

Nor dare the Actions of crown'd Heads to ſcan:

(At leaſt within the Memory of Man)

If th' Errors of *Copernicus* may be

Apply'd to ought within this Century,   160.

When e'er the want of underſtanding Laws,

In Government, might ſome wrong Meaſures

    cauſe,

His Bodies rightly plac'd ſtill rolling on,

Will repreſent our fix'd Succeſſion,

To which alone th' united *Britons* owe,   165.

All the ſure Happineſs they feel below.

                               Nor

   A s the Comet recedes from the Sun, its apparent Magnitude decreaſes, till at laſt both Comet and Tail become inviſible, when they are about as far from us as *Jupiter*, but ſtill we muſt make allowance for the bigneſs of the Comet, ſome being nearly as big as the Earth, and others very little bigger than the *Moon*.

Nor let the Whims of the Cartefian Scheme,

In Politicks be taken for thy Theme,

Nor fay that any Prince fhou'd e'er be meant,

By *Phœbus*, in his *Vortex*, indolent,   170.

Suff'ring each Globe a *Vortex* of his own,

Whofe jarring Motions fhook their Mafter's
    Throne,

Who governing by Fear, inftead of Love,

Comets, from ours, to other Syftems drove.

But boldly let thy *perfeƈt Model* be,   175.

NEWTON's (the only true) *Philofophy*:

Now fing of Princes deeply vers'd in Laws,

And Truth will crown thee with a juft Applaufe;

                        Roufe

VERSE 174. *Comets, from ours, to other Syftems drove.*

SEE the Note on *Verfe* 94, concerning *Cartefius*'s Account of Comets.

Roufe up thy Spirits, and exalt thy Voice

Loud as the Shouts, that fpeak the People's

    Joys;   180.

When MAJESTY diffufive Rays imparts,

And kindles Zeal in all the *Britifh* Hearts,

When all the Powers of the Throne we fee

Exerted, to maintain our *Liberty*:

When Minifters within their Orbits move,   185.

Honour their King, and fhew each other Love:

When all Diftinctions ceafe, except it be

Who fhall the moft excell in Loyalty:

Comets from far, now gladly wou'd return,

And, pardon'd, with more faithful Ardour

    burn.   190.

                  F   *ATTRA-*

ATTRACTION now in all the Realm is feen,

To blefs the Reign of GEORGE and

CAROLINE.

Voltaire:

Introduction to the Philosophy of Newton

Voltaire, *The Elements of Sir Isaac Newton's Philosophy … Translated from the French. Revised and corrected by J. Hanna … With explication of some words in alphabetical order,* Introductory poem, 'M. Voltaire to the Marchioness du Ch**' (London: Stephen Austen, 1738). pp. iii–viii.

Voltaire's poem is a celebration of Newtonian philosophy that is also a poem in praise of a lady, Emilie du Châtelet, Voltaire's friend and lover. She was a great enthusiast for the new science and the first translator of Newton's *Principia* from Latin into French. The poem first appeared in French as a prefatory epistle to the Amsterdam edition of *Eléments de la Philosophie de Neuton* (1738). This edition was published without Voltaire's permission and contained additional chapters not written by him. In the same year there appeared Voltaire's own edition in Paris and an English translation in London, *The Elements of Sir Isaac Newton's Philosophy. By Mr. Voltaire. Translated from the French. Revised and Corrected by John Hanna.* In the Advertisement, Hanna, a teacher of mathematics, explained that the translation was from the unauthorized Amsterdam edition, which contained several errors which he had amended.

The complicated publishing history of the *Eléments* has its origins in Voltaire's ambivalent relationship with France. In 1726 Voltaire arrived in England in voluntary exile and, on 8 April 1727, attended Newton's funeral at Westminster Abbey. On his return to Paris in 1728, Voltaire wrote his *Letters Concerning the English Nation*, first published in London in 1733, in which he marvelled at how Newton's 'Countrymen honour'd him in his Life-Time, and interr'd him as tho' he had been a King who had made his People happy' (Nicholas Cronk (ed.), *Letters Concerning the English Nation, Voltaire* (Oxford: Oxford University Press, 1994), p. 62). Voltaire's *Letters Concerning the English Nation* first appeared in London in 1733. Published the following year in France as *Lettres Philosophiques,* the work caused a scandal because of what was seen as Voltaire's contempt for his own country and excessive praise of England, a 'Country of Liberty' (Cronk, *Letters Concerning the English Nation,* p. 64). Voltaire fled Paris and took refuge at Madame du Châtelet's chateau at Cirey.

In the company of Madame du Châtelet, Voltaire immersed himself in the study of experimental philosophy in preparation for writing the *Eléments*, intended to be an 'easy and intelligible' account of Newton's physics (Voltaire, *The Elements of Sir Isaac Newton's Philosophy* (London, 1738), p. 3). He wrote a philosophical poem, the *Discours en Vers sur l'Homme* (1738), partly inspired by Pope's *Essay on Man*. In early 1737 Madame du Châtelet persuaded Voltaire to publish his *Eléments* first in Paris rather than in Amsterdam, as planned, as a way of seeking a reconciliation with the French authorities. Voltaire's Amsterdam publishers lost patience with him and went ahead with publication. When Voltaire failed to gain a license to publish his work in France he published it in Paris, giving London as the place of publication. The work was a critical success and won him elections to the Royal Society in London and in Edinburgh, as well as many other European academies. In 1743 he portrayed himself in his letter of thanks to the President of the Royal Society as a 'confessor' and 'martir' to Newton's faith (Theodore Besterman (ed.), *Voltaire: Correspondance* (13 vols, Paris: Gallimard, 1977-1993), Vol. 2, p. 816).

Voltaire's highly emotive response to Newtonian philosophy reflected, in part, his feeling of being an intellectual outsider. His enthusiasm was also typical of devotees to the new science. In his exposition of Newtonian physics, philosophical study is represented as an ecstatic experience: 'From Truth to Truth the human Mind rises insensibly to such sublime Points of Knowledge, as seem to be entirely out of its Sphere' (Voltaire, *Elements of Sir Isaac Newton's Philosophy*, p. 241). In the epistle to Madame du Châtelet below, Voltaire marvels at the power of the new philosophy not only to transform celestial mechanics but also the mind: 'How beautiful these Objects! how the Mind/ Flies to these Truths, enlighten'd and refin'd!'

The iconoclasm of Newton's philosophy had tremendous appeal for Voltaire. In his *Letters Concerning the English Nation* Voltaire celebrates Newton as the 'Destroyer of the Cartesian System' (Cronk, *Letters Concerning the English Nation*, p. 62). In the epistle Voltaire portrays himself as Newton's self-appointed champion, entering the philosophical lists to dispel Descartes's vortices, 'Those learned Phantoms'. He praises Madame du Châtelet's defiance of convention in studying science, linking her, in the introduction to his *Elements*, with Newton's philosophy: 'Madam, Neither your Title, nor the Philosophy here treated, are imaginary' (Voltaire, *Elements of Sir Isaac Newton's Philosophy*). In this barbed reference to Fontenelle's *Entretiens*, Voltaire mocked Fontenelle's Cartesianism and his doubts that a philosophical lady could ever exist in reality. Like Desaguliers's *Newtonian System of the World*, Voltaire's poem is a striking example of the extension of scientific models into polite culture. Its singularity lies in Voltaire's rebuke to traditionalists who saw the combination of women and philosophy as incongruous.

M. VOLTAIRE

TO THE

MARCHIONESS du CH**.

IMMORTAL Emily, vaſt, pow'rful Mind,
Pallas of *France*, and Glory of thy Kind,
Surpaſſing Age, ev'n in thy Bloom of
Youth,
The Pupil, Friend, of *Newton*, and of Truth.
Thy Fires tranſpierce me, and thy Charms
controul ;   5
I feel the Force, the Brightneſs of thy Soul !
To Thee attracted, I renounce the Bays
Sought on the Stage, while yet I liv'd on
Praiſe.
My Wit, corrected, roves not as before,
Of vain Applauſe, idolatrous no more !   10
  Let Earth-born *Rufus* with Reſentment
rave,
And drag his ſenſeleſs Fury to the Grave.
In Rhyme ſtill ſtraining, coldly to encloſe
Some trivial Thought, that would depreciate
Proſe,

A 2   That

15   That harmlefs Thunder let him hurl at me,
Which firft his Rage for others might decree.
To blaft my Fame let Pedant *Zoilus* feek,
And fpread unmeaning Malice once a Week.
With me their Envy withers in the Bud;
20   I fee no Tracts imprinted in the Mud.

     Philofophy, all-charming, pow'rful Queen,
Lifts the wife Mind above corroding Spleen.
Happy on high, where *Newton* now remains,
Knows He on Earth if. Enmity yet reigns?
25   Not more than He my Enemies I know,
While Truth auguft invites me from below.

     Already fee! fhe opes the Gate of Day!
The Lifts I enter, and purfue my Way!
The maffy Whirlpools, heaving ftill for Place,
30   Heap'd without Rule, and moving without
       Space,
Thofe learned Phantoms vanifh from my
       Sight,
And Day comes on me with her genuine Light!
That vaft Expanfe, of Being the Abode,
Space, which contains th' Infinity of God,
35   Sees in her Breaft this bounded Syftem move
Of Planets, Worlds, beneath us and above,
Whofe whole Extent, fo wondrous to our Senfe,
Is but a Point, an Atom in th' Immenfe.

                      Go

God-speaks, and Chaos at his Voice subsides;
In various Orbs the mighty Mass divides: 40
At once they gravitate, they strive to fall,
One Center seeki ng, which attracts them all.
That Soul of Nature, that all-moving Spring,
Lay long conceal'd, an unregarded Thing;
'Till *Newton's* Compass, moving thro' the   45
   Space
Measures all Matter, all discover'd Place;
Finds Motion's Cause, Philosophy unleavens,
Lifts up the Veil, and open'd are the Heavens.
   His learned Hand unfolds the glitt'ring
   Robe,
That clothes yon lucid, animated Globe,   50
Who guides the Seafons, and who rules the
   Day.
Mine Eyes distinguish each emitted Ray.
With Purple, Azure, Emerald, and Rose,
Th' immortal Tissue of his Habit glows.
Each Emanation, in pure Substance, bears   55
The various Colours that all Nature wears;
Those blended Taints illuminate our Eyes,
Give Life to Matter, fill th' expanded Skies.
   Eternal Pow'rs, who, near the King of
   Kings,
Burn with his Fires, and cover with your Wings 60

A 3   His

His Throne; O tell us! viewing *Newton's* Plan,
Were you not jealous of that wond'rous Man?
    The Sea too hears him. With stupendious
      Dance
I see the humid Element advance!
65 Tow'rds Heav'n it rises; Heav'n attracts it
    high:
But central Pow'r, more potent, as more nigh,
Each Effort stops: The Sea recoils; it roars;
Sinks in its Bed, and rolls against the Shores.
    Ye Comets, dreaded like the Bolts of Jove,
70 In vast Ellipses regularly rove!
Cease with your Motion Mortals to affright:
Remount, descend near the great Orb of Light:
Elance your Fires; fly; and, as each appears,
Restore the Vigour of exhausted Spheres!
75   Thou, Sister of the Sun, who, in the Skies,
Of dazzled Sages mock'd the feeble Eyes
Newton has mark'd the Limits of thy Race:
March on; illumine Night; we know thy
    Place.
    Earth, change thy Form; let the great Law
    of Matter,
80 The Pole depressing, elevate th' Equator!
Pole, fix'd to Sight, avoid the frozen Car,
The Constellation of the Northern Bear:
                      Embrace,

Embrace, in each of thy immenſe Careers,
Almoſt two thouſand Centuries of Years *!

How beautiful theſe Objects! how the Mind   85
Flies to theſe Truths, enlighten'd and refin'd !
Yes, in the Breaſt of God, from Matter free,
It hears the Voice of that eternal He.

Thou, whom that Voice familiarly invites,
Say, ev'n in Youth, the Seaſon of Delights,   90
How haſt Thou dar'd, in ſpite of Cuſtom's
    Force,
To move ſo boldly, thro' ſo vaſt a Courſe?
To follow *Newton* in that boundleſs Road,
Where Nature's loſt, and ev'ry Thing but God?

Purſuing Thee, I venture to advance,   95
And bring home Truth, that Wanderer, to
France.

While *Algaroti* †, ſure to pleaſe and teach,
Conducts the Stranger to the Latian Beach,
With native Flow'rs adorns the beauteous Maid,
And *Tyber* wonders at ſuch Worth diſplay'd; 100

---

  * *Almoſt two thouſand Centuries.*] Mr. *Voltaire's* Line is
    Deux cens ſiecles entiers par delà ſix milleans.

  But the Period he is ſpeaking of, according to his own
Account of it, conſiſts of 194000 Years, which is almoſt
two thouſand Centuries.

  † *Algaroti.*] A young *Venetian*, who is now printing at
Venice a Treatiſe on Light, in which he explains Attraction.

I grasp the Compass, and the Out-lines trace,
And with coarse Crayons imitate her Face.
Th' immortal Fair, all simple, noble, grand,
Should I attempt it, my unskilful Hand
105 To Her, as Thee, no Lustre could impart,
Above all Praise, and far above my Art.

ALGAROTTI:

Sir Isaac Newton's Philosophy. Explained for the Use of the Ladies

Francesco Algarotti, *Sir Isaac Newton's Philosophy. Explain'd for the Use of the Ladies in Six Dialogues on Light and Colours.* From the Italian, 2 volumes, translated by Elizabeth Carter, (London: E. Cave, 1739), pp. 1–xvi, Preface pp. 3–5, the First Dialogue pp. 1–42.

Francesco Algarotti early set about achieving his aim of becoming a cosmo-politan man of letters. He came from a wealthy family and, at the age of twenty he travelled to France and England, meeting famous writers, wits and learned ladies, in particular, Voltaire, Madame du Châtelet, Lady Mary Wort-ley Montagu and Lord John Hervey. He later became a favourite of the Polish King Augustus III and was made a Prussian count by Frederic the Great. Algarotti's *Il Newtonianismo per le Dame* was published in Milan in December 1737 and was soon afterwards translated into French. Like Fontenelle's *Entre-tiens sur la Pluralité des Mondes*, it was placed on the Papal index with the result that Algarotti left Italy shortly after its publication. *Il Newtonianismo* was less enthusiastically received in Italy than elsewhere, the main criticism being that it too closely imitated Fontenelle. The English translation by Eliza-beth Carter, one of the century's most learned women, appeared in 1739 under the title *Sir Isaac Newton's Philosophy. Explained for the Use of the Ladies in Six Dialogues on Light and Colours*. Carter was twenty-two at the time and this was one of her first published works. Her translation was republished in 1742 and 1765.

It was over fifty years since the publication of Fontenelle's *Entretiens*, yet Algarotti chose Fontenelle as his dedicatee. His ambition was to do for New-tonianism what Fontenelle had done for Cartesianism. In his dedication he praises Fontenelle's *Plurality of Worlds* as the work which 'first softened the savage Nature of Philosophy, and called it from the solitary Closets and Libraries of the Learned, to introduce it into the Circles and Toilets of Ladies'. Algarotti followed Fontenelle's format, with six dialogues between a philosopher and a marchioness, but his work made for more difficult reading, since it included more hard science. Nevertheless, it came close to matching Fontenelle's in popularity.

Madame du Châtelet had expected that Algarotti's *Newtonianismo* would be dedicated to her, which, in part, accounts for Voltaire's promotion of Algarotti's forthcoming work in the prefatory epistle to his *Elements*. On leaving France, Algarotti travelled to London where, shortly after his arrival in 1736, he was elected a Fellow of the Royal Society. Thanks to Voltaire's initial recommendation, he met Lord John Hervey and Lady Mary Wortley Montagu, who both fell in love with him. In a new edition of *Il Newtonianismo* published in Naples in 1739, Lady Mary's laudatory verses, which appeared alongside others by Voltaire and Hervey, highlighted Algarotti's success in targeting polite society: 'While Life so short, and Art so long we mourn, / Science in you appears not taught, but born. / While Newton's deep Philosophy you tell/ You show the pleasing gift to trifle well' (Algarotti, *Il Newtonianismo per le Dame* (Naples, 1739)).

Algarotti follows Fontenelle in so far as his intended readers are gentlemen. Although he pays tribute to ladies for having inspired him, he is forthright in expressing his low opinion of their intellectual abilities. In the light of this, it is interesting, now, that Carter should have taken on the translation. Algarotti's handling of the flirtation between his philosopher and lady is less subtle than Fontenelle's. Gallantry shades into condescension and, at the end, his philosopher boasts of his 'fine Conquest' (Vol. 2, p. 247).

The dedication to Fontenelle is beguiling. For a work dedicated to one of Descartes's greatest apologists, it is peppered with anti-Cartesian remarks, such as the philosopher's rebuke to the Marchioness: 'You are throughly possessed, Madam, with the Spirit of Cartesianism: This Sect places its Glory in Conjectures' (Vol. 1, p. 57). Algarotti's novelty lay in his vehemently post-Newtonian perspective, which he shared with his mentor Voltaire. At the same time, in his interest in establishing the proper language for philosophy, his championing of the moderns and his depiction of philosophers as heroes, he had much in common with the first apologists for the Royal Society. The success of *Il Newtonianismo* is reflected in its influence on later works, in particular, Benjamin Martin's *The Young Gentleman and Lady's Philosophy* (1759).

T O

Monf. de FONTENELLE.

IF you addreſſed your ingenious and entertaining *Dialogues* to the illuſtrious *Dead*, who had firſt given you the Idea of that Work, and therefore thought yourſelf obliged to ſeek your Hero even in the Obſcurity of the Tomb; how much greater Reaſon have I to dedicate theſe Diſcourſes to one of the moſt illuſtrious among the *Living*, whom I am indebted to for the Example which firſt ſet me upon compoſing them, and who has given me ſo perfect a Model of polite Wit and agreeable Writing?

A 3 Your

Your *Plurality of Worlds* firſt ſoftened the ſavage Nature of Philoſophy, and called it from the ſolitary Cloſets and Libraries of the Learned, to introduce it into the Circles and Toilets of Ladies.   You firſt interpreted to the moſt amiable Part of the Univerſe thoſe Hieroglyphics, which were at firſt only for Initiates; and found a happy Method to imbelliſh and interſperſe with the moſt beautiful Flowers a Field, which once ſeemed incapable of producing any Thing but the moſt rugged Thorns and perplexing Difficulties. You may be ſaid to have committed the Care of revolving the Heavens to *Venus*, and the Graces, inſtead of thoſe Intelligences to whom Ignorance had anciently aſſigned that Office.

The

The Succefs was anfwerable to the Beauty and Novelty of the Undertaking. That half of our World, which always commands the Votes of the other, has given its Approbation to your Book, and in the moft agreeable manner confecrated it to Pofterity.

May I venture to flatter myfelf, that my *Light* and *Colours* will have the fame Fate as your Worlds ? If a Defire of pleafing thofe who afford us fo much Pleafure, were fufficient to make its Fortune, I fhould have nothing to envy you. But I am too fenfible of the very many Defects that attend my Performance, Defects that I cannot help lamenting; for not to fay any Thing of your Talents, and that happy Art of rendering every Thing you undertake entertaining and agreeable, the Plu

A 4   rality

rality of Worlds, which you have chose for your Subject, seems of all others to present the most pleasing and elegant Images, and is therefore the most agreeable to your Dialogists, that the vast Field of Philosophy could ever supply you with. It presents to the Mind nothing less than the Stars and Planets, the grandest and most shining Objects of the Universe. There are but few of the subtile Enquiries of Science, into which you are obliged to enter. The Arguments, upon which your Opinion is founded, do not carry such a Certainty in them, as to make the Conversation grow languid.

I have endeavoured to set Truth, accompanied with all that is necessary to demonstrate it, in a pleasing Light,

Light, and to render it agreeable to that Sex, which had rather *perceive* than *underſtand. Light* and *Colours* are the Subject of my Dialogues; a Subject, which, however lively and agreeable it may ſeem, is not in itſelf either ſo pleaſing or ſo extenſive as your Worlds. I am obliged to deſcend to many difficult and minute Particularities of Knowledge; and my Arguments are unhappily inconteſtable Experiments, which muſt be explained with the greateſt Accuracy imaginable. It was indeed juſt, that the Ladies, who by your Work had been made acquainted with the great Change introduced by *Des Cartes* into the thinking World, ſhould not be ignorant of the new, and 'tis probable the laſt Change, of which the illuſtrious Sir *Iſaac Newton* was the Author. But it was extremely difficult to recivilize

A 5   this

this favage Philofophy, which in the Paths of Calculation and the moft abftrufe *Geometry* was returning more than ever to its ancient Aufterity. You have embellifhed the *Cartefian* Philo-fophy; and I have endeavoured to foften the *Newtonian*, and render its very Severities agreeable.

However, the abftrufe Points, upon which I have been obliged to treat, were only fuch as are abfolutely necef-fary, and always interfperfed with fomething that may relieve the Mind from that Attention which they re-quire. In the moft delightful Walk we are fometimes glad to find a ver-dant Turf to repofe ourfelves upon. Lines and mathematical Figures are entirely excluded, as they would have given thefe Difcourfes too Scientific an

3   Air,

Air, and appeared formidable to thofe, who to be inftructed muft be pleafed. Mathematical Terms are as much as poffible avoided; and if ever any do occur, they are explained by the Affiftance of the moft familiar Objects. The Difficulties raifed againft any particular Experiment, the Hiftory of optical Inventions, metaphyfical Doubts, and the various Opinions of different Philofophers, preferve the Subject from that continued Uniformity, which would make it difagreeable and tedious. I have endeavoured as much as poffible to render it lively, and make my Readers intereft themfelves in it as they would in a Compofition for the Theatre. Is there any Thing (efpecially where Ladies are concerned) in which a Writer fhould omit any Endeavours to move the Heart?

A 6　　　　　　The

The *marvellous*, of which the Heart always defirous of being affected is fo fond, happily arifes in true Philofophy of itfelf, without the help of Machines. I have made a fort of Change or Cataftrophe in the Philofophy of my Marchionefs, who is at firft a *Cartefian*, afterwards a Profelyte to *Malebranche*, and at laft obliged to embrace the Syftem of that Perfon, who ought to be placed at the Head of his Speeies, if Superiority and Rank among Mankind were determined by Strength of Genius and the moft comprehenfive Knowledge. This great Philofopher's general Syftem of Attraction is not omitted, becaufe it has a natural Connexion with the particular Attraction obferved betwixt Bodies and Light. Thus thefe Dialogues may be confidered as a complete

plete Treatife of the *Newtonian* Philofophy. The Sanctuary of the Temple will always be referved for the
Priefts and Favourites of the Deity;
but the Entrance and its other lefs
retired Parts will be open to the pro-
fane.

The Style I have endeavoured to follow is what I believed moft proper for
Dialogue, clear, concife, interrupted,
or interfperfed with Images and Turns
of Wit. I have taken the utmoft
Care to avoid thofe perplexed and
long Periods clofed by the Verb,
which only ferve to run the Reader
out of Breath, and are befides re-
pugnant to good Senfe, and much
lefs agreeable to the Genius of our
Language than is generally believed, and certainly cannot be agreeable

able to the Genius of thofe, who write with an Intention of being underftood. I have left them entirely to thofe, who forfake the [a] *Saggiatore* for the [b] *Fiammetta*, together with thofe antique and obfolete Words which conftitute fo great a Part both of their Knowledge and Delight. The Count *di Caftiglione*, in his *Courtier*, two Centuries ago, ventured to write in fuch a Manner, as to be underftood by his Contemporaries, and throwing afide the Affectation of *Gothic* Terms, adapted his manner of writing to the Forms of Speech in Ufe among the polite and well bred Perfons of his Time. *Cuftom*, the fovereign Judge in all Languages, (except perhaps our own) was

[a] An Epiftle from *Galileo* to *Virginius Cæfarinus*, in which the Author gives a very elegant Expofition of his Syftem of Phyfics and Aftronomy.
[b] A Romance, by *Boccace*.

his

his Guide ; and thus he enriched us with the fineſt Piece (as far as regards the Style) which the *Italian* Language has to boaſt of. For what Reaſon ſhould I think myſelf obliged to make uſe of the antiquated Diſcourſes of ſome clamorous Haranguer of four hundred Years ſtandıng, as a Model for a Work of Philoſophy and Politeneſs ; and rather than talk to Ladies in the Language of the preſent Age, addreſs my Diſcourſe to the Devotees of the thirteenth Century ?

This minute Diſſertation I thought in ſome Meaſure due to yourſelf, to let you ſee how little I have neglected in a manner of Writing, which may be regarded as your own. Nor was it leſs due to my Countrymen, ſince

this

this Work, whatever it be, is written in their original Language. Young Mathematicians, in giving the Solution of a Problem, generally defcribe the Steps by which they inveftigated it : It is only thofe of an eftablifhed Reputation who are permitted to give the fimple Solution, and leave to others the Care of finding by what Means they attained it.

I would not however appear to fet a greater Value upon this Work than perhaps the World will think it deferves, or fuppofe myfelf to have given a perfect Solution of this Problem. I am too well acquainted both with myfelf, and the Difficulty of the Enterprize, to entertain fo high an Opinion of the Performance. I have perhaps only

                                        feen

feen the Method, which ought to be followed, and yet have not followed it myfelf. *Raphael* and *Guercino* had nearly an equal Knowledge of the Preparations neceffary for the right Defigning of a Figure, and yet were extremely unequal in the Execution of it.

Whatever may be the Succefs of my Undertaking, the Ladies, for whom this Work is principally intended, ought at leaft to think themfelves obliged to me, if I have procured them a new kind of Amufement, which others may perhaps carry to a greater Degree of Perfection ; and if I have brought into *Italy* a new Mode of cultivating the Mind, rather than the prefent momentary Fafhion of adjufting their Head-drefs and placing

their

their Curls. Travellers fhould be the *Importers* of Wit, and of thofe reciprocal Advantages, which different Nations even in this refpect have over each other. Happy the Society formed upon the *Italian* Fancy, the *French* Politenefs, and *Britifh* good Senfe !

We ought to think ourfelves obliged to your Nation, and yourfelf in particular, for giving us an Example to render common and eafy what was once myfterious and difficult, and to write in our own Language what by a fuperftitious Veneration was appropriated to the *Latin*, and at the fame Time perplexed with *Greek*, that moft formidable Weapon of Pedantry. We may in this refpect caft the fame Reproach on the *Italians* as

Mr.

Mr. *Pope* does in another Cafe on the *Englifh* in his fine Prologue to *Cato*.

Our Scene precarioufly fubfifts too long

On French *Tranflation and* Italian *Song,*

Dare to have Senfe yourfelves, affert the Stage,

Be juftly warm'd with your own native Rage.

If we except fome Tranflations from the *French,* there is nothing among us but Songs and Collections of Verfes, which every Day overfpread us like a Deluge, and are the Torments of our Age. In the modern Books, written in the *Italian* Language, the Ladies can find nothing but Sonnets full of a metaphyfical Love, which I fuppofe muft affect them as little as the antiquated

quated Expreſſions of ſuperannuated *Cicisbei.* Let the Age of Realities once more ariſe among us, and Knowledge inſtead of giving a rude and ſavage Turn to the Mind, and exciting endleſs Diſputes and wrangling upon ſome obſolete Phraſe, ſerve to poliſh and adorn Society. I have at leaſt opened the Way to ſomething, which is neither Grammar nor Sonnet; and I ſhall flatter myſelf to have done much more, if what the Ladies inſpired me with, has the good Fortune to meet with your Approbation.

CON-

CONTENTS.

The FIRST DIALOGUE.

The SECOND DIALOGUE.

3　　　　　　　　*The*

The THIRD DIALOGUE.

Several Particulars relating to Vifion, Difcoveries in Optics, and a Confutation of the Cartefian Syftem.

Page 148

Errata in Volume I.

PAGE 26. *L.* 15. *for* Spread, *read* overfpread *p* 40. *l.* 16. *for* below, *r.* below ; *p.* 46. *L* 9. *for* examine, *r.* profecute. *p* 103 *l.* 12 *for* Appearances, *r.* Appearances? *p* 106 *l* 18, 19 *for* which were capable, *r.* capable *p.* 131. *l* 16 *for* , that is *r.* that is, *p* 150 *l* 11. *for* of *r.* to. *p* 178. *l.* 18. *for* given, *r* given ? *p* 182 *l* 22. *for* Ounce, *r.* Inch. *p* 219 *l* 26, *for* I, an, *r.* I. An.

C O N-

CONTENTS.

Vol. II.

The Fourth Dialogue.

The FIRST DIALOGUE.

A general Idea of Phyſics, and an Explanation of the moſt remarkable Hypotheſes concerning Light *and* Colours.

T H E very ſame Reaſon that led me every Day to a Concert of Muſic, a gay and elegant Entertainment, a Ball, or the Theatre, induced me to write an Account of the Manner in which I paſſed my Time laſt Summer in the Country with the Marchioneſs of *E* ——, and has thus from an idle and uſeleſs Member of Society, rendered me an Author. And the natural Deſire that every Author has to appear in print (whatever theſe Gentlemen may tell us in their long Pre-

B   faces)

faces) engages me at prefent to publifh
this Account. It is entirely philofophical, and compofed of certain Difcourfes which I had with that polite Lady
on the Subject of Light and Colours.
Some will, I make no doubt, condemn
me for having paffed my Time fo ill
with a Lady ; and indeed I have condemned myfelf for it. But if they knew
what an engaging Manner the Marchionefs has of obliging every one to whatfhe
defires, I am perfuaded they would for-
give me, even if I had read her *Guicciardini*'s [a] Hiftory of the Wars of *Pifa*, if
fhe could have defired it. But however
inexcufable my Error might be, I conftantly endeavour'd to amend it, whenever I could difengage myfelf a little
from Light and Colours: And indeed
both the Beauty of the Marchionefs
and the Nature of the Place (which
feemed formed to fupport what fhe had

[a] An *Italian* Hiftorian very prolix and tedious.
It was a Saying of Dr. *Donne's*, that if *Mofes* had
wrote like *Guicciardini*, the whole World would not
have been big enough to contain the Hiftory of its
own Creation.

every

every where given Birth to) infpired a
Difcourfe quite different from that of
Philofophy. The little Peninfula of
Sirmione, (the Country of the polite
Catullus) and thofe Mountains which
have fo often repeated the fine Verfes
of [a] *Fracaftorius*, two remarkable Points
(if I may ufe the Expreffion) in the
poetical Geography, formed a diftant
Profpect to a fine Seat placed on an eafy
Afcent that was watered below with
the clear Streams of the *Benaco* [b], which
by its great Extent and the roaring of
its Waves, feems to rival the Ocean.

[a] *Jerom Fracaftorius* was born of a noble Family
at *Verona* in *Italy*, about the Year 1483. He ftudied Phyfic, 'till a few Years before his Death, when
he devoted himfelf entirely to the Study of polite
Learning Mathematics, Aftronomy and Cofmography.
He died of an Apoplexy in 1553, and was interred in
the Church of St. *Euphemia* at *Verona*, where in 1559
he had a Statue erected to him by Order of that City.
His poetical Works are much admired, the principal
of which are his *Syphilis*; *Jofeph* an Epic Poem in
2 Books, but left unfinifhed at his Death; and his
Alcon feu de Curâ Canum Venaticorum. See *his Life
prefixed to his Works, Joann. Imperialis Mufæum Hifto-
ricum*. Pag. 16. *Les Eloges des Hommes Savans, tirez de
l'Hiftoire de M. de* Thou. *Tom*. 1. Pag. 189.
[b] A Lake in the Territories of *Venice*, now called
Lagodi Garda.

B 2   The

The Orange Trees that diffused, their Odours along the Banks, and perfumed the Air all around with a delightful Fragrance, the Coolness of the Woods, the Murmur of Fountains, the Vessels that spread their Sails along the crystal Lake, each of these agreeable Objects would have alternately ravished my Senses, if the Goddess of this delightful Place had not wholly engaged my Attention.

To the Charms of Wit, and the most polite Imagination she joined an uncommon Strength of Judgment, and to the most refined Sentiments a learned Curiosity. Superior to the rest of her Sex, without being solicitous to appear so, she could talk of Ornament and Dress whenever there was Occasion for it, and ask proper Questions upon more important Subjects. A natural Negligence, an easy Unaffectedness imbellished all she said. She had Beauty enough to gain her Consort many Friends, and was judicious enough not to shew any one a particular Regard. and these Accomplishments being seldom
dom

dom found united except in Books and the Imagination of Authors, is the Reaſon, I believe, that Learning in Ladies does not meet with ſo univerſal an Applauſe from the World as their Beauty.

When impertinent Viſitors gave us ſome Reſpite from Play, that Relief and Plague of Society, we paſſed ſome part of the Day in reading ancient and modern Authors contrary to the Opinion of that Monarch [a] who preferred old Books like old Friends. Our principal reading was Poetry, as this ſeemed of all others moſt agreeable to the Country from whence the *Genealogiſts* of polite Literature tell us it derived its Original. But, however, that we might preſerve a certain Spirit of Liberty, upon which all our Converſation was grounded, we did not entirely exclude that Sort of Poetry which is formed expreſly for the Town, as Satire,

---

[a] *Alphonſus* the 10th King of *Arragon*, ſirnamed the Wiſe, who uſed to ſay, he deſired little more than four *old* Things, *viz. old* Wood to burn, *old* Wine to drink, *old* Books to read, and *old* Friends to live with. He began his Reign in 1252, and died in 1284.

B 3   Comedy

Comedy, and Epic. This Spirit had a more particular Influence upon our Criticifm, which regarded an *Italian*, a *French*, an ancient and a modern Author, with an equal Impartiality. The fober Dignity and Purity of the *Eneid*, the Variety and Perfpicuity of *Orlando Furiofo*, the noble finifhing of the *Gierufalemme Liberata*, the Juftnefs, the philofophical Spirit, and the peculiar Beauties of the *Henriade*, the Invention of the *Mandragora* [a], the Characters of the *Mifanthrope*, the Sweetnefs of Verfe in [b] *Sannazarius*, and the happy

[a] *Mandragora* or *Mandragola*, an *Italian* Comedy written by the famous *Nicolas Machiavel*.

[b] *Actius Sincerus Sannazarius* was born at *Naples* of a noble Family in 1488, He was Secretary to *Ferdinand* King of *Naples*, who honoured him with a great Share of his Confidence and Efteem He was eminent for his *Italian* and *Latin* Verfes. He fpent twenty Years in correcting and polifhing his Poem *De Partu Virginis*, but his pifcatory Eclogues in *Latin* which he wrote when he was young, were preferred to all his other poetical Writings He was rewarded by the *Venetians* with a Prefent of 600 Crowns for his celebrated Epigram,

Viderat Hadriacis Venetam, &c.

He

happy Negligence of *Chappelle*; all these
we compared in such a Manner, that
we neither esteemed a Verse the more
harmonious for its Antiquity, nor a
Thought less sublime or elegant from
any Difference of Country. We in-
terspersed our Discourse with Episodes
and Digressions, which the Marchioness did not think herself less obliged to
me for, than if I had given her an Encomium upon her Beauty.

In one of these Digressions I spoke of
the Force and Advantages of *English*
Poetry, which gave her a strong Inclination to be acquainted with it, imagining
that a Nation, on whom *Minerva* had
lavished her Favours in so profuse a
Manner, could not be destitute of
those of *Apollo*.

As I desired nothing more than to
give Pleasure to a Person who continually afforded so much to me, I was

He died in 1530 of Grief, because the Prince of
Orange, who was General of the Imperial Army, had
demolished a Tower belonging to his Country-house.
He lies interred near *Virgil's* Tomb. See *Paulus Jo-
vius in Elogiis*, &c.

ex-

extremely forry that I could trace her only a very low and imperfect Idea of *Dryden*'s harmonious Copioufnefs, *Waller*'s Softnefs, *Prior*'s various and eafy Style, the lively Wit and Fire of *Rochefter* and *Dorfet*, the correct Majefty of *Addifon*, the ftrong and manly Strokes of *Shakefpeare*, and the aftonifhing Sublimity of *Milton*. To fpeak of the Merit of a Poet, is the fame Thing as endeavouring to defcribe the Beauty of a Face, which can be judged of only by the Sight; and to quote, even in its original Language, only one particular Paffage feparate from the reft, would be the fame as fhewing an Eye, a Lip, or a Dimple of a Face of which we defire to fee, not fingle Features, but the whole, whofe Beauty and Symmetry are the Refult of innumerable Charms. However it gave me a little Confolation when I remembred, that, among fome Papers which I happened to bring with me into the Country, I had Mr. *Pope*'s Ode on St. *Cæcilia*'s Day. None can be unacquainted with the Name of this great Author,

Author, without being at the fame Time ignorant that there is any fuch Thing as Poetry in the *Englifh* Language. The next Morning I carried this fine Ode with me into a Grove dedicated to our poetical Converfation, and now become the *Parnaffus* of all Nations. After having begged Pardon of the *Englifh* Mufes, I tranflated it as well as I could, and began to read. The Marchionefs liftened to me with an Attention that fine Ladies feldom give themfelves the Trouble of, When I came to this Paffage ——

While in more lengthen'd Notes and flow
The deep Majeftic folemn Organs blow.

fhe interrupted me, and could not enough admire the Propriety of thefe *Epithets*, which (added fhe) defcribe that Inftrument in fuch a Manner that I really hear it play. I cannot tell whether you hear it too, but I think I

ᵃ Mentre con tarde ed allungate Note
Il profundo, Solenne, e Maeftofo
Organo Soffia ——

B 5   may

may reasonably conclude it from a certain Pleasure you shewed, perhaps insensibly, in reading this Passage to me. You are so well acquainted, *Madam*, with the most secret Motions of my Heart, that it is impossible for you to be deceiv'd; and you commend a Thing that certainly renders the Imagery, which is the Support of Poetry, extremely lively and expressive. These Sort of *Epithets* are the Strokes that give Life to the Picture. A *white* Hand, a *serene* Brow, and *bright* Eyes, are at best but the rough Draught of it.

Now we are speaking of Epithets, is not *the sevenfold Light*, which I read of some Time ago, (replied the Marchioness) in an Ode made in Honour of the philosophical Lady [a] of *Bologna*, some *Chinese* Hieroglyphic? at least it is so to me and many others whom I have desired to explain it. You mean, answered I,

[a] *Laura Maria Katherina Barsi*, a learned Lady in *Italy*, who in 1732, at 19 Years old, held a philosophical Disputation at *Bologna*, upon which she was admitted to the Degree of Doctor in that University.

—— *The*

—— *The* ſevenfold *Light*
Whence ev'ry pleaſing Charm of Colour
  ſprings,
And forms the gay variety of Things[a].

If you knew the Force of this Epithet, you would ſee a *Newtonian* Picture inſtead of a *Chineſe* Hieroglyphic,
though perhaps a little too philoſophical
for Poetry. What (anſwered ſhe, interrupting me with an Air of Surprize)
you underſtand this Paſſage as well, as
if it was the Production of an *Engliſh*
Author. I am of Opinion, *Madam*,
anſwered I, that the Verſes of an *Italian* who has the Honour to be a great
Admirer of you, are infinitely preferable to thoſe of an unfortunate *Briton*,
who has the Unhappineſs of being at ſo
great a Diſtance from you. I underſtand you, continued ſhe, and I need
not deſire a better Encomiaſt than you,

---

[a] O dell, aurata
  Luce Settemplice.
  I varioardenti, e miſti almi Colori.

if it be true, that no one understands,
the Sense of an Author so well as himself. Come then, since you are the
Author of this Piece, deliver me from
the Perplexity I am under about this.
sevenfold Light, and the rest of your
Newtonian Picture, which gives me
great Reason to believe, that in praising
one Lady, you have used your utmost
Endeavours that no other should understand your Meaning. It is certainly,
that profound Respect that I have for
you, *Madam*, (answered I) which has
made you find me out. Afterwards
reflecting that it was impossible to give
her in few Words an Explication of
Sir *Isaac Newton's* Opticks to which
these Verses allude, a Thing which
she had not the least Idea of, had not
we better follow the Example of the
Theatre, *Madam* said I, where the
Play is generally at an End when the
Persons come to a Knowledge of one
another? And besides, we should finish
Mr. *Pope's* Ode, which will certainly
give you a far greater Pleasure, than
any Comment upon mine. No, no,
said

faid fhe, we will finifh that another Time, and for the prefent we will act contrary to the Theatre, but without forgetting the Cataftrophe, or finding myfelf in as much Ignorance as ever.

Being willing to give her fome Idea of the Syftem to which thefe Verfes refer, and thinking that the Marchionefs would for once be like other Ladies, who are often defirous of feeming to underftand what they are not fuppofed to have the leaft Notion of, I told her, as briefly as I could, That according to Sir *Ifaac Newton*'s Opinion, or rather as the Thing really is, every Ray of Light is compofed of an infinite Number of other Rays, fome of which are red, fome orange-colour, others green, fome blue, fome indigo, and others violet; and that from the Compofition of thefe feven Colours in a direct Ray from the Sun, arifes the white or rather golden Colour of Light : That if this direct Ray from the Sun is refracted by a certain Glafs called a Prifm, thefe Rays, of which it is compofed differing in Colour, differ alfo in Degrees of Refrangibility.

frangibility.——I fee (faid the Marchionefs, interrupting me in a Manner very
different from what I expected) that
your Comment has more need of an
Explanation than perhaps the Text itfelf. But this is my Fault in not being
able to underftand your *Refraction, different Degrees of Refrangibility,* and
the like, which quite confound the Idea
I had begun to form. But pray explain yourfelf in fuch a Manner that I
may not have any farther Reafon to
accufe you with Obfcurity, nor my
own Dulnefs with being the Caufe of
it.

You will not be fatisfied, anfwered I,
unlefs I make you a Comment at leaft
as long as that of the *Malmantile,* which,
I obferved to you the other Day, feemed
to be dictated by the agreeable *Mathanafius.*[a] who was formerly the *Moliere* of

[a] Monfieur de' St. *Hyacinthe,* under the fictitious
Name of Dr. *Mathanafius,* publifhed a Piece intituled,
Chef d'Oeuvre d'un Inconnu avec des Remarques, in
order to ridicule the Impertinence of fome Critics and
Commentators. The *Malmantile* is an *Italian* Piece
wrote after the manner of this Author.

the

the Commentators; at leaft, faid fhe, *Newton* will enter more properly here than *Micheli* does there, whofe Difcoveries are of no fort of Service to illuftrate this Poem; and fince all you faid was fpoke with an Air of Serioufnefs and fuch Confidence that you did not fcruple faying, *according to* Sir Ifaac Newton's *Opinion*, *or rather as the Thing really is*, you have made me extremely defirous of becoming a *Newtonian*. This, anfwered I, is a very ready Method of propagating Sir *Ifaac Newton's* Philofophy and bringing it into Fafhion. *Pemberton*, *Gravefand*, and *Dunch*, the zealous Propagators of this Syftem, would be very glad to give the Care of it to you. But what will Mr. *Pope* fay (fhewing her the Book which I had ftill in my Hand) if you leave him in the Beginning of this fine Ode, for a fudden Fancy that you have taken to Light and Colours? Mr. *Pope*, anfwered fhe, cannot be offended at my leaving him for a Philofopher, and fuch a Philofopher as Sir *Ifaac Newton*, one of his own Countrymen too.

Do

Do not you know, said I smiling, that
the Poets look upon themselves as
sacred, and when they have once got
this Enthusiasm into their Heads, they
regard neither Country nor Relations,
but think themselves greater than any
Philosopher, even if he had discovered
wherein consists the Union of the
Soul and Body ? 'Tis well for us, said
she, that the Poets have more Modesty than to declare this in their Writings.

It signified nothing for me to plead
Incapacity and many other Excuses,
which are made use of on the like Occasions, and which occurred to me upon this. The Marchioness insisted upon seeing my *Newtonian* Picture as she
called it. I begged she would at least
have Patience till Evening, telling her
that the Night had always been the
Time consecrated to philosophical Affairs ; and that the most polite Philosopher in *France* had made use of it in a
Circumstance resembling mine, and made
no Scruple of entertaining a fine Lady
with philosophical Discourses in a Wood
at

at Mid-night. But we, Sir, replied the Marchioness, ought to make use of the Day, which is certainly more proper than the Night for a Discourse on Light and Colours. She spoke this with an Air of Authority that inforced her Commands in the most amiable Manner, and made it a Pleasure to obey.

Thus I was absolutely obliged to begin, but the Difficulty was how to do it; for she had not the least Notion of Physics, which it was necessary to give her a general Idea of, before I proceeded to a Discourse upon Light and the *Newtonian* System. At last, after having again in vain reminded her of Mr. *Pope* and other Subjects that required less Application and afforded greater Pleasure, when the Heat of the Sun, which was now almost at his Meridian, obliged us to retire into the House, I began after the following Manner.

It is natural to suppose that after Society was so well established among Mankind, that some of them had nothing to do (which I look upon as the
Epocha.

Epocha of its Perfection) thefe Perfons either from that Curiofity, which we naturally have about thofe Things that concern us leaft, or perhaps for fear of being charged with Idlenefs by the reft, applied themfelves to confider that Variety of Things of which this Univerfe is compofed, their Differences and Effects. It is probable too, that one of the firft Speculations that thefe idle People, who afterwards affumed the Name of *Philofophers*, employed themfelves about, was concerning the Nature of Light, which is certainly the moft beautiful and confpicuous Object of our Sight, and indeed the Means by which we fee every Thing elfe. This confequently led them to the Colours which this Light depictures upon Objects, and which diffufe fuch a Variety and Beauty on our World. Thus, I believe, that *Opticks*, which is that Part of Natural Philofophy that regards Light and Colours, and in general all Natural Philofophy, had their Origin among Men at the fame Time with their Idlenefs; indeed it was of a later Date than fome Parts

Parts of Morality and Geometry, which
were abſolutely neceſſary in the earlieſt
Ages of the World, but contemporary
to Poetry, if you will, and antecedent
to Metaphyſics, which required a ſtill
greater Vacation from Buſineſs.

I am pleaſed, replied the Marchioneſs, that Poetry and Natural Philoſophy have one common Date ; ſince for
that Reaſon you will not perhaps think
this Tranſition ſo ſtrange, that we have
made from one to t'other upon my Account.   The Tranſition, (anſwered I)
that our Philoſophers made from a ſlight
Knowledge of Things to an Ambition
of unfolding Nature and penetrating its
Effects, was much ſtranger.   This, in
the Language of Philoſophy, is called
making *Syſtems*.   This is juſt as if any
one, after having had a curſory Diſcourſe
with a ſubtile Miniſter of State about
good or bad Weather, ſhould attempt
to write his Character, and pretend that
he had penetrated his moſt profound
Secrets.   They ſhould have begun with
a very attentive Examination of Things,
drawn from frequent Obſervations and
diligent

diligent Experiments before they ventured upon the least System. They were to act, if possible, like those two antient Philosophers; one [a] of whom, in order to write on the Nature of Bees, retired into a Wood, that he might have the better Opportunity of considering them; and the other [b] spent sixty Years in making Observations upon these Insects. But the Misfortune is, that Experiments and Observation require Patience and Time, and very often we are indebted to mere Chance for the most useful and entertaining among them. On the other Hand, Men are always in haste to arrive at Knowledge, or at least to have the Appearance of it.

After this, the Revolutions of States, the rude and uncultivated Manners of the People, the Temper of Nations, and the Profession of those, among whom Philosophy had formerly flourished, did not a little retard its Progress. From the *Indian* Traditions

[a] *Philiscus, vid.* Plin *N H. L.* xi *C* 9.
[b] Aristomachus *Id ibid.*

which

which their Priefts kept to themfelves
with as much Jealoufy as they did their
Genealogies, and from the *Egyptian*
Temples, where it had long lain hid under Myfteries and Hieroglyphics, Philofophy at Length took its Seat in the
Portico's and Gardens of *Greece*, where
it was very foon imbellifhed and cor-
rupted with Allegory, Fables, and all
the Ornaments of Eloquence. Imagination, which is the Characteriftic of
the *Grecian* Genius, prevented Philofophy from taking any deep Root, and
indeed it was attempted to have been
totally extirpated by the Eloquence of
a Man whofe Difcourfes were diftinguifhed by a certain grave and elegant
Pleafantry, which made him Mafter of
the moft powerful Arts of Perfuafion,
and who had been judged by the
Oracle the wifeft among Mortals He
afferted, that we have nothing to do
with what is above us, and ftrove to
reclaim our Curiofity and Studies from
natural to moral Objeds ; from the
Combinations of the Univerfe, to the
little Chaos of human Extravagancies,

I   and

and from that Rapture with which we are tranfported by the Contemplation of vaft and diftant Objects, to the melancholy Confideration of our own Emptinefs. And this Perfon, who, more deftructive than *Pandora*, engaged Mankind in a Confideration of that Train of Evils which had iffued from her fatal Box, without giving them [a] any Hopes of a Cure, was had in the higheft Veneration as the Father of a new Philofophy called *Moral*, which is of all others the moft treated of and the leaft underftood.

Philofophy after this, together with Luxury, Riches, and Corruption, was tranfported from *Afia* to *Rome*. It could make but little Progrefs among a People who cultivated hardly any other Art but thofe of pardoning the vanquifhed, and depreffing the proud. In the firft Ages of Chriftianity, Philofophy lent its Affiftance to combat *Pa-*

[a] It is probable that the greater Part of thofe, who are acquainted with the Character of *Socrates*, will think Signor *Algarotti* has paffed too fevere a Cenfure

ganifm,

ganism, and after this was subdued, it
raised so many civil Wars and Diffen-
tions among those who by its Affiftance
had triumphed over *Jupiter* and *Olym-
pus,* that the ecclefiaftical Ship seemed
in Danger of perishing when it was
hardly loosed from the Port. To this
fatal War of Words succeeded that
which the *Barbarians* raised against
Learning and the Roman Empire,
wherein both were equal Sufferers; for it
deftroyed the one, and sunk the other.
'till from the profound Darkness, which
afterwards followed, some Sparks of antient Knowledge were re-kindled a-
mong the *Arabians.* The Doctrine of
Ariftotle revived, and being spread
through the *Eaft,* was gladly embraced
by the Monks, as it was the moft fuitable to their Manner of Life. How
much Pains and Study are neceffary to
frame a right Philofophy! It requires
no lefs Art and Labour, than to make
thofe fine Silks which you Ladies are
adorned with. But the Philofophy, in
which the Name of *Ariftotle* supplied
the

the Place of Reaſon, did not greatly diſturb the Monaſtic Tranquillity.
This Philoſopher who was baniſhed
ᵃ from *Athens* by the antient Prieſts,
was (but with ſome Variety of Fortune) received by ours; who, though

ᵈ *Ariſtotle* retired from *Athens*, in order to avoid
a Proceſs of Irreligion which the *Athenian* Prieſts carried on againſt him. The Circumſtances of this Affair
are unknown: Some aſſert, that he was charged with
Impiety on Account of a Hymn which he had made
in Honour of his Friend *Hermius*. This Hymn is
ſtill extant, but there is not the leaſt Impiety diſcoverable in it; but his Accuſers urged that he had prophaned divine Songs by proſtituting them to the
Honour of a mortal Man. *Ariſtotle* not thinking it
ſafe to truſt to the Interpretation this little Poem might
meet with, retired very privately to *Chalcis*, where
he pleaded his Cauſe at a diſtance by Writing, which
was the ſafeſt Way he could take; for his Accuſers
were a Set of Men who would never have let him
been at reſt. Others affirm that he was driven from
Athens for the Goodneſs of his Morals. Some Authors report, that this Philoſopher drowned himſelf in
the *Euripus*, a narrow Sea near *Eubœa*, becauſe he
could not find out the Reaſon of its ebbing and flowing ſeven Times in one Day. But the more received
Opinion is, that his very great Application in the
Study of this Phænomenon, brought an Illneſs upon
him, which occaſioned his Death. *See* Bayle's
Life of Ariſtotle *in the* General Dictionary, Vol.
II.

they

they once condemned him as a [a] pernicious Author, yet afterwards carried
their Zeal for him to such a Height, as
to believe him not ignorant even of
those Things which are above the Reach
of human Reason. Religion at this
Time was more than ever united with

---

[a] The *French*, who took *Conſtantinople* about the Beginning of the 13th Century, having brought the
Books of *Ariſtotle* into their own Country, his Doctrine began to be publickly taught in the Univerſity
of *Paris*, and continued ſo for ſome Time. But
Arnaury, a Student in that Univerſity, having advanced
ſeveral obnoxious Opinions, and endeavoured to defend them from the Principles of *Ariſtotle*, the Phyſics
and Metaphyſics of that Philoſopher were burnt by
order of a Council held at *Paris* in 1209. and the
reading of them prohibited under Pain of Excom-
munication. This Prohibition was confirmed about
the Year 1215, by the Pope's Legate, who was employed to reform the Univerſity of *Paris* ; but he allowed the Logic of *Ariſtotle* to be taught. *Gregory* VII.
renewed this Prohibition in 1231, but with this Addition, that he only forbid the reading of *Ariſtotle's*
Works till they ſhould be corrected. In 1261, *Simon* the Legate of the See of *Rome* in his Reformation
of the Univerſity confirmed the Regulation of the
Year 1215, relating to *Ariſtotle's* writings without
mentioning the Correction of them. But in the Reformation of the Univerſity in 1366, this Philoſopher's Phyſics, as well as his other Works, were allowed to be read. *Vid. Father* Rapin's *Compariſon of*
Plato *and* Ariſtotle, Du Pin's *Nouvelle Bib.* &c.

C   Phi-

Philofophy, which could not fail to produce the utmoft Confufion in the one, and Ignorance in the other, fince both their Nature and End are extremely different.

A Chaos of vain and ufelefs Difputes, a Chain of unintelligible Definitions, a blind Zeal for wrangling, and a ftill blinder Devotion for *Ariftotle* whom they called by Way of Diftinction, *the Philofopher*, or a fecond Nature, and above all a certain Jargon of indeterminate, obfcure, and hard Expreffions, either without any Meaning, or confufed, fpread like a deftroying Deluge the Face of the whole Earth, and for many Ages ufurp'd the pompous Name of Science. As among the *Chinefe* he is efteemed the moft learned who can read and write more Words or Figures than the reft, fo he was counted to have moft Learning among us, who in a particular Habit, could pronounce in certain Places, and with certain Geftures, and feemed to underftand the greater Number of Expreffions in this vain
and

and pedantic Jargon. Their Diſtinctions and Anſwers might be as eaſily foreſeen by any one who had a little examined their Memoirs, as the Turns of Muſic in Country Scrapers, or the Jingling of Rhyme in bad Poets. Such were the Vails under which they hid, from the Eyes of the World, that Ignorance which very often they could not hide from themſelves. The Pride of Schools was ſupported by the Noiſe of empty Words, and the Tyranny of Names. It was imagined that they really contended for Truth, but theſe gray-headed Children in Reality amuſed themſelves only in fighting with Bubbles.

This obſtinate Veneration for the Antients, which for a long while paſſed among the Philoſophers as hereditary from one Generation to another, was the Cauſe that the Knowledge of Phyſics made little or no Progreſs till the laſt Age. At length among ſome few others, who were to fall as it were Martyrs to Reaſon, there appeared in

Tuſcany

Tuscany a Perſon named ª *Galileo*, who had the Courage not only to ſay, but what is worſe, to demonſtrate with the cleareſt Evidence, that Men, who had perhaps for ſixty Years been honoured with the Title of Doctors, or ſat in the Chair of Philoſophy, had taken very great Pains all their Life long to know nothing. And this Boldneſs coſt him

---

ª *Galileo* was born at *Florence* in 1564. He was put into the Inquiſition for maintaining the Diurnal Motion of the Earth, and aſſerting the Sun and not the Earth to be the Center of the World. Theſe Propoſitions were condemned by the Inquiſitors as falſe and heretical. He was not diſcharged till he had promiſed to renounce his Opinions, and not to defend them either by Word or Writing, or inſinuate them into the Mind of any Perſon. Upon his publiſhing his Dialogues upon the two chief Syſtems of the World, the *Copernican* and *Ptolemaic* in 1632, he was again cited before the Holy Office. The ſame Year the Congregation convened, and in his Preſence pronounced Sentence againſt him and his Book, committing him to the Priſon of the Holy Office during Pleaſure, and commanding him as a ſaving Penance for three Years to come to repeat once a Week the ſeven Penitential Pſalms, but reſerving to themſelves the Power of moderating, changing, and taking away, altogether or in Part, the above-mentioned Puniſhment and Penance. He was diſcharged from his Confinement in 1634, but the Impreſſion of his Dialogues *of the Syſtem of the World* was burnt at *Rome*. *Vid.* The General Dictionary.

dear;

dear; for to venture to make ufe of his
Reafon was the fame Thing as reproach-
ing them with the general Abufe they
had made of theirs; and to endeavour
at the Promotion of Knowledge was
as dangerous as an Attempt to change
the Boundaries of antient *Rome,* which
the *Augurs* took fuch a religious Care
in the Prefervation of. After fuch a
Courfe of Ages, he fhewed them what
ought to have been done at firft, and
began to make a Search into Nature
by Obfervations and Experiments, re-
ducing himfelf to that Ignorance which
is ufeful for arriving to fome Knowledge at laft.

I think it not improper to call this
Man the Czar, *Peter the Great,* in
Natural Philofophy; each of them had
to do with a Nation of pretty near the
fame Character. No one People ever
ufed fuch Endeavours for Knowledge,
as the *Mufcovites* did to know nothing.
They forbid all Strangers to come into
their Country, and all the Natives to
go out of it, for fear they fhould introduce fomething new. Thus was it
C 3 with

with thefe Philofophers, who, jealous of
their Tenets, renounced every Experiment, and more certain Demonftration
of the Moderns, rather than introduce
any Novelty or Reformation into their
own Syftems; but as Force has generally more Influence upon Men than
Reafon, the Czar compaffed his Defigns fooner than *Galileo*, who was at
the fame Time obftructed by another
Species of Philofophers, who were by
fo much the more formidable as they
too defpifed the Antients, (which now
began to be the Fafhion) and afferted
Things in Oppofition to them of which
every one had a clear and diftinct Idea.
They introduced Exactnefs and Order
into Writing, which were then as uncommon as they are natural and neceffary, and by Means alone of certain
Motions and Figures, which they knew
how to give to Bodies at proper Times
and on proper Occafions, promifed
to unfold what feemed the moft un-
explicable in Nature. You may eafily imagine that the magnificent Promifes of thefe Philofophers, which fo
agreeably

agreeably flattered the Ambition of the human Mind (which *Galileo*'s Obfervations ferved rather to humble) joined to a certain Simplicity that gave fuch an Air of Wonder to their Syftems, as it does to a well concerted Romance, muft naturally feduce many People, and form a Sect. And it indeed had this Effect; fo that thefe Moderns too began to have Expofitors, and Followers as obftinate and zealous as thofe of the Antients had been before; and thefe made themfelves the more ridiculous by laughing at the fame Fault in others. But it was a melancholy Thing to fee an Experiment fometimes offer itfelf, which had never before been known or thought on; and the fineft and moft artificial Syftems, which had perhaps coft their Inventors whole Months of Labour and Study, fhamefully fall to the Ground.

In order then to avoid thefe forrowful Reflexions, faid the Marchionefs, it is neceffary for thofe, who would form a Syftem in any Thing, to be careful firft to take Notice of all that is obfervable in it,

C 4   that

that it may not be expofed to the Mercy
and Infults of Experiments. This is exactly what the *Newtonians* fay, anfwered
I, and certainly, *Madam*, you muft
have fome fecret Intelligence with them
to be fo well informed of their Sentiments. It would be ridiculous for a Mechanic to take it in his Head, to guefs
how the famous Clock of *Strasbourg* is
made within Side, if he had not firft
acquainted himfelf with its outfide;
the manner in which it ftrikes, and
thofe many other Things it does befides telling the Hour. Thus, fay they,
if we can ever hope to make Syftems
that carry fome Appearance of being
durable, it will be then only when by
the Means of Experiments and Obfervations we fhall know all, that in Terms
of Art is called *Phænomenon*, which
fignifies the Appearance of Things,
and the Laws which refult from thefe
Phænomena, and by which Nature conftantly performs all her Operations. How
then could *Des Cartes* for Example, who
was the chief Author of this enterpri-
fing Sect of Philofophers, make a rational

tional Syſtem concerning *Light* and *Co-lours*, when he was entirely ignorant of ſo many of their Qualities, which Sir *Iſaac Newton* afterwards diſcovered by Obſervations? How could he form the Statue, when he had not the Marble? This is the manner in which the reſt of the Philoſophers of our Time, and thoſe learned Societies founded and maintained by the Liberality of Princes, or the Genius of Nations, proceed; they make Obſervations and prepare Materials for Poſterity to build Syſtems upon, more fortunate in their Duration, than thoſe that preceded the preſent Age. This Profeſſion indeed is not ſo pompous as that of thoſe who will build you a World in the twinkling of an Eye; but on the other Hand it has this Advantage, that it is able to make good its Promiſes, which is as great an Obligation upon a Philoſopher, as a Miſtreſs.

I, who am a Woman, replied the Marchioneſs, confeſs that I love thoſe who have the Courage to venture upon grand and difficult Enterpriſes. Is-

not

not this the Reaſon why we intereſt our-
ſelves ſo much in the Adventures of
Heroes? The Courage of thoſe philoſophical Heroes has ſomething ſublime
and ſuperior in it : If they do not attain
to all they promiſe, muſt there not be
given ſome Indulgence to the Imperfections of Human Nature? On the other
hand, if, as you ſay, there cannot be any
good Syſtems, till all the Phænomena
are fully known, when ſhall we have
them? They will happen as ſeldom
with us, as the ſecular Games anciently among the *Romans :* And I cannot flatter myſelf that I ſhall live long
enough to ſee ſo much as one in my
time. I muſt be contented then with
thoſe Syſtems that we have, be they
what they will. I believe, Madam,
anſwered I, that no one could have
more ſpecious Reaſons to alledge in favour of Trifles, I ſhould ſerve you
right, if I put you on proving theſe
Reaſons ; but as I will act more merci-
fully with you, than you perhaps would
with regard to me, (ſince you have a
mind that we ſhould reaſon away that

Time,

Time, which might be better employ'd on Pleaſure) I will not make
uſe of that Right which theſe Reaſons
of yours give me, to propoſe to your
ſeriouſly the important Queſtions, Whether Light be a Subſtance, or an Accident, or an Act of the Pellucid, as
far as it is pellucid ? Whether Colours
are the firſt Configurations of Matter,
or a certain little Flame that ariſes from
Bodies, whoſe Parts are proportioned
to our Sight ? I might gravely aſk
you too (that you may ſee how many things I ſpare you the Trouble of
conſidering at once) Whether Light, or
its Spirit, be the Soul that *Plato* places
between Nature and Ideas, to connect
the ſenſible and intellectual World ? and
Whether it was for this Reaſon that
Plato repreſented the Element of Fire,
which is the Seat of Light, under the
Figure of a Pyramid, which in ſome
meaſure agrees with that ſublime and
myſtic Triangle which is the Symbol of
this Soul ? idle Enigmas of the learned Ignorance of paſt Ages ! And who
can tell but if you had fallen into o-

B 6   ther

ther hands than mine, you might have been set a yawning with some *Gothic* Paſſages out of *Dante?* Or perhaps by this Light, you would have been gradually conducted to Divinity; at leaſt you could not have got free from an Explication of the myſtic Senſe hid under the Fable of *Prometheus,* who ſtole Light from the Sun to animate his Statue.

I ſee, ſaid the Marchioneſs, that Philoſophers are to be dealt with in a very circumſpect manner, who know how to improve every thing to their own Advantage. You act juſt like Tyrants, who think they confer a great Favour on any one, whom they have not injured. However, I am much obliged to you, for ſparing me the Trouble of hearing all theſe fine Things, which, I confeſs, are quite a-bove my Underſtanding.

Let us ſee, anſwered I, whether you can underſtand the Doctrines of ſome among the Ancients who were more prudent and humane than the reſt. Theſe labour'd to explain every thing by a Vacuum,

3 and

and the Motion and Figure of certain very little Particles, which they called Atoms, and from thence gave their Schools the Name of *Atomiſts*, which was perhaps the moſt antient of all other Sects, and lately try'd by the Splendor of Eloquence to riſe upon the Ruines of the *Ariſtotelian*, in op-poſition to that of *Deſcartes*. Theſe Phi-loſophers aſſerted that the Light of the Sun, for Example, was nothing but a perpetual and copious Stream of the very little Particles, or Atoms, which flowing from the Sun himſelf, ſpread themſelves every way with an incredi-ble Velocity, and fill the immenſe ae-rial Space; ſo that Light is always followed by new Light, and one Ray is as it were impelled by a ſecond. You may eaſily underſtand this by the Similitude of a Fountain. —— I un-derſtand it mighty well, interrupted the Marchioneſs, without the Fountain; but I am greatly afraid that theſe A-tomiſts of yours, by making ſo many Particles continually proceed from the Sun, will at laſt turn ſome fine Day

into

into Midnight. Truly, anſwered I, that would be playing us a villainous Trick, which no one would get any thing by, unleſs perhaps ſome few Beauties, who would then always be ſeen by Candle-light: But do not fear it. Revolutions of this Importance require more time to be brought about, than the Revolution of a Monarchy. And beſides theſe Atomiſts give us ſo great a Security that it would be a Shame to dread it. For, in the firſt place, they tell us, that the Rarity and incredible Smalneſs of theſe little Particles that proceed from the Sun (which Sun they make to be of a denſe and cloſe Matter as you will ſee hereafter) in a very long courſe of Years will produce only a very little Diminution in his Light. And to make you ſtill more ſecure, this may be confirmed by the Example of a little Grain of Colour, which is ſufficient to tinge a very great Quantity of Water. An Example drawn from odorous Bodies, may ſerve to ſhew you how very much the Parts of Matter may be ſubtiliſed; as, for inſtance, inftance, a Grain of Mufk, which, though it continually emirs a prodigious Quantity of Particles yielding a Perfume fo ftrong and quick that at a certain Diftance it is able to ftupify Serpents of a monftrous Size, and quite deprive them of Motion, yet in a confiderable time its Weight is but very little diminifhed. And Amber-greafe, in the fame manner, for a long while lofes hardly any thing of its agreeable Scent. From Light's paffing thro' the denfeft Bodies, fuch as Diamonds and Gold when it is beaten into thin Plates, we muft neceffarily infer, that the Particles of Light are extremely fubtile. All this is mighty well, replied the Marchionefs; but that fuch a Quantity of Light fhould continually proceed from the Sun, as is fufficient to fill and illuminate this whole World, puts me into terrible Apprehenfions, notwithftanding all your fine Examples of Mufk, Amber-greafe,. and Diamonds.

Have not you fome Inclination, anfwered I, to the learned Melancholy of the Inhabitants of *Dean Swift's* flying

flying Ifland ? Who in the moft Poetical Allegories has given us the moft
philofophical Satyr upon Mankind.
This Ifland, which, in the Language
of the Country, is called *Laputa*, as it
is different from all that have hitherto been difcovered by our Voyagers,
fo it is inhabited by a very fingular
Species of Men : Always abftracted and
immerfed in the profoundeft Speculations, they give themfelves up to Spleen
and the Mathematics, fo that they
have always need of a *Flapper*, who, by
ftriking them from time to time with
a Bladder, may bring them back to
the World below, their Knowledge
fills them with thofe continual Fears
and Difquietudes which the Vulgar by a
happy Privilege of their Ignorance are
quite free from.   They are afraid that a
Comet, by approaching a little too near
the Earth, may in an inftant reduce us
to Afhes ; or, that the Sun one Day
or other will fwallow us up ; or, that
this immenfe Source of Light and Heat
will at length be exhaufted and leave us
involved in a profound and eternal
Night.

Night. May not your Fears, Madam, be faid a little to refemble thofe of the *Laputian* School ?

As to the *Flapper*, anfwered fhe, I have nothing to do with that, efpecially when I am with you. But do you not think that there is fome Reafon for me to be frighted at the terrible Threatning of a perpetual Night? Ought you not rather to think yourfelf obliged to me for interefting myfelf fo much in the Caufe of *Light*, which you have made your Heroine? It would be quite fhameful that I fhould fhew more Regard and Concern for it, than yourfelf. You fhall fee, *Madam*, anfwered I, that thefe Atomifts have taken Care to fecure your Repofe, and preferve what you fhew fuch a Regard for. They will find you a Method to recruit the Sun with that Facility which a Philofopher is Mafter of, who knows how to make all Nature fubfervient to his Schemes. They will make the Seeds of Light and Heat which are diffufed through the Univerfe, continually return back again into the Sun, in order to repair
his

his Loffes. They will place fomething round him with which he is fuftained and reftored juft as a Lamp is fed by Oil or fome other Matter. We will call certain Syftems to our Affiftance which will lend us Comets that from Time to Time fhall fall into the Sun and afford him frefh Supplies : And if this be not fufficient, we will have Recourfe to fome Philofopher, who may find Means to make a Star fall into him. And if you have not Confidence enough in human Syftems, we will call a Celeftial one to your Aid, revealed to *Adam* by an Angel in *Milton*, who affures us, that the Sun draws his Aliment from humid Exhalations, and in a regular Manner takes his Supper every Night with the Ocean. Will you have any more ? No, no, faid fhe, the one half of thefe Things is fufficient to diffipate the Fears of a *Laputian* himfelf. And I hope there will be no need at prefent to trouble any Philofopher, much lefs a fuperior Being.

Jones:

'Philosophy, a Poem,
Addressed to the Young Ladies who Attended
Mr. Booth's Lectures in Dublin'

Henry Jones, 'Philosophy, A Poem, Addressed to the Young Ladies who Attended Mr. Booth's Lectures in Dublin' (1749), pp. 3–8.

This poem was first published in Dublin, 1746, under the title 'Philosophy. A Poem Address'd to the Ladies who Attend Mr. Booth's Lectures', with the tag 'By the Bricklayer'. Born at Beaulieu, County Louth, in 1721, Jones was apprenticed to a bricklayer. His versifying was his fortune. 'Philosophy' is one of Jones's earliest poems, written during his employment in Dublin. The 'Mr. Booth' of the title is probably John Booth of Glasgow, an itinerant lecturer, whose *Course of Experiments* covered optics and electrical attraction, topics described in Jones's poem.

Jones's early verse won him a patron in Lord Chief Justice Singleton. Not long afterwards, Singleton presented to Chesterfield Jones's poem celebrating Chesterfield's appointment as Lord-Lieutenant of Ireland. His fortunes improved still further when Chesterfield invited him to follow him to England in 1748. In London Chesterfield organized a subscription edition of Jones's *Poems on Several Occasions*, from which the poem in this volume is taken. John Booth is listed as a subscriber. It was a lucrative venture but Jones's greatest success was still to come. Chesterfield introduced him to Colley Cibber, the poet laureate, who in 1753 staged his play 'The Earl of Essex', starring Barry, at Covent Garden. The play, described as of the 'poorest' literary quality by Gordon Goodwin (*DNB*), had gone through four editions by 1770. Cibber showed his esteem for Jones by recommending him at Court as his successor as poet laureate. Wealth and success, however, brought out the worst in Jones's character. He alienated his patrons with his drunken and obnoxious behaviour. Reduced to a life of poverty, he ended his days in a parish workhouse.

Jones's 'Philosophy' is interesting in taking as its theme a series of public lectures and specifically addressing the ladies who attended. Stewart has written of 'the rage of public lectures on science in which the century reveled', contending that the public lecturers 'helped to erode the social distinctions the Royal Society maintained' (Stewart, *The Rise of Public Science*, p. 27, p. 144). In 'Philosophy' Jones recalls Booth's lectures by addressing his fictional female readership in the manner of a lecturer performing a series of experiments.

In the pattern of earlier poems written in celebration of Newtonianism, 'Philosophy' is full of exclamations. What is striking is Jones's extension of wonder to the technology of the new science and phenomenon of public lectures. In the orrery, by 'wondr'ous Art', the maker of scientific instruments has created 'A boundless System in a small Machine'. Demonstrations, scientific instruments and the audience's response are treated as fit subjects for poetry. Whereas Voltaire, in his poem 'To the Marchioness du Ch**', published in this volume, addresses his friend and lover, who has learnt about science by reading and discussion with gentlemanly scientists, Jones's addressees are anonymous ladies who pay fees to attend public lectures. Jones presents his ladies' application to philosophical study as a sign of virtue but his exaggerated language belies his encouragement. His ladies are 'ye FAIR' and 'bright Nymphs', superior to those who 'squander' their youth on 'empty Toys'. Like Algarotti, he concentrates on visual perception rather than understanding and his closing lines identify his readers as gentlemen.

'Philosophy', like Desaguliers's 'Newtonian System of the World', demonstrates the uneven quality of poetry about philosophy. Equally, though, it shows that a poem celebrating experimental philosophy had become a set-piece in an aspiring poet's repertoire. In Jones's *Poems on Several Occasions*, 'Philosophy' takes its place alongside other genre poems, such as his lines 'On Mr. Pope's Death' and his eulogy to Chesterfield. The success of the campaign to make experimental philosophy matter to polite society would seem to be reflected in such a poem as Jones's 'Philosophy'. However, Jones contradictorily included in his collection a poem expressing scepticism about the powers of the new philosophy. If this was a case of his hedging his bets, it indicates that, by the mid-century, the new science still had some way to go to secure public approval.

PHILOSOPHY,

A

P O E M.

TO Science facred, Mufe, exalt thy Lays,
    Science of Nature, and to Nature's Praife.
Attend ye Virtuous, and rejoice to know
Her myftic Labours, and her Laws below;
Her ways above with curious Eyes explore,
Admire her Treafures, and her God adore.

A 2   BEHOLD

BEHOLD ye FAIR how radiant Colours glow,

What dyes the Rose, what paints the Heav'nly Bow,

The purpling Shade, the rich refracted Ray,

And all the bright Diversity of Day.

Lo ! here the Magnet's Magic charms the Sight,

And fills the Soul with Wonder and Delight,

In her coy Nature turns her Face aside,

And mocks th' enquiring Sages learned Pride,

Here less reserv'd she shows her plainer Course

In mutual Contest of Elastic Force,

Saving each vital Frame from crushing Fate,

For inward Act sustains external Weight,

Which holds reciprocal in ballanc'd Strife,

The Shield of Nature, and the Fence of Life :

The ambient Atmosphere embracing all

The wide Circumf'rence of this circling Ball,

The Vehicle of Life to those that breath

On solid Land, or liquid Waves beneath,

The Universe pervading, filling Space,

And like its Maker unconfin'd to Place.

WHAT

WHAT pleafing Fervours in my Bofom rife,

What fix'd Attention and what deep Surprize,

When quick as Thought th' electric Vigour fprings,

Swifter than Light'ning on its rapid Wings,

A Flight fo inftant to no Space confin'd,

Eludes Ideas, and outftrips the Mind?

Lo! to the Brain the bright Effluvium flies,

Glows in the Heart and flafhes from the Eyes:

Here the fond Youth with raptur'd Eye fhall gaze,

And proudly warm, enjoy th' extatic Blaze:

See the proud Nymph partake his Flame by Turns,

See! like a Seraph, how fhe fmiles and burns.

Contracted here by wond'rous Art is feen

A boundlefs Syftem in a fmall Machine;

Here human Skill to proud Perfection brought,

The mortal Mimic of Omnific Thought,

Th' Almighty's Model to the Mind conveys,

The Univerfe, and all it's Pow'rs difplays:

How wander Planets, how revolves the Year,

The Moon how changes, and how Comets glare.

The

The Sun's bright Globe illumes th' unmeaſur'd Space,

While waiting Worlds enjoy by Turns his Face,

From his bright Preſence drink enliv'ning Rays,

From him their Seaſons gain, from him their Days;

See Wiſdom here her brighteſt Beams diſplay,

To fill the Soul with philoſophic Day,

The Springs unfolding of mechanic Laws,

Tracing through known Effects th' eternal Cauſe,

Whoſe pow'rful *Fiat*, whoſe creative Will

Firſt founded Nature, and ſupports her ſtill.

Here godlike *N E W T O N*'s all capacious Mind,

(The Glory and the Guide of human Kind)

Shows wedded Worlds far diſtant Worlds embrace

With mutual Bands, yet keep their deſtin'd Space,

Roll endleſs Meaſures through th' etherial Plain,

Link'd by the ſocial ſtrong attractive Chain,

Whoſe latent Springs exert all Nature's Force,

Inwrap the Poles, and point the Stars their Courſe.

Myſterious Energy ! ſtupendous Theme !

Immediate Mover of this boundleſs Frame,

Who

Who can thy Effence, or thy Pow'r explain?

The Sons of Wifdom feek thy Source in vain;

Thyfelf invifible, yet feen thy Laws,

This goodly Fabrick thy Effect, and GOD thy Caufe.

THRICE happy few who wifely here attend

The Voice of Science, and her Caufe befriend:

Let others, heedlefs of their youthful Prime,

Squander on empty Toys their fleeting Time;

'Tis yours with Reafon's fearching Eye to view

Great Nature's Laws, and trace her winding Clue;

Behold her Book the op'ning Page expand,

Fill'd with the Wonders of her Maker's Hand,

In awful Characters, which clearly fhine,

Worthy of Wifdom, and of Pow'r divine.

Perufe GOD's Ways, his perfect Workings trace,

In Nature's Mirrour fhines his heavenly Face.

To you, bright Nymphs, where Goodnefs charms
        us moft,

The Pride of Nature, and Creation's Boaft,

To you Philofophy enamour'd flies,

And triumphs in the Plaudit of your Eyes.

                      When

When Worth like yours her sapient Throne sustains,

The Queen of Science with true Splendour reigns;

By Beauty aided she extends her Sway,

And, won by you, Mankind glad Homage pay.

F I N I S.

MARTIN:

'The Life of Newton'

Benjamin Martin, 'The Life of Sir Isaac Newton', *Biographia Philosophica. Being an Account of the Lives, Writings, and Inventions, of the Most Eminent Philosophers and Mathematicians Who have flourished from the earliest Ages of the World to the present Time* (London: W. Owen, 1764), pp. 360–76.

Benjamin Martin (1704–82), resident of Fleet Street, was an optician, an amateur natural philosopher, and a London hack. Born in Surrey, a bequest enabled him to devote himself to study; he bought books and instruments with which he toured the country, giving lectures on natural philosophy. After a successful and happy life, Martin ended his days by becoming bankrupt and committing suicide. There are over eighty entries to his name in the British Library catalogue, from *The Philosophical Grammar* (London, 1735, which was still being reprinted in 1778) to *The Mariner's Mirror* (London, 1782). In between, he simplified trigonometry for the student, explained the eclipse, wondered at the microscope, observed the sight of Venus in the sun, campaigned for a new system of philology, examined the sextant and the octant, and eulogised Newton.

The extract chosen here is from *Biographia Philosophica* (Lives of the Philosophers), a work written under the patronage of the King. The book begins with Thales and ends, over 550 pages later, with Benjamin Robins, in the process presenting accounts of over a hundred philosophical lives. Roger Bacon gets twenty pages, Paracelsus only one. Copernicus, Brahe, Kepler, Galileo are all here; but so is Christopher Columbus and Christopher Wren. Of those mentioned in his account of Newton's life, we find biographies of John Collins, Robert Hooke, Lord Brounker (*sic.*), Huygens, Isaac Barrow, Mercator, Oldenburg, Flamsteed, and Leibnitz (*sic.*). The accounts of Flamsteed and Leibniz avoid mentioning Newton's dispute with the two men. Newton's life appears between Mercator and Flamsteed. The only illustration in the book is an image of Newton.

He could grasp Newton's mathematics, but lacked the stylistic felicity and intellectual clarity that would bring Newton and his work to life for the reader. The language is knotty, convoluted and excessively confused. To take one example, his account of Newton's studies of the 1680 comet renders a fairly straightforward matter weirdly complex. He makes numerous errors, and undertakes no biographical research of his own. Perhaps it is unfair to expect him to have done so. There were, after all, other books to be written.

For a man who devoted his life to writing popular natural philosophy, Martin had little obvious aptitude for the task. Sometimes he is better than this. In *The Young Gentleman and Lady's Philosophy* (London, W. Owen, 1763), he employs the dialogue form as Euphrosyne and Cleon debate such matters as the use of the celestial globe: 'the happiest Invention sure that every Mankind was blest with! And it is no wonder, when we see those noble Instruments in the Study of every Gentleman and Lady of Taste' (1, 62). Even here Euphrosyne has a hard time of it, lectured unremittingly and inelegantly for 412 pages. However, his *Miscellaneous Correspondence* (London, W. Owen, 1759–64) in four volumes is worth looking at, being a compendious and illogical treasure trove of trivia, inquiries, bad verse, competent verse, geometry, meteorology, maritime news, and gossip.

Martin's account of Newton's life is one of many published in the long eighteenth century. It follows: Bernard le Bovier de Fontenelle's *Eloge de M. Neuton* in *Histoire et Mémoires* (Paris, Académie Royale des Sciences, 1727), pp. 151–72, translated as *The Life of Sir Isaac Newton* (London, J. Woodman and D. Lyon, 1728); Thomas Birch, 'Sir Isaac Newton', *General Dictionary*, Vol. 7 (London, 1738), pp. 232–3; and the article on Newton in *Biographia Britannica* (London, William Innys, etc, 1760) written by the anonymous 'P'. Martin's work seems to have made use particularly of Fontenelle and also Thomas Pemberton's *A View of Sir Isaac Newton's Philosophy* (London, 1728).

It would be pointless picking out all the errors and fictions in Martin's text. Martin simply follows the legends that were already clinging to Newton's name. We have the apple story (a true legend, it would seem), as you'd expect, and the more unlikely legend of Newton's amiability, modesty and eagerness to avoid dispute. When the 'Marquis *de l'Hospital*' asks if Newton eats, drinks and sleeps like other men, the comment cuts to the heart of Martin's, and polite culture's, image of Newton. He is both the godlike genius and the absolutely ordinary Englishman; the hero who ascends to heights of intellectual genius and the man who seeks a life of unremarkable quietness. The legend is, of course, untrue. Yet polite culture needed legends; its history proceeded on the strength of them.

Martin's life of Newton intends to obscure the one obvious lesson of Newton's life and character: that is, the one thing that scientific culture didn't possess was politeness. Newton's selfishness and paranoia made him needily disputatious. Yet sometimes Martin just had to share the pugnacious bravado of his hero's brutal victories. It's a great story of his facing Leibniz's challenge of the fiendishly difficult Problem of the Trajectories as 'nothing more than an Amusement to our etherial Genius, as he solved it the same Evening he received it, though he had been fatigued that Day with the Business of the Mint' (below, p. 200).

SIR ISAAC NEWTON KT.

The LIFE of

Sir ISAAC NEWTON.

SIR *Isaac Newton*, defcended from an antient and honourable Family in *Lincolnfhire*, was born on *Chriftmas-day*, O. S. 1642, at the Manor of *Woolftrope* in that County, his Anceftors enjoying the Title and Eftate of that Lordfhip for more than 200 Years, his Father being the elder Son of Sir *John Newton*, Bart. and his Mother of the antient and opulent Family of *Afcoughs* in that County. Our Author's Father dying when he was young, the Care of his Education devolved on his Mother, who, notwithftanding fhe married again after his Father's Death, in her great Wifdom, took Care to improve his diftinguifhing Genius by an early and liberal Education.——— In 1654, when he was but 12 Years of Age, fhe fent him to the Grammar-fchool at *Grantham*, where he made great Profieiency in the Knowledge of Language, and laid the Foundation of his future Studies. In 1660, at the Age of 18, he was removed to *Trinity College, Cambridge*, where he principally devoted himfelf to the Study of the Mathematics, wherein Mr. (afterwards Doctor) *Ifaac Barrow*, then Fellow of that College, was very eminent. He began his Studies, in the ufual Method, with *Euclid's* Elements: The moft difficult Problems of which (from his penetrating Genius) foon became eafy and familiar to him. He then proceeded to the Study of *Des Cartes's* Geometry, with *Oughtred's* Clavis, *Kepler's* Optics, and *Schooten's* Mifcellanies, in which he made feveral Improvements, which he inferted in marginal Notes as he went along, which was his common Method of ftudying: By Means of thefe Notes, and other original Papers of

Z z z   his,

We have thought it requifite to diftinguifh the PRINCE of PHILOSOPHERS with an *Engraving*, (of an Octavo Size) which we have the Satisfaction to affure the Reader, is extremely like Sir *Ifaac*, as we are informed by thofe who knew him many Years ——— This Plate will be prefixed as a Frontifpiece to the Volume of Biographia

his, it is eafy to fhew, in fome Meafure, the Progrefs by which the Methods of Series and Fluxions were invented by him: And this continued to be his Employment and Study till 1664. —— The fame Year, at the Age of 22, he took the Degree of Bachelor of Arts: And obferving, at this Time, many Perfons of. Genius engaged in the Bufinefs of improving Telefcopes, by grinding Glaffes in fuch manner as might beft fubferve to that Purpofe, he applied himfelf to the grinding of Optic Glaffes of other Figures than fpherical, having as yet no Apprehenfion of the heterogeneous Nature of Light · But not fucceeding at once in the Attempt, he procured a Glafs Prifm, in order to try the celebrated Phænomena of Colours, difcovered by *Grimaldi* not long before. He was much pleafed at firft with the vivid Brightnefs of the Colours produced by this Experiment; but, after a while, applying himfelf to confider them in a philofophical Way, with that Accuracy which was natural to him, he became immediately furprized to obferve them in an oblong Form; which, according to the received Rule of Refractions, ought to be circular. At firft, he thought the Irregularity might poffibly be no more than accidental; but, as this excited his Enquiry, he foon invented an infallible Method of deciding the Queftion, and the Refult was, his new *Theory of Light and Colours.*

However, the Theory alone, unexpected and furprizing as it was, did not fatisfy him; he rather confidered the proper Ufe that might be made of it, for improving Telefcopes, which was his firft Defign. To this End, having now difcovered that Light was not homogeneal, but an heterogeneous Mixture of differently refrangible Rays, he computed the Errors arifing from this different Refrangibility; and finding them to exceed, fome hundreds of Times, thofe occafioned by the circular Figure of the Glaffes, he threw afide his Glafs-works, and took the Nature of Reflectors into Confideration. He was now fenfible, that optical Inftruments might be brought to any Degree of Perfection defired, in Cafe there could be found a reflecting Subftance which would polifh as finely as Glafs, and reflect as much Light as Glafs tranfmits, and the Art of giving it a parabolical Figure be alfo attained: But, in this Enquiry, he met with confiderable Difficulty, and it received, at leaft for fome Time, no fmall Check, by the breaking out of the Plague in 1665.

1665. ———— He then retired from *Cambridge*, and was, in some Measure, secluded from Conversation and Books. However, his active Genius found some important Subjects for his mental Facilties; and, in the Midst of his Solitude, started that Hint which gave Rise to the System of the World, which is the main Subject of his *Principia*. ———— He was sitting alone; in a Garden, when some Apples falling from a Tree, led his Thoughts to the Subject of Gravity ; and reflecting on the Power of that Principle, he began to consider; that as this Power is not found to be sensibly diminished at the remotest Distance from the Center of the Earth to which we can rise, neither at the Tops of the loftiest Buildings, nor on the Summits of the highest Mountains, it appeared to him reasonable to conclude, that this Power must extend much farther than is usually thought : " Why not " as high as the Moon ? said he to himself, and if so, her Mo- " tion must be influenced by it : Perhaps she is retained in her " Orbit thereby. However, though the Power of Gravity is " not sensibly weakened in the little Change of Distance, at " which we can place ourselves from the Center of the Earth, " yet it is very possible that; as high as the Moon this Power " may differ in Strength much from what it is here." To make an Estimate what might be the Degree of this Diminution; he considered with himself that, if the Moon be retained in her Orbit by the Force of Gravity, no doubt the primary Planets are carried about the Sun by the like Power : And by comparing the Periods of the several Planets with their Distances from the Sun, he found, that if any Power like Gravity held them in their Courses, its Strength must decrease in the duplicate Proportion of the Increase of Distance. This he concluded, by supposing them to move in perfect Circles concentric to the Sun, from which the Orbits of the greatest Part of them do not much differ. Supposing therefore, the Power of Gravity; which extended to the Moon; to decrease in the same Manner, he computed whether that Force would be sufficient to keep the Moon in her Orbit. ———— But in this Computation (attempting it in a common Method, and absent from Books) he did not make the Power of Gravity, decreasing in a duplicate Proportion to the Distance, answerable to the Power which retained the Moon in her Orbit : Whence he concluded, that some other Cause must at least join

with

with the Action of the Power of Gravity on the Moon. However, some Incidents suspended any farther Thoughts on that Subject.

On his Return to *Cambridge*, in 1667, he was chosen Fellow of his College, and, in 1668, advanced to the Degree of Master of Arts. ——— At this Time, *Nicholas Mercator*, who was born in *Holstein*, but spent most of his Time in *England*, published his *Logarithmotechnia*, in which he gave the Quadrature of the Hyperbola by an infinite Series. This was the first Appearance, in the learned World, of a Series of this Sort drawn from the particular Nature of the Curve, and that in a Manner very new and abstracted. ——— The famous Dr. *Barrow*, then at *Cambridge*, where Mr. *Newton*, who was about 26 Years of Age, resided, recollected, that he had met with the same Thing in the Writings of that young Gentleman, and there not confined to the Hyperbola only, but extended by general Forms to all Sorts of Curves, even such as are mechanical, to their Quadratures, their Rectifications, and their Centers of Gravity, to the Solids formed by their Rotations, and to the Superficies of those Solids; so that supposing their Determinations to be possible, the Series stopped at a certain Point, or at least their Sums were given by stated Rules. But if the absolute Determinations were impossible, they could yet be infinitely approximated; which is the happiest and most refined Method, says *Monsieur Fontenelle*, of supplying the Defects of human Knowledge, that Man's Imagination could possibly invent. To be Master of so fruitful and general a Theory, was a Mine of Gold to a Geometrician; but it was a greater Glory to have been the Discoverer of so surprizing and ingenious a System So that Sir *Isaac* finding, by *Mercator*'s Book, that he was in the Way to it, and that others might follow in his Track, should naturally have been forward to open his Treasures, and secure the Property, which consisted in making the Discovery. But he contented himself with the Treasure he had found, without regarding the Glory. He modestly observes, in a Letter printed in the *Commercium Epistolicum*, that he thought *Mercator* had intirely discovered his Secret, or that others would, before he was of a proper Age for writing. ——— His Manuscript upon infinite Series was communicated to none but Mr. *John Collins*, F. R. S. and the Lord

Broun-

Brounker; and even this had not been done but for Dr. *Barrow*, who would not suffer him to indulge his Modesty so much as he desired. This Manuscript was taken out of our Author's Study in 1669, intitled, *A Method which I formerly found out, &c.* and supposing this formerly to mean no more than three Years, he must then have discovered this admirable Method of his Series, when he was not 24 Years of Age. But what is still more, this Manuscript contains both the Discovery and Method of Fluxions, or those infinitely small Quantities, which have occasioned so great a Contest between Mr. *Leibnitz* and him, or rather between *Germany* and *England*.

In 1669, he was chosen Professor of the Mathematics in the University of *Cambridge*, upon the Resignation of Dr. *Barrow*; and the same Year, and the two following Years, he read a Course of optical Lectures, in *Latin*, in the public Schools of the University: He had not finished them when he was elected a Fellow of the *Royal Society* in *January* 1671-2, and having now brought his Theory of Light and Colours to a great Degree of Perfection, he communicated it to that Society first, to have their Judgment upon it, and it was afterwards published in their *Transactions* of *February* 19, 1672. In the same *Transactions* of *March* 28, 1672, N°. 81, he published an Account of a new *Catadioptrical Telescope* of his own Invention, which Account *Monsieur Gallois* inserted in the *Journal des Sçavans*, with a Letter of *Monsieur Huygens*, shewing the Advantages of this Kind of Telescope. From this Time, till 1679, our Author maintained a Correspondence, by Letters, with Mr. *Henry Oldenburg*, Secretary of the *Royal Society*; Mr. *John Collins*, Mr. *John Flamstead*, and Dr. *Edmund Halley*; which Letters contain a Variety of curious and useful Observations, which are published in the *general Dictionary*, including near 20 Pages, to which therefore we shall refer the Reader.

In 1676, at the Request of Mr. *Leibnitz*, he explained his Invention of infinite Series, and took Notice how far he had improved it by his Method of Fluxions, which, however, he still concealed, and particularly, on this Occasion, by a Transposition of the Letters that make up the two fundamental Propositions of it into an alphabetical Order.

4 A   In

In the Winter between 1676 and 1677, as Mr. *Jones* informs us, he investigated the grand Proposition, that by a centripetal Force, acting reciprocally as the Squares of the Distance a Planet must revolve in an Ellipsis about the Center of Force placed in the lower Focus of the Ellipsis, and, with a Radius drawn to that Center, describe Area's proportional to the Times.

In 1680, he made several astronomical Observations upon the Comet that then appeared, which, for some considerable Time, he took not to be one and the same, but two different Comets. He was at an Uncertainty in this Matter, when he received a Letter from Mr. *Hooke* on the Nature of the Line described by a falling Body, supposed to be moved circularly by the diurnal Motion of the Earth, and perpendicularly by the Power of Gravity : This led him farther to enquire what was the real Figure in which such a Body moved, and, as *Picart* had not long before, *viz.* in 1679, measured a Degree of the Earth with sufficient Accuracy, by using his Measures, that Planet appearing to be retained in her Orbit by the sole Power of Gravity, and consequently that this Power decreases in the duplicate Proportion of the Distance, as he had formerly conjectured : Upon this Principle he found the Line described by a falling Body, to be an Ellipsis, of which the Center of the Earth is one Focus. And finding, by this Means, that the primary Planets really moved in such Orbits as *Kepler* had supposed, he had the Satisfaction to find the Result of his Enquiries to answer some valuable Purposes : Accordingly, he drew up sundry Propositions relative to the Motion of the primary Planets round the Sun, which were communicated to the *Royal Society* in 1683, and, with much Solicitation, printed in 1687, under the Title of *Philosophiæ naturalis principia Mathematica*, containing, in the third Book, what is now denominated his *Cometic Astronomy*, or rather his *System of the World*.

In the Height of all these profound philosophical Researches, the Privileges of the University being attacked by King *James* II. our Author appeared among the most hearty Defenders, and was, on that Occasion, appointed one of their Delegates to the high Commission Court, when he made such a rational and vigorous

gorous Defence, that King *James* thought proper to drop the Affair, and continue their Privileges.

In 1688, our Author was chosen one of their Members for the Convention Parliament, in which he sat till it was dissolved.

Obstructions being in a great Measure removed, he reassumes his former Studies, on the Motion of the primary Planets round the Sun, to which he was somewhat led by Conversation with Dr. *Halley* (who paid him a Visit at *Cambridge :*) It gave Occasion to his writing the above mentioned Treatise of *Mathematical Principles of natural Philosophy*, a second Edition whereof was afterwards published at *Cambridge*, with great Additions, under the Care of Mr *Roger Cotes*, Professor of Astronomy and experimental Philosophy. *Monsieur de Fontenelle* tells us, that this Book, in which our Author had built a new System of natural Philosophy upon the most sublime Geometry, was wrote with so great Profoundness of Judgment, and withal so concise, that it required some Time and Skill thoroughly to understand it ; on which Account, it was not so generally read and admired : But at Length, when its Worth came to be sufficiently known, nothing was to be heard from all Quarters but one general Shout of Admiration. This Work seems to be the Production of a Genius, or of a celestial Intelligence, rather than a Man, says the Marquis *de l'Hospital*, one of the greatest Mathematicians of the Age. And when he was visited by some *English* Gentleman, it is said, he asked "if Mr. *Newton*, eat, drank, or "slept like other Men ?" I represent him to myself (says he) as a celestial Genius, intirely disengaged from Matter. The *Principia Mathematica* are founded chiefly on two Theories, *viz.* the Doctrine of central Forces, and that of the Resistance of Mediums to Bodies moving in them, both almost entirely new, and treated according to our Author's sublime Geometry. ———
Kepler had found from the celestial Observations of *Tycho Brahe*, I. That the same Planets described about the Sun equal Areas in equal Times. II. That their Orbits were Ellipses, the Sun being in the common Focus. III. That in different Planets, the Squares of periodic Times were, as the Cubes of the transverse Axes of their Orbits. From the first Phænomenon our Author demonstrated, that the Planets were attracted towards

the

the Sun in the Center; from the Second, that the Force of this Attraction was reciprocally as the Squares of the Distances of the Planet from this Center; and from the Third, that all the Planets were influenced by the very same centripetal Force.

Our Author's Merit became now so well known, that even Men of the highest Rank, as well as Genius, caressed him: And in 1696, when the Earl of *Hallifax* undertook the great Work of recoining the Money, he made Choice of Mr. *Newton* for his Assistant; and, accordingly, he was appointed Warden of the Mint, in which Employment he did very signal Service to the Nation. About three Years after, he was promoted to be Master of that Office, a Place worth 12 or 1500*l. per Ann.* which he held till his Death; for which he appears to be peculiarly qualified, by his Tables of the Essays of Foreign Money, printed at the End of Dr. *Arbuthnot's* Book. ——— Upon this Promotion, he appointed Mr. *William Whiston,* then M. A. of *Clare Hall,* his Deputy in the mathematical Professorship at *Cambridge,* giving him the full Profits of the Place, which, too, he procured for him in 1703.

The same Year, our Author was chosen President of the *Royal Society,* in which Chair he sat for 25 Years; and he had been chosen a Member of the *Royal Academy of Sciences* at *Paris* in 1699, upon the new Regulation made of admitting Foreigners into that Society.

In 1704, our Author published, in 4to, his Treatise of the *Reflections, Refractions, Inflections, and Colours of Light:* Which was afterward translated into a Variety of Languages, and passed through several Editions. *Monsieur Fontenelle* observes, that the constant Object of this Work is the Anatomy of Light. ——— The smallest Ray of Light admitted into a perfectly dark Room, which yet can never be so small but that it is, like a *Fasciculus,* composed of an infinite Number of Rays, is divided and dissected, so as to leave the Elementary Rays, which composed it, distinct from each other, each tinged with a particular Colour, and incapable of being farther altered after this Separation.———The Whiteness of the whole Beam, before its Dissection, arose from the Mixture of all the particular Colours of the original Rays. The primitive and coloured Rays could not possibly be separated, if their Nature were not such, that in passing through the same
Me-

Medium, through the fame Glafs-prifm, they are refracted under different Angles, and by that Means appear difunited, when received at convenient Diftances. This different Refrangibility of red, yellow, green, blue, violet, and the infinite Variety of intermediate coloured Rays, a Property which had never been dreamed of, and to which no Conjecture could ever lead us, is the fundamental Difcovery of our Author's Treatife. The different Refrangibility leads us to the different Reflexibility, and, which is ftill more curious, Rays, falling upon a Surface under the fame Angle of Incidence, are alternately refracted and reflected, with a Kind of Play, which could never have been diftinguifhed but by a very good Eye, affifted by an excellent Judgment. Befides (and in this Point only the firft Notion was not our Author's) thofe Rays, which pafs near the Extremity of a Body without touching it, are neverthelefs thereby turned afide out of the Right-line; and this he calls Inflexion. He fhews likewife, that the Caufe why Bodies appear of different Colours, arifes from the Magnitude of the conftituent Particles of Bodies. From all thefe Obfervations together, he has formed a Body of Optics fo new, that this Science may be confidered as entirely owing to our Author.———— It has been remarked, that our Author's Hypothefis of Light and Colours frees the Corpufcularian Philofophy from the Embarrafs of an Argument, which *Ariftotle* brought againft that Doctrine, of fenfible Qualities being the Refult of the Figures and Difpofitions of the infenfible Parts, or Atoms:———— But Sir *Ifaac*'s Hypothefis, which makes Colours the innate Property of the Rays of Light, and that different Kinds of Rays originally and immutably affert a Colour peculiar to themfelves, entirely takes off the Force of this Argument.

In Reality, the Affair that chiefly employed his Refearches for fo many Years, was far from being confined to the Subject of Light alone: On the contrary, all that we know of natural Bodies feem to be comprehended in it: He had found out, that there was a mutual Action, a Diftance between Light and other Bodies, by which both the Reflections and Refractions, as well as Inflexions of the former, were conftantly produced. He has, indeed, opened a Way of paffing from Optics to an entire Syftem of Phyfics; and if we only look upon his Queries, as containing the Hiftory of a great Man's firft Thoughts, even in that View they muft be always entertaining and curious.

In 1705, he had the Honour of Knighthood conferred upon him by Queen *Ann*, in Confideration of his great Merit.——— In 1707, he publifhed, at *Cambridge*, in Octavo, his *Arithmetica Univerfalis, five de Compofitione & Refolutione Arithmeticæ Liber.* ——— In 1711, his *Analyfis per Quantitatum Series, Fluxiones, & Differentias, cum Enumeratione Linearum tertii Ordinis*, was publifhed at *London*, by *William Jones*, Efq; F. R. S. who met with the firft of thofe Pieces amongft the Papers of Mr. *John Collins.* ——— In 1712, feveral Letters of Sir *Ifaac* were publifhed in the *Commercium Epiftolicum*.

Soon after the Acceffion of his Majefty King *George* I. our Author's Talents were fo confpicuous that he was introduced to his Majefty, with peculiar Marks of Efteem ; and that Year he was applied to, by Parliament, for his Opinion upon a new Method of difcovering the Longitude at Sea, by Signals, which had been propofed by *Ditton* and *Whifton*, in order to procure their Incouragement. But his Remarks, and Reafons affigned for his Difapprobation of it, in a Paper delivered to the Committee, was fo entirely Satisfactory, that the Project was thrown afide.

The following Year, *viz.* 1715, Mr. *Leibnits*, with a View of bringing the World more eafily into the Belief, that Sir *Ifaac* had borrowed his *Method of Fluxions* from his *differential* Method, attempted to try his mathematical Genius by the famous Problem of the Trajectories, which, though it was the moft difficult Propofition the Wit of his Antagonift could propofe, was nothing more than an Amufement to our etherial Genius, as he folved it the fame Evening he received it, though he had been fatigued that Day with the Bufinefs of the Mint. But the Greatnefs of our Author's Abilities, and his Popularity on that Account, were very often likely to occafion Difputes as to their firft Difcovery or Improvement, which he carefully avoided whenever the Importance of Truth, or his own juft Vindication did not render it neceffary.

He was now more than ever at Court. The Princefs of *Wales*, afterwards Queen Confort to King *George* II. had fuch a Tafte for philofophical Enquiries, and fo excellent an Underftanding therein, that fhe frequently converfed with him on thofe Subjects,

jects, and propofed fuch Queries, as none but himfelf could an-
fwer to her Satiffaction. And fhe was often heard to declare in
Public, that fhe thought herfelf happy in living at the fame
Time, and enjoying the Opportunities of Improvement by him.
———— He had then written a Treatife of ancient Chronology,
or was about it in 1718, when he communicated to that Princefs the chief Particulars of his Plan, which fhe thought fo new
and ingenious, that fhe defired to have an Abftract of the whole
Work, which fhe would never part with. Neverthelefs, a
Copy of it ftole abroad, and was carried over to *France*, by
the Abbé *Conti*, where it was tranflated and printed, with fome
Obfervations upon it. ———— Upon this Sir *Ifaac* publifhed in
the *philofophical Tranfactions*, N°. 389, v. 33, p. 315, *Remarks
thereon*, which were afterwards tranflated into *French* by the Ob-
fervator. And the Abbe *Conti* and Father *Souciet* attacked our
Author's Chronological Index. And a full Reply was foon after given to it by Dr. *Edmund Halley*, who was the King's Aftro-
nomer, efpecially to that Part of it which related to Aftronomy.
———— This Work at Length was publifhed in *Englifh*, and of
the Few that were Judges there were Diverfity of Opinions.
The main Defign was evidently this, to find out, by following
with Abundance of Sagacity fome of the Tracks, however faint
they are of the moft ancient *Greek* Aftronomy, what was the Pofition of the equinoctial Colures with refpect to the fixed Stars,
in the Time of *Chiron* the *Centaur*. As it is now known that
thefe Stars have a Motion in Longitude of one Degree in 72
Years, and if it is once known through what fixed Stars the Co-
lure paffed in *Chiron*'s Time, by taking the Diftance of thefe
Stars from thofe through which it now paffes, we might determine what Number of Years is elapfed fince *Chiron*'s Time. As
Chiron was one of thofe who went along with the *Argonauts* in
their famous Expedition, this would therefore fix the Epocha of
that Expedition, and confequently that of the *Trojan* War; two
great Events, upon which all ancient Chronology depends.
After having been fo ferviceable to all the learned Part of *Europe* in fpeculative Sciences, he devoted himfelf more entirely to
the Service of his Country, in Affairs to which he was more efpecially called; but his Leifure-time he devoted to gratify the
Curiofity of his Mind: He thought no kind of Knowledge beneath

neath his Confideration, and he knew how to improve himfelf
by even a fuperficial View of Things. After his Death there
were found amongft his Papers, feveral Writings upon Antiquity, Hiftory, and Divinity, Subjects widely different from each
other, and from thofe for which he was fo much diftinguifhed.
He never fuffered Time to pafs unemployed, nor ever fpent it
after a trifling Manner, or with flight Attention to what he was
about. He all along enjoyed a fettled and equal State of Health,
until he was fourfcore Years of Age, a very effential Circumftance of the extraordinary Happinefs he enjoyed. ———— He
then began to be afflicted with an Incontinence of Urine, and
yet the five Years following, which preceded his Death, he enjoyed long Intervals of Health, or was tolerably well, owing,
next to Providence, to that Care and Regularity he obferved
with regard to his Diet. ———— The laft twenty Days of his
Life were attended with much Pain, at fome Intervals, and it
was concluded he had the Stone in his Bladder, and that he
could not recover. In thofe Fits of Pain, which were fo violent that Drops of Sweat fell from his Face, he never cried
out nor expreffed the leaft Impatience; and as foon as he had
a moment's Eafe, he would fmile, and talk with his ufual
Chearfulnefs. Till this Time he had always read and wrote feveral Hours in a Day: And on *Saturday* Morning, *March* 18,
1726, difcourfed a long Time with Dr. *Mead*, his Phyfician,
having then the perfect Ufe of all his Senfes and Underftanding;
but that Night he entirely loft them, and did not recover them
any more, and died on *Monday*, *March* the 20th, in the 85th
Year of his Age. His Corpfe lay in State in the *Jerufalem* Cham-
ber, and on the 28th was conveyed into *Weftminfter Abbey*, the
Lord Chancellor, the Dukes of *Montrofe* and *Roxburgh*, and
the Earls of *Pembroke*, *Suffex*, and *Macclesfield* fupporting the
Pall. He was interred near the Entrance into the Choir, on
the Left-hand, where a ftately Monument is erected to his Memory, with the following Infcription:

H. S. E.
Ifaacus Newton, Eques Auratus,
Qui animi vi prope divina
Planetarum motus, figuras,

Co-

Cometarum femitas, Oceanique æftus,
Sua mathefi facem præferente,
Primus demonftravit.
Radiorum lucis diffimilitudines,
Colorumque inde nafcentium proprietates,
Quas nemo antea vel fufpicatus erat, perveftigavit.
Naturæ, Antiquitatis, S. Scripturæ,
Sedulus, fagax, fidus interpres,
Dei. Opt. Max. majeftatem philofophia afferuit,
Evangelii fimplicitatem moribus expreffit.
Sibi gratulentur mortales, tale tantumque extitiffe,
HUMANI GENERIS DECUS.
Natus xxv. Decemb. MDCXLII. Obiit. xx. March,
MDCCXXVI.

His Character has been attempted by many, more efpecially by *Monfieur Fontenelle*, Dr. *Pemberton*, and feveral others, the Subftance whereof is as follows:

He was of a middling Stature, and fomewhat inclined to be fat in the latter Part of his Life. His Countenance was pleafing and venerable. He never made ufe of Spectacles, and during his whole Life never loft but one Tooth. Bifhop *At-
terbury* defcribes him as having fomething rather Languid in his Look and Manner, than lively and piercing. ———— He was of a very meek Difpofition, and a great Lover of Peace. He would rather have chofen to remain in Obfcurity, than to have the Calm of Life ruffled by thofe Storms and Difputes, which Genius and Learning often draw upon thofe that are eminent for them. In contemplating his Genius, it prefently becomes a Doubt which of thefe Endowments had the greateft Share, Sagacity, Penetration, Strength, or Diligence; and after all, the Mark that feems moft to diftinguifh it, that he himfelf made the jufteft Eftimation of it, declaring, if he had done the World any Service, it was owing to Induftry and patient Thought, that he kept the Subject under Confideration conftantly before him, and waited till the firft Dawning opened gradually into a full and clear Light: And hence, no Doubt, arofe that Averfion he had to all Difputes, a fteady uninterrupted Attention, free

4 C   from

from thofe frequent Recoilings infeparable from many others, was his peculiar Felicity. He knew it, and he knew the Value of it ; and fpeaking of fome Errors which he had too haftily publifhed, which occafioned fome Difpute, he fays, I blame my own Imprudence for parting with fo real a Bleffing as my Quiet, to run after a Shadow. Though, as *Fontenelle* juftly obferves, this little Foible at firft proved the Occafion of his much greater Sollicitude to be exact in his future Productions, and thereby proved the Inftrument of much greater Ufefulnefs.

After all, notwithftanding his anxious Care to avoid every Occafion of breaking his intenfe Application to Study, he was far from being fwallowed up and loft in it ; he could lay afide his Thoughts, though engaged in the moft intricate Refearches, when his other Affairs required his Attendance, and, as foon as he had Leifure, refume the Subject at the Point where he had left it. This he feems to have done, not from any extraordinary Strength of Memory as by the Force of his inventive Faculties, to which every Thing opened itfelf again with Eafe, if nothing intervened to ruffle him ; the Readinefs of his Invention made him not think of putting his Memory much to the Rack: But this was the Offspring of a vigorous Intenfenefs of Thought, out of which he was but a common Man. He fpent, therefore, the Prime of his Life in thofe abftrufe Refearches, when his Situation in a College gave him Leifure, and even while Study was his proper Profeffion : But, as foon as he removed himfelf to the Mint, he principally attended to the Bufinefs of that Office.

Dr. *Pemberton* obferves, that he read but few modern Authors, or, at leaft, but fuperficially : But, as curfory as it might feem, it appears, he could form his Judgment of them with great Accuracy. He often cenfured handling geometrical Subjects by Algebraic Calculation, and therefore called his Book of Algebra *Univerfal Arithmetic*, in Oppofition to *Des Cartes*'s Book of Geometry. ———— He frequently praifed *Slufius*, *Barrow*, and *Huygens*, for not being influenced by the falfe Tafte that then began to prevail: ———— He commended the laudable Attempt of *Hugh de Omerique*, to reftore the ancient Analyfis ; and very much efteemed *Apollonius*'s Book *de Sectione Rationis*, for giving us a clearer

clearer *Notion* of that Analyfis than we had before. ————
Dr. *Barrow* he efteemed, as having ſhewn a Compaſs of Invention equal, if not ſuperior, to any of the Moderns. ————
Sir *Ifaac* commended *Huygens*'s Stile and Manner of Writing;
and thought him the moſt Elegant of any mathematical Writer
in modern Times, and the moſt juſt Imitator of the Ancients,
of whoſe Taſte and Form of Demonſtration Sir *Ifaac* always
profeſſed himſelf a great Admirer, and often cenſured himſelf
for not following them more exactly than he did.

It is farther obſerved of him, that he feldom talked much of
himſelf, or others; nor ever behaved in ſuch Manner as to
give the moſt malicious Cenfurers the leaſt Occaſion to charge
him with Vanity. ————— He was candid and affable, and always put himſelf upon a Level with his Company. He never
thought either his Merit or Reputation ſufficient to excuſe him
from any of the common Offices of ſocial Life ; no Singulari-
ties, either natural or affected, diſtinguiſhed him from other
Men. Though he was ſteadily attached to the Church of
England, he was greatly averſe to the Perſecution of Noncon-
formiſts. He judged of Men by their Manners; and the true
Schiſmatics, in his Opinion, were the vicious and immoral:
Not that he confined his Principles to natural Religion ; for
he was thoroughly perſuaded of the Truth of Revelation, and,
amidſt the great Variety of Books which he had conſtantly before him, that which he ſtudied with the greateſt Application
was, the *Bible*. He did not neglect the Opportunities of doing Good, which the plentiful Revenues of his Patrimony, and
a profitable Employment, improved by a prudent Oeconomy,
put into his Power. " He thought a Legacy, ſays *Monſieur
de Fontenelle*, was no Gift, and, therefore, left no Will; for
he would even ſtrip himſelf, as often as he had Occaſion, to
aſſiſt either his Relations or others, who ſtood in Need of it:
The Inſtances of his Liberality, in both theſe Reſpects, were
neither few nor inconſiderable." ————— He died poſſeſſed of
Thirty-two Thouſand Pounds, which was in Eſtate, and is
ſaid to devolve, as the Law directed, to his next of Kin. ————
When Decency, upon any Occaſion, required Expence and
Shew, he was magnificient without grudging it; and, with a
very

very good Grace, at all other Times, that Pomp, which feems great to low Minds only, was utterly retrenched, and the Expence faved for better Ufes. He never married; which was always attributed to his being fo deeply immerfed in profound and continual Studies during the prime Part of his Life, and his other important Employments.

Mr. *Hume*, in his Hiftory of *England*, fpeaks of Sir *Ifaac* to the following Purport : " In *Newton* (fays he) this Ifland may boaft of having produced the greateft and rareft Genius that ever arofe, for the Ornament and Inftruction of the Species in philofophical, aftronomical, and mathematical Knowledge; cautious in admitting no Principles but fuch as were founded on Experiment; but refolute to adopt every fuch Principle, however new or unfual; from Modefty, ignorant of his Superiority above the reft of Mankind, and thence lefs careful to accommodate his Reafonings to common Apprehenfions, more anxious to Merit than acquire Fame. He was from thefe Caufes long unknown to the World; but his Reputation at laft broke out with a Luftre which fcarce any Writer before his Time ever attained : While *Newton* feemed to draw off the Veil from fome of the Myfteries of Nature, he fhowed at the fame Time the Imperfections of the mechanical Philofophy, and thereby reftored her ultimate Secrets from that Obfcurity in which they had before lay, and in which, without his Affiftance, would probably ever have remained.

And another ingenious Author, in a Kind of Rhapfody, fays, the *Newtonian* Philofophy alone, to what fublime Sentiments does it lift the Mind ! what noble Ideas does it give us of Immenfity, filled with innumerable Worlds revolving round innumerable Suns ! thofe Worlds themfelves the Centres of others, Secondary to them all, all attracting or attracted, enlightening or receiving Light, at Diftances unmeafurable ! but all under one Law. ———— How do thefe Ideas tend to raife our Conceptions of the great Author, and firft Caufe of thofe Worlds, and excite our Admiration !

PRIESTLEY:

The History of Electricity

Joseph Priestley, *The History of Electricity*, 3rd edn, 'The Preface to the First Edition', pp. i–xxvi; 'Volume I, Period IX, Section I: Dr Franklin's Discoveries Concerning the Similarity of Lightning and Electricity', pp. 204–18; 'Volume II, Section VII. Experiments on Animals', pp. 253–9 (London, 1775).

When, in 1767, Joseph Priestley (1733–1804) came to write *The History and Present State of Electricity*, he wanted to celebrate the progress of scientific discovery. It seemed to him that a boundless opportunity was opening up for mankind. Here in electricity was a power whose application might be endless; a force that might generate a thousand inventions.

Priestley himself was a radical in politics, a dissenter in religion, and a keen practitioner of natural philosophy. He supported the French Revolution; he was one of the original members of the Unitarian Society; and discovered oxygen, hydrochloric acid, nitric oxide, and sulphur dioxide, among other gases. He is a quintessential figure of the late English enlightenment; a polymath; a ceaseless experimenter; a tester of received opinions. Although not Priestley's first book, *The History and Present State of Electricity* was his first major published work in the field of natural philosophy. It appeared a couple of years after his arrival in London, and his entry into a scientific and dissenting circle of friends.

The first volume of the book traces experiments with electricity from the early seventeenth century (with a glance back to classical knowledge) to the present day. The second volume examines theories of electricity, offers desiderata for the further exploration of the field, presents descriptions of useful electrical machines, and writes of experiments that Priestley himself had performed. Interestingly, he describes the sight of the electrical current as very beautiful. Perhaps Priestley's first task was to give the discoveries of natural philosophy a history. In creating a narrative of the onward progress of science, he could provide a model for later experimenters and discoverers. Writing a history would make history.

Priestley's style is one that is delightfully simple to read. In writing of his experiments, Priestley also takes care to describe his failures as much as his successes. The effect of these things is a consciously democratic one. Natural philosophy does not appear a mystery open only to the elect, but a subject that could become the property of any interested person. At the start of the preface, Priestley addresses both 'electricians' and 'persons who have a taste for Natural Philosophy'. This openness is one of the great strengths of the work: it both advances knowledge, and presents that knowledge to anyone wishing to receive it.

Priestley knew the need for a genuinely informed communicator of discoveries. Already he was uttering the complaint, so familiar to us today, that rapid increases in knowledge and the multiplicity of scientific discoveries were making it impossible for one person to grasp the whole field of science. He both argues for what we would call 'specialisation' (and he calls 'subdivision') and asserts the value of knowing the broader picture. The writing of works such as *The History and Present State of Electricity* would be vital in allowing natural philosophers easily to survey their whole field of study, and also to examine potentially useful discoveries in other apparently unrelated fields. He admires adventurers in experimentation as much as he praises the great thinkers. Priestley sees natural philosophy as a field of practical activity; it is about doing things. The book aims to make its readers become part of the history; real discoveries are promised a place in later editions.

Lastly, in the Preface, Priestley affirms the moral value of such experiments: natural philosophy disciplines the heart. Science is valuable in itself, and for the practical power it gives us over nature. Yet, Priestley remembers that we should be interested in things other than science; that we must be men or women thinking, and not just thinkers. Science ultimately belongs to our leisure; a polite and noble pursuit for those resting from the sterner and more pre-emptory duties of life.

The description of Franklin's experiments with lightning using a kite return us to Priestley's delight in the adventurous and the practical. As with Newton and the apple, the story became a symbolic anecdote in the history of natural philosophy. With each story, the combination of the homespun and the exciting discovery is what motivates our interest. In Newton's case, the thoughts range far beyond us, but the situation that inspired them is cosily familiar. Newton asks the child's question – why should apples fall to the ground? – and so defamiliarises the fact we all knew, but none of us could understand. Franklin's tale of the kite is crazier, an image of recklessness in the pursuit of knowledge that nonetheless remains endearingly eccentric and cosy.

The last extract from this book shows Priestley describing some of his own experiments. In the summer of 1765, Priestley's work on the nature of electricity led him to perform a series of experiments on the effects of electrical current on animals. The results were, in every sense, explosive. Experimenting with animals was a standard practice among the electricians of the day; Franklin prophetically imagined a world in which a turkey would be killed with an electric shock and then cooked electrically. Priestley stands here at one crux of our relationship with animals, caught between the requirements of knowledge and the desire for compassion.

THE

PREFACE

TO THE

FIRST EDITION.

IN writing the *History and Present State of Electricity*, I flatter myself that I shall give pleasure, as well to persons who have a taste for Natural Philosophy in general, as to electricians in particular; and I hope the work will be of some advantage to the science itself. Both these ends would certainly be answered in a considerable degree, were the execution at all answerable to the design.

THE History of Electricity is a field full of pleasing objects, according to all the genuine and universal principles of taste, deduced from a knowledge of human nature. Scenes like these, in which we see a gradual rise and progress in things, always exhibit a pleasing spectacle to the human mind. Nature, in all her delightful walks, abounds with such views, and they are in a more especial manner connected with every thing that relates to human life and happiness; things, in their own nature, the most interesting to us. Hence it is, that the power of association has annexed crouds of pleasing sensations to the contemplation of every object, in which this property is apparent.

VOL. I.   a   THIS

THIS pleasure, likewise, bears a considerable resemblance to that of the sublime, which is one of the most exquisite of all those that affect the human imagination. For an object in which we see a perpetual progress and improvement is, as it were, continually rising in its magnitude; and moreover, when we see an actual increase, in a long period of time past, we cannot help forming an idea of an unlimited increase in futurity; which is a prospect really boundless, and sublime.

THE pleasures arising from views exhibited in *civil*, *natural*, and *philosophical* history, are, in certain respects, different from one another. Each has its advantages, and each its defects: and both their advantages and defects contribute to adapt them to different classes of readers.

CIVIL history presents us with views of the strongest passions and sentiments of the human mind, into which every man can easily and perfectly enter, and with such incidents, respecting happiness and misery, as we cannot help feeling, would alarm and affect us in a very sensible manner; and therefore, we are at present alarmed and affected by them to a considerable degree. Hence the pleasure we receive from civil history arises, chiefly from the exercise it affords our passions. The imagination is only entertained with scenes which occasionally start up, like interludes, or episodes, in the great drama, to which we are principally attentive. We are presented, indeed, with the prospect of gradual

gradual improvement during the rife of great empires; but, as we read on, we are obliged to contemplate the difagreeable reverfe. And the hiftory of moft ftates prefents nothing but a tedious uniformity, without any ftriking events, to diverfify and embellifh the profpect. Befides, if a man have any fentiment of virtue and benevolence, he cannot help being fhocked with a view of the vices and miferies of mankind; which, though they be not all, are certainly the moft glaring and ftriking objects in the hiftory of human affairs. An attention, indeed, to the conduct of divine Providence, which is ever bringing good out of evil, and gradually conducting things to a more perfect and glorious ftate, tends to throw a more agreeable light on the more gloomy parts of hiftory; but it requires great ftrength of mind to comprehend thofe views; and, after all, the feelings of the heart too often overpower the conclufions of the head.

NATURAL hiftory exhibits a boundlefs variety of fcenes, and yet infinitely analogous to one another. A naturalift has, confequently, all the pleafure which the contemplation of uniformity and variety can give the mind; and this is one of the moft copious fources of our intellectual pleafures. He is likewife entertained with a profpect of gradual improvement, while he fees every object in nature rifing by due degrees to its maturity and perfection. And while new plants, new animals, and new foffils are per-

petually

petually pouring in upon him, the moſt pleaſing views of the unbounded power, wiſdom,
and goodneſs of God are conſtantly preſent
to his mind. But he has no direct view of
human ſentiments and human actions; which,
by means of their endleſs aſſociations, greatly heighten and improve all the pleaſures of
taſte.

THE hiſtory of philoſophy enjoys, in ſome
meaſure, the advantages both of civil and
natural hiſtory, whereby it is relieved from
what is moſt tedious and diſguſting in both.
Philoſophy exhibits the powers of nature, diſcovered and directed by human art. It has,
therefore, in ſome meaſure, the boundleſs
variety with the amazing uniformity of the
one, and likewiſe every thing that is pleaſing
and intereſting in the other. And the idea
of continual riſe and improvement is conſpi-
cuous in the whole ſtudy, whether we be attentive to the part which nature, or that which
men are acting in the great ſcene.

IT is here that we ſee the human underſtanding to its greateſt advantage, graſping
at the nobleſt objects, and increaſing its own
powers, by acquiring to itſelf the powers of
nature, and directing them to the accom-
pliſhment of its own views; whereby the ſecurity, and happineſs of mankind are daily
improved. Human abilities are chiefly con-
ſpicuous in adapting means to ends, and in
deducing one thing from another by the method of analogy; and where ſhall we find
inſtances of greater ſagacity, than in philo-
                                        ſophers

fophers diverfifying the fituations of things, in order to give them an opportunity of fhowing their mutual relations, affections, and influences; deducing one truth and one difcovery from another, and applying them all to the ufeful purpofes of human life.

IF the exertion of human abilities, which cannot but form a delightful fpectacle for the human imagination, give us pleafure, we enjoy it here in a higher degree than while we are contemplating the fchemes of warriors, and the ftratagems of their bloody art. Befides, the object of philofophical purfuits throws a pleafing idea upon the fcenes they exhibit; whereas a reflection upon the real objects and views of moft ftatefmen and conquerors cannot but take from the pleafure, which the idea of their fagacity, forefight, and comprehenfion would otherwife give to the virtuous and benevolent mind. Laftly, the inveftigation of the powers of nature, like the ftudy of Natural Hiftory, is perpetually fuggefting to us views of the divine perfections and providence, which are both pleafing to the imagination, and improving to the heart.

BUT though other kinds of hiftory may, in fome refpects, vie with that of philofophy, nothing that comes under the denomination of hiftory can exhibit inftances of fo fine a rife and improvement in things, as we fee in the progrefs of the human mind, in philofophical inveftigations. To whatever height we have arrived in natural fcience, our be—

a 3   ginnings

ginnings were very low, and our advances have been exceedingly gradual. And to look down from the eminence, and to fee, and compare all thofe gradual advances in the afcent, cannot but give the greateft pleafure to thofe-who are feated on the eminence, and who feel all the advantages of their elevated fituation. And confidering that we ourfelves are, by no means, at the top of human fcience; that the mountain ftill afcends be- yond our fight, and that we are, in fact, not much above the foot of it, a view of the manner in which the afcent has been made, cannot but animate us in our attempts to ad- vance ftill higher, and fuggeft methods and expedients to affift us in our farther progrefs.

GREAT conquerors, we read, have been both animated, and alfo, in a great meafure, formed by reading the exploits of former conquerors. Why may not the fame effect be expected from the hiftory of philofophy to philofophers? May not even more be ex- pected in this cafe? The wars of many of thofe conquerors, who received this advan- tage from hiftory, had no proper connection with former wars : they were only analogous to them. Whereas the whole bufinefs of philofophy, diverfified as it is, is but one ; it being one and the fame great fcheme, that all philofophers, of all ages and nations, have been conducting, from the beginning of the world; fo that the work being the fame, the labours of one are not only analogous to thofe
of

of another, but in an immediate manner fubfervient to them; and one philofopher fuc-
ceeds another in the fame field; as one Roman proconful fucceeded another in carrying on the fame war, and purfuing the fame
conquefts, in the fame country. In this cafe,
an intimate knowledge of what has been done
before us cannot but greatly facilitate our future progrefs, if it be not abfolutely neceffary
to it.

THESE hiftories are evidently much more
neceffary in an advanced ftate of fcience, than
in the infancy of it. At prefent philofophical difcoveries are fo many, and the accounts
of them are fo difperfed, that it is not in the
power of any man to come at the knowledge
of all that has been done, as a foundation for
his own inquiries. And this circumftance appears to me to have very much retarded the
progrefs of difcoveries.

NOT that I think philofophical difcoveries
are now at a ftand. On the other hand, as
quick advances feem to have been made of
late years, as in any equal period of time
paft whatever. Nay, it appears to me, that
the progrefs is really accelerated. But the
increafe of knowledge is like the increafe of
a city. The building of fome of the firft
ftreets makes a great figure, is much talked
of, and known to every body; whereas the
addition of, perhaps, twice as much building, after it has been fwelled to a confiderable fize, is not fo much as taken notice of,

and

and may be really unknown to many of the inhabitants. If the additions which have been made to the buildings of the city of London, in any fingle year of late, had been made two or three centuries ago, it could not have efcaped the obfervation of hiftorians; whereas, now, they are fo fcattered, and the proportion they bear to the whole city is fo fmall, that they are hardly noticed. For the fame reafon, the improvements that boys make at fchool, or that young gentlemen make at an academy, or the univerfity, are more taken notice of than all the knowledge they acquire afterwards, though they continue their ftudies with the fame affiduity and fuccefs.

THE hiftory of experimental philofophy, in the manner in which it ought to be written, to be of much ufe, would be an immenfe work; but it were much to be wifhed, that perfons who have leifure, and fuffieient abilities, would undertake it in feparate parts. I have executed it, in the beft manner I have been able, for that branch which has been my own favourite amufement; and I fhall think myfelf happy, if the attempt excite other perfons to do the like for theirs.

I CANNOT help thinking myfelf to have been peculiarly fortunate, in undertaking the hiftory of electricity, at the moft proper time for writing it, when the materials were neither too few, nor too many to make a hiftory; and when they were fo fcattered, as
to

to make the undertaking highly defirable, and the work peculiarly ufeful to Englifh-men.

I LIKEWISE think myfelf exceedingly happy in my fubject itfelf. Few branches of Natural Philofophy would, I think, make fo good a fubject for a hiftory. Few can boaft fuch a number of difcoveries, difpofed in fo fine a feries, all comprifed in fo fhort a fpace of time, and all fo recent, the principal ac-tors in the fcene being ftill living.

WITH feveral of thefe principal actors it has been my fingular honour and happinefs to be acquainted; and it was their approba-tion of my plan, and their generous encou-ragement that induced me to undertake the work. With gratitude I acknowledge my obligations to Dr. Watfon, Dr. Franklin, and Mr. Canton, for the books, and other mate-rials with which they have fupplied me, and for the readinefs with which they have given me any information in their power to pro-cure. In a more efpecial manner am I oblig-ed to Mr. Canton, for thofe original commu-nications of his, which will be found in this work, and which cannot fail to give a value to it, in the efteem of all the lovers of electri-city. My grateful acknowledgements are al-fo due to the Rev. Dr. Price, F. R. S. and to the Rev. Mr. Holt, our profeffor of Natural Philofophy at Warrington, for the attention they have given to the work, and for the many important fervices they have rendered me with refpect to it.

To

To the gentlemen above mentioned the public is, likewife, indebted for whatever they may think of value in the *original experiments* which I have related of my own. It was from converfing with them that I was firft led to entertain the thought of attempting any thing new in this way, and it was their example, and favourable attention to my expériments, that animated me in the purfuit of them. In fhort, without them, neither my experiments, nor this work would have had any exiftence.

THE hiftorical part of this work, the reader, I hope will find to be full and circumftantial, and at the fame fuccinct. Every new fact, or important circumftance, I have noted as it arofe; but I have abridged all long details, and have carefully avoided all digreffions and repetitions. For this purpofe, I have perufed every original author, to which I could have recourfe; and every quotation in the margin points to the authority that I myfelf confulted, and from which the account in the text was actually taken. Where I could not procure the original authors, I was obliged to quote them at fecond hand, but the reference will always fhow where that has been done. That I might not mifreprefent any writer, I have generally given the reader his own words, or the plaineft tranflation I could make of them; and this I have done, not only in direct quotations, but where, by a change of perfon, I have made the language my own.

I MADE

I MADE it a rule to myfelf, and I think I have conftantly adhered to it, to take no notice of the miftakes, mifapprehenfions, and altercations of electricians; except fo far as, I apprehended, a knowledge of them might be ufeful to their fucceffors. All the difputes which have no way contributed to the difcovery of truth, I would gladly confign to eternal oblivion. Did it depend upon me, it fhould never be known to pofterity, that there had ever been any fuch thing as envy, jealoufy, or cavilling among the admirers of my favourite ,ftudy. I have, as far as my beft judgment could direct me, been juft to the merits of all perfons concerned. If any have made unjuft claims, by arrogating to themfelves the difcoveries of others, I have filently reftored them to the right owner, and generally without fo much as giving a hint that any injuftice had ever been committed. If I have, in any cafe, given a hint, I hope it will be thought, by the offending parties themfelves, to be a very gentle one; and that it will be a *memento*, which will not be without its ufe.

I THINK I have kept clear of any mean partiality towards my own countrymen, and even my own acquaintance. If Englifh authors are oftener quoted than foreign, it is becaufe they were more cafily procured; and I have found a difficulty I could not have expected, in procuring foreign publications upon this fubject.

I FIND

I FIND it impossible to write a preface to this work, without discovering a little of the enthusiasm which I have contracted from an attention to it, by expressing my wishes, that more persons, of a studious and retired life, would admit this part of experimental philosophy into their studies. They would find it agreeably to diversify a course of study, by mixing something of action with speculation, and giving some employment to the hands and arms, as well as to the head. Electrical experiments are, of all others, the cleanest, and the most elegant, that the compass of philosophy exhibits. They are performed with the least trouble, there is an amazing variety in them, they furnish the most pleasing and surprising appearances for the entertainment of one's friends, and the expence of instruments may well be supplied, by a proportionable deduction from the purchase of books, which are generally read and laid aside, without yielding half the entertainment.

THE instruction we are able to get from books is, comparatively, soon exhausted; but philosophical instruments are an endless fund of knowledge. By philosophical instruments, however, I do not here mean the globes, the orrery, and others, which are only the means which ingenious men have hit upon, to explain their own conceptions of things to others; and which, therefore, like books, have no uses more extensive than the

views

views of human ingenuity; but such as the air-pump, condensing engine, pyrometer, &c. (with which electrical machines are to be ranked) and which exhibit the operations of nature, that is of the God of nature himself, which are infinitely various. By the help of these machines, we are able to put an endless variety of things into an endless variety of situations, while nature herself is the agent that shows the result. Hereby the laws of her action are observed, and the most important discoveries may be made; such as those who first contrived the instrument could have no idea of.

In electricity, in particular, there is the greatest room to make new discoveries. It is a field but just opened, and requires no great stock of particular preparatory knowledge: so that any person who is tolerably well versed in experimental philosophy, may presently be upon a level with the most experienced electricians. Nay, this history shows, that several raw adventurers have made themselves as considerable, as some who have been, in other respects, the greatest philosophers. I need not tell my reader of how great weight this consideration is, to induce him to provide himself with an electrical apparatus. The pleasure arising from the most trifling discoveries of one's own, far exceeds what we receive from understanding the much more important discoveries of others; and a mere reader has no chance of finding new truths, in comparison of him who now and then amuses

amuſes himſelf with philoſophical experiments.

HUMAN happineſs depends chiefly upon
having ſome objeƈt to purſue, and upon the
vigour with which our faculties are exerted
in the purſuit. And, certainly, we muſt be
much more intereſted in purſuits wholly our
own, than when we are merely following the
track of others. Beſides, this pleaſure has re-
inforcements from a variety of ſources, which
I ſhall not here undertake to trace; but
which contribute to heighten the ſenſation,
far beyond any thing elſe of this kind that
can be experienced by a perſon of a ſpecula-
tive turn of mind.

IT is a great recommendation of the ſtudy
of eleƈtricity, that it now appears to be, by
no means, a ſmall objeƈt. The eleƈtric fluid
is no local, or occaſional agent in the theatre
of the world. Late diſcoveries ſhow that its
preſence and effeƈts are every where, and
that it aƈts a principal part in the grandeſt
and moſt intereſting ſcenes of nature. It is
not, like magnetiſm, confined to one kind of
bodies, but every thing we know is a con-
duƈtor or non-conduƈtor of eleƈtricity. Theſe
are properties as eſſential and important as
any they are poſſeſſed of, and can hardly
fail to ſhow themſelves wherever the bodies
are concerned.

HITHERTO philoſophy has been chiefly
converſant about the more ſenſible properties of bodies; eleƈtricity, together with chy-
miſtry, and the doƈtrine of light and colours,

ſeems

feems to be giving us an inlet into their internal ftructure, on which all their fenfible
properties depend. By purfuing this new
light, therefore, the bounds of natural fcience
may poffibly be extended, beyond what we
can now form an idea of. New worlds may
open to our view, and the glory of the great
Sir Ifaac Newton himfelf, and all his contemporaries, be eclipfed, by a new fet of philofophers, in quite a new field of fpeculation.
Could that great man revifit the earth, and
view the experiments of the prefent race of
electricians, he would be no lefs amazed than
Roger Bacon, or Sir Francis, would have been
at his. The electric fhock itfelf, if it be
confidered attentively, will appear almoft as
furprifing as any difcovery that he made;
and the man who could have made that difcovery, by any reafoning *a priori*, would
have been reckoned a moft extraordinary genius : but electrical difcoveries have been
made fo much by accident, that it is more
the powers of nature, than of human genius,
that excite our wonder with refpect to them.
But if the fimple electric fhock would have
appeared fo extraordinary to Sir Ifaac Newton, what would he have faid upon feeing
the effects of a modern electrical battery, and
an apparatus for drawing lightning from the
clouds ! What inexpreffible pleafure would it
give a modern electrician, were the thing
poffible, to entertain fuch a man as Sir Ifaac
for a few hours with his principal experiments !

To

To return from this excurſion to the buſineſs of a preface: beſides relating the hiſtory
of electrical diſcoveries, in the order in which
they were made, I thought it neceſſary, in
order to make the work more uſeful, eſpecially to young electricians, to ſubjoin a me-
thodical treatiſe on the ſubject, containing the
ſubſtance of the hiſtory in another form, with
obſervations and inſtructions of my own. The
particular uſes of theſe parts of the work are
expreſſed at large in the introductions to
them. And, in the laſt place, I have given
an account of ſuch original experiments as
I have been ſo fortunate as to hit upon
myſelf.

I INTITLE the work the *Hiſtory and Preſent State of Electricity*; and whether there be
any more additions of the whole work or not,
care will be taken to preſerve the propriety of
the title, by occaſionally printing ADDI-
TIONS, in the ſame ſize, as new diſcoveries
are made; which will always be ſold at
a reaſonable price to the purchaſers of the
book; or given *gratis*, if the bulk be inconſiderable.

CONSIDERING what reſpectable perſons
have already honoured this work with their
valuable communications, I hope it will not
be deemed arrogance in me, if I here ad-
vertiſe, that if any perſon ſhall make diſcoveries in electricity, which he would chuſe to
ſee recorded in this hiſtory, he will oblige
me by a communication of them; and if
they be really original, a proper place ſhall

ccr-

I

certainly be affigned to them in the next edition, or paper of additions. And I hope that,
if electricians in general would fall into
this method, and make either a periodical,
or occafional, but joint communication of
their difcoveries to the public, the greateft
advantage would thence accrue to the
fcience.

THE bufinefs of philofophy is fo multi-
plied, that all the books of general philofophical tranfactions cannot be purchafed by
many perfons, or read by any perfon It is
high time to *fubdivide* the bufinefs, that
every man may have an opportunity of feeing every thing that relates· to his own
favourite purfuit; and all the various branches
of philofophy would find their account in
this amicable feparation. Thus the numerous branches of a large overgrown family, in
the patriarchal ages, found it neceffary to feparate; and the convenience of the whole, and
the ftrength, and increafe of each branch
were promoted by the feparation. Let the
youngeft daughter of the fcience fet the example to the reft, and fhow that fhe thinks
herfelf confiderable enough to make her appearance in the world without the company
of her fifters.

BUT before this general feparation, let
each collect together every thing that belongs
to her, and march off with her whole ftock.
To drop the allufion: let hiftories be written
of all that has been done in every particular
branch of fcience, and let the whole be feen

VOL. I. b at

at one view. And when once the entire progrefs, and prefent ftate of every fcience fhall
be fully and fairly exhibited, I doubt not but
we fhall fee a new and capital *æra* commence
in the hiftory of all the fciences. Such an
eafy, full, and comprehenfive view of what
has been done hitherto could not fail to give
new life to philofophical inquiries. It would
fuggeft an infinity of new experiments, and
would undoubtedly greatly accelerate the progrefs of knowledge; which is at prefent retarded, as it were, by its own weight, and
the mutal entanglement of its feveral parts.

I WILL juft throw out a farther hint, of
what, I think, might be favourable to the
increafe of philofophical knowledge. At prefent there are, in different countries in Europe, large incorporate focieties, with funds
for promoting philofophical knowledge in
general. Let philofophers now begin to fubdivide themfelves, and enter into fmaller combinations. Let the feveral companies make
fmall funds, and appoint a director of experiments. Let every member have a right to
appoint the trial of experiments in fome proportion to the fum he fubfcribes, and let a periodical account be publifhed of the refult of
them all, fuccefsful or unfuccefsful. In this
manner, the powers of all the members
would be united and increafed. Nothing
would be left untried, which could be compaffed at a moderate expence, and it being
one perfon's bufinefs to attend to thefe experiments, they would be made, and reported
without

without loſs of time. Moreover, as all in-corporations in theſe ſmaller ſocieties ſhould be avoided, they would be encouraged only in proportion as they were found to be uſeful; and ſucceſs in ſmaller things would excite them to attempt greater.

I by no means diſapprove of large, general, and incorporated ſocieties. They have their peculiar uſes too; but we ſee by experience, that they are apt to grow too large, and their forms are too ſlow for the diſpatch of the *minutiæ* of buſineſs, in the preſent multifarious ſtate of philoſophy. Let recourſe be had to rich incorporated ſocieties, to defray the ex-pence of experiments, to which the funds of ſmaller ſocieties ſhall be unequal. Let their tranſactions contain a ſummary of the more important diſcoveries, collected from the ſmaller periodical publications. Let them, by rewards, and other methods, encourage thoſe who diſtinguiſh themſelves in the inferior ſo-cieties; and thus give a general attention to the whole buſineſs of philoſophy.

I wish all the incorporated philoſophical ſocieties in Europe would join their funds (and I wiſh they were ſufficient for the purpoſe) to fit out ſhips for the complete diſcovery of the face of the earth, and for many capital expe-riments which can only be made in ſuch ex-tenſive voyages.

Princes will never do this great buſineſs to any purpoſe. The ſpirit of adventure ſeems to be totally extinct in the preſent race of merchants. This diſcovery is a grand deſide-

ratum

ratum in fcience; and where may this pure and noble enthufiafm for fuch difcoveries be expected but among philofophers, men uninfluenced by motives either of policy or gain? Let us think ourfelves happy if princes give no obftruction to fuch defigns. Let them fight for the countries when they are difcovered, and let merchants fcramble for the advantage that may be made of them. It will be an acquifition to philofophers if the feat of war be removed fo far from the feat of fcience; and frefh room will be given to the exertion of genius in trade, when the old beaten track is deferted, when the old fyftem of traffic is unhinged, and when new and more extenfive plans of commerce take place. I congratulate the prefent race of philofophers on what is doing by the Englifh court in this way *; for with whatever view expeditions into the South Seas are made, they cannot but be favourable to philofophy.

NATURAL PHILOSOPHY is a fcience which more efpecially requires the aid of wealth. Many others require nothing but what a man's own reflection may furnifh him with. They who cultivate them find within themfelves every thing they want. But experimental philofophy is not fo independent. Nature will not be put out of her way, and fuffer her materials to be thrown into all that variety of fituations which philofophy requires, in order to difcover her wonderful powers, with-

---

* Written in the year 1756.

out

out trouble and expence. Hence the patronage of the great is effential to the flou-
rifhing ftate of this fcience. Others may project great improvements, but they only have
the power of carrying them into execution.

BESIDES, they are the higher claffes of men
which are moft interefted in the extenfion of
all kinds of natural knowledge; as they are
moft able to avail themfelves of any difcoveries, which lead to the felicity and embellifh-
ment of human life. Almoft all the elegancies
of life are the produce of thofe polite arts,
which could have had no exiftence without
natural fcience, and which receive daily improvements from the fame fource. From the
great and the opulent, therefore, thefe fciences
have a natural claim for protection; and it is
evidently their intereft not to fuffer promifing
inquiries to be fufpended for want of the
means of profecuting them.

BUT other motives, befides this felfifh one,
may reafonably be fuppofed to attach perfons
in the higher ranks of life to the fciences;
motives more exalted, and flowing from the
moft extenfive benevolence. From Natural
Philofophy have flowed all thofe great inventions, by means of which mankind in general are able to fubfift with more eafe, and
in greater numbers upon the face of the earth.
Hence arife the capital advantages of men
above brutes, and of civilization above barba-
rity. And by thefe fciences alfo it is, that
the views of the human mind itfelf are enlarged, and our common nature improved
and ennobled. It is for the honour of the

b 3   fperies,

fpecies, therefore, that thefe fciences fhould be cultivated with the utmoft attention.

AND of whom may thefe enlarged views, comprehenfive of fuch great objects, be expected, but of thofe whom divine providence has raifed above the reft of mankind. Being free from moft of the cares peculiar to individuals, they may embrace the interefts of the whole fpecies, feel for the wants of mankind, and be concerned to fupport the dignity of human nature.

GLADLY would I indulge the hope, that we fhall foon fee thefe motives operating in a more extenfive manner than they have hitherto done; that by the illuftrious example of a few, a tafte for natural fcience will be excited in many, in whom it will operate the moft effectually to the advantage of fcience and of the world; and that all kinds of philofophical inquiries will, henceforward, be conducted with more fpirit, and with more fuccefs than ever.

WERE I to purfue this fubject, it would carry me far beyond the reafonable bounds of a preface. I fhall therefore conclude with mentioning that fentiment, which ought to be uppermoft in the mind of every philofopher, whatever be the immediate object of his purfuit; that fpeculation is only of ufe as it leads to *practice*, that the immediate ufe of natural fcience is the power it gives us over nature, by means of the knowledge we acquire of its laws; whereby human life is, in its prefent flate, made more comfortable and happy; but that the greateft, and nobleft

ufe

use of philofophical fpeculation is the difcipline of the heart, and the opportunity it affords of inculcating benevolent and pious fentiments upon the mind.

A PHILOSOPHER ought to be fomething greater, and better than another man. The contemplation of the works of God fhould give a fublimity to his virtue, fhould expand his benevolence, extinguifh every thing mean, bafe, and felfifh in his nature, give a dignity to all his fentiments, and teach him to afpire to the moral perfections of the great author of all things. What great and exalted beings would philofophers be, would they but let the objects about which they are converfant have their proper moral effect upon their minds! A life fpent in the contemplation of the productions of divine power, wifdom, and goodnefs, would be a life of devotion. The more we fee of the wonderful ftructure of the world, and of the laws of nature, the more clearly do we comprehend their admirable ufes, to make all the percipient creation happy: a fentiment, which cannot but fill the heart with unbounded love, gratitude, and joy.

EVEN every thing painful and difagreeable in the world appears to a philofopher, upon a more attentive examination, to be excellently provided, as a remedy of fome greater inconvenience, or a neceffary means of a much greater happinefs; fo that, from this elevated point of view, he fees all temporary evils and inconveniences to vanifh, in the glorious profpect of the greater good to which they are fubfervient. Hence he is able to venerate and

b 4   rejoice

rejoice in God, not only in the bright fun-
fhine, but alfo in the darkeft fhades of nature,
whereas vulgar minds are apt to be difcon-
certed with the appearance of evil.

NOR is the cultivation of piety ufeful to us
only as *men,* it is even ufeful to us as *philofophers:* and as true philofophy tends to promote piety, fo a generous and manly piety is
reciprocally, fubfervient to the purpofes of philofophy; and this both in a direct and indirect
manner. While we keep in view the great
final caufe of all the parts and the laws of nature, we have fome clue, by which to trace the
efficient caufe. This is moft of all obvious in
that part of philofophy which refpects the animal creation. As the great and excellent Dr.
Hartley obferves. " Since this world is a
" fyftem of benevolence, and confequently its
" author the object of unbounded love and a-
" doration, benevolence and piety are our on-
" ly true guides, in our inquiries into it; the
" only keys which will unlock the myfteries
" of nature, and clues which lead through her
" labyrinths. Of this all branches of natural
" hiftory, and natural philofophy afford abun-
" dant inftances. In all thefe inquiries, let the
" inquirer take it for granted previoufly, that
" every thing is right, and the beft that can be
" *ceteris manentibus;* that is, let him, with
" a pious confidence, feek for benevolent
" purpofes, and he will be always directed to
" the right road; and after a due continuance
" in it, attain to fome new and valuable truth:
" whereas every other principle and motive of
" examination, being foreign to the great plan
" on

" on which the univerfe is conftructed, muft lead
" into endlefs mazes, errors, and perplexities*."

WITH refpect to the indirect ufe of piety, it
muft be obferved, that the tranquility, and
chearfulnefs of mind, which refults from devotion forms an excellent temper for conducting philofophical inquiries; tending to make
them both more pleafant, and more fuccefsful.
The fentiments of religion and piety tend to
cure the mind of envy, jealoufy, conceit, and
every other mean paffion, which both difgrace
the lovers of fcience, and retard the progrefs of
it, by laying an undue bias upon the mind,
and diverting it from the calm purfuit of truth.

LASTLY, let it be remembered, that a tafte
for fcience, pleafing, and even honourable as
it is, is not one of the higheft paffions of our
nature, that the pleafures it furnifhes are even
but one degree above thofe of fenfe, and therefore that temperance is requifite in all fcientifical purfuits. Befides the duties of every man's
proper ftation in life, which ought ever to be
held facred and inviolate, the calls of piety,
common friendfhip, and many other avoca-
tions ought generally to be heard before that
of ftudy. It is, therefore, only a fmall fhare of
their leifure, that moft men can be juftified in
giving to the purfuit of fcience; though this
fhare is more or lefs, in proportion to a man's
fituation in life, his natural abilities, and the opportunity he has for conducting his inquiries.

I SHALL conclude with another paffage from
Dr. Hartley to this purpofe. " Though the pur-

* Hartley's Obfervations on Man, Vol. ii. p. 245.

fuit

" fuit of truth be an entertainment and em-
" ployment fuitable to our rational natures, and
" a duty to him who is the fountain of all
" knowledge and truth, yet we muft make fre-
" quent intervals and interruptions; elfe the
" ftudy of fcience, without a view to God and
" our duty, and from a vain defire of applaufe,
" will get poffeffion of our hearts, engrofs
" them wholly, and by taking deeper root
" than the purfuit of vain amufements, be-
" come, in the end, a much more dangerous,
" and obftinate evil than that. Nothing can
" eafily exceed the vain-glory, felf-conceit,
" arrogance, emulation, and envy, that are
" found in the eminent profeffors of the fciences,
" Mathematics, Natural Philofophy, and even
" Divinity itfelf. Temperance in thefe ftudies
" is, therefore, evidently required, both in or-
" der to check the rife of fuch ill paffions, and
" to give room for the cultivation of other ef-
" fential parts of our natures. It is with thefe
" pleafures as with the fenfible ones; our ap-
" petites muft not be made the meafure of
" our indulgence, but we ought to refer all
" to a higher rule.

" But when the purfuit of truth is directed
" by this higher rule, and entered upon with a
" view to the glory of God; and the good of
" mankind, there is no employment more
" worthy of our natures, or more conducive to
" their purification and perfection *."

* Hartley's Obfervations on Man, Vol. ii. p. 255, &c.

Warrington,
March 1767.

I SHALL digeſt all Dr. Franklin's obſervations concerning lightning under the ſeveral points of reſemblance which he obſerved between it and electricity, mentioned theſe points of ſimilarity in the order in which he himſelf remarked them; only bringing into one place the obſervations which may happen to lie in different parts of his letters, when they relate to the ſame ſubject.

1. FLASHES of lightning, he begins with obſerving, are generally ſeen crooked, and waving in the air. The ſame, ſays he, is the electric ſpark always, when it is drawn from an irregular body at ſome diſtance †. He might have added, when it is drawn by an irregular body, or through a ſpace in which the beſt conductors are diſpoſed in an irregular manner, which is always the caſe in the heterogeneous atmoſphere of our globe.

2. LIGHTNING ſtrikes the higheſt and moſt pointed objects in its way preferably to others, as high hills, and trees, towers, ſpires, maſts of ſhips, points of ſpears, &c. In like manner, all pointed conductors receive or throw off the electric fluid more readily than thoſe which are terminated by flat ſurfaces ‡.

3. LIGHTNING is obſerved to take the readieſt and beſt conductor. So does electri-

‡ Ibid. p. 47.

† Ibid. p. 46.

city

city in the difcharge of the Leyden phial. For this reafon, the Doctor fuppofes that it would be fafer, during a thunder ftorm, to have one's cloaths wet than dry, as the lightning might then, in a great meafure, be tranfmitted to the ground, by the water, on the outfide of the body. It is found, fays he, that a wet rat cannot be killed by the explofion of the electrical bottle, but that a dry rat may *.

4. LIGHTNING burns. So does electricity. Dr. Franklin fays, that he could kindle with it hard dry rofin, fpirits unwarmed, and even wood. He fays, that he fired gun-powder, by only ramming it hard in a car-tridge, into each end of which pointed wires were introduced, and brought within half an inch of one another, and difcharging a fhock through them †.

5. LIGHTNING fometimes diffolves metals. So does electricity, though the Doctor was miftaken when he imagined it was by a cold fufion, as will appear in its proper place. The method in which Dr. Franklin made elec-tricity melt metals was by putting thin pieces of them between two panes of glafs bound faft together, and fending an electric fhock through them. Sometimes the piece of glafs, by which they were confined, would be fhattered to pieces by the difcharge; and be broken into a kind of coarfe fand, which once happened with pieces of thick looking-glafs; but if they remained whole, the piece

* Franklin's Letters, p. 47.   † Ibid. p. 48, 92.

P 2   of

of metal would be miffing in feveral places where it had lain between them, and inftead of it, a metallic ftain would be feen on both the glaffes, the ftains on the under and upper glafs being exactly fimilar in the minuteft ftroke *.

A PIECE of leaf gold treated in this manner appeared not only to have been melted, but, as the Doctor thought, even vitrified, or otherwife fo driven into the pores of the glafs, as to be protected by it from the action of the ftrongeft aqua regis. Sometimes he obferved that the metallic ftains would fpread a little wider than the breadth of the thin pieces of metal. True gold, he obferved, made a darker ftain, fomewhat reddifh, and filver a greenifh ftain †.

MR. WILSON fuppofes that, in this experiment, the gold was not driven into the pores of the glafs, but only into fo near a contact with the furface of the glafs, as to be held there by an exceedingly great force; fuch an one, he fays, as is exerted at the furface of all bodies whatever ‡.

6. LIGHTNING rends fome bodies. The fame does electricity §. The Doctor obferves, that the electric fpark would ftrike a hole through a quire of paper. When wood, bricks, ftone, &c. are rent by lightning, he takes notice, that the fplinters will fly off on that fide where there is the leaft refiftance.

---

* Franklin's Letters, p. 48, 65.   † Ibid. p. 68.
‡ Hoadley and Wilfon, p. 68.
§ Franklin's Letters, p. 49.

In

In like manner, he fays, when a hole is ftruck through a piece of pafteboard by an electrified jar, if the furfaces of the pafteboard are not confined and compreffed, there will be a bur raifed all round the hole on both fides of the pafteboard ; but that if one fide be confined, fo that the bur cannot be raifed on that fide, it will all be raifed on the other fide, which way foever the fluid was directed. For the bur round the outfide of the hole is the effect of the explofion, which is made every way from the center of the electric ftream, and not an effect of its direction *.

7. LIGHTNING has often been known to ftrike people blind. And a pigeon, after a violent fhock of electricity, by which the Doctor intended to have killed it, was obferved to have been ftruck blind likewife †.

8. IN a thunder ftorm at Stretham, defcribed by Dr. Miles ‡, the lightning ftripped off fome paint which had covered a gilded molding of a pannel of wainfcot, without hurting the reft of the paint. Dr. Franklin imitated this, by pafting a flip of paper over the filleting of gold on the cover of a book, and fending an electric flafh through it. The paper was torn off from end to end, with fuch force, that it was broken in feveral places ; and in others there was brought away part of the grain of the Turkey leather in which the book was bound. This convinced

---

* Franklin's Letters, p 124. † Ibid. p. 63.
‡ Phil. Tranf. abridged, Vol. xlv. p. 3£7.

P 3   the

the Doctor, that if it had been paint, it would have been ſtripped off in the ſame manner with that on the wainſcot at Stretham *.

9. LIGHTNING deſtroys animal life. Animals have likewiſe been killed by the ſhock of electricity. The largeſt animals which Dr. Franklin and his friends had been able to kill were a hen, and a turkey which weighed about ten pounds †.

10. MAGNETS have been obſerved to loſe their virtue, or to have their poles reverſed by lightning. The ſame did Dr. Franklin by electricity. By electricity he frequently gave polarity to needles, and reverſed them at pleaſure. A ſhock from four large jars, ſent through a fine ſewing needle, he ſays, gave it polarity, ſo that it would traverſe when laid on water. What is moſt remarkable in theſe electrical experiments upon magnets is, that if the needle, when it was ſtruck, lay Eaſt and Weſt, the end which was entered by the electric blaſt pointed North, but that if it lay North and South, the end which lay towards the North, would continue to point North, whether the fire entered at that end or the contrary ; though he imagined, that a ſtronger ſtroke would have reverſed the poles even in that ſituation, an effect which had been known to have been produced by lightning. He alſo obſerved, that the polarity was ſtrongeſt when the needle was ſtruck ly-

* Phil. Tranſ. abridged, Vol. xlv. p. 64.
† Franklin's Letters, p. 86, 153.

ing

ing North and South, and weakeſt when it lay Eaſt and Weſt. He takes notice that, in theſe experiments, the needle, in ſome caſes, would be finely blued, like the ſpring of a watch, by the electric flame; in which caſe the colour given by a flaſh from two jars on‐ ly might be wiped off, but that a flaſh from four jars fixed it, and frequently melted the needles. The jars which the Doctor uſed held ſeven or eight gallons, and were coated and lined with tinfoil *.

To demonſtrate, in the completeſt manner poſſible, the ſameneſs of the electric fluid with the matter of lightning, Dr. Franklin, aſtoniſhing as it muſt have appeared, contriv‐ ed actually to bring lightning from the heavens, by means of an electrical kite, which he raiſed when a ſtorm of thunder was perceived to be coming on. This kite had a pointed wire fixed upon it, by which it drew the lightning from the clouds. This lightning deſcended by the hempen ſtring, and was re‐ ceived by a key tied to the extremity of it; that part of the ſtring which was held in his hand being of ſilk, that the electric virtue might ſtop when it came to the key. He found that the ſtring would conduct electricity even when nearly dry, but that when it was wet, it would conduct it quite freely; ſo that it would ſtream out plentifully from the key, at the approach of a perſon's finger †.

* Franklin's Letters, p. 90, &c. † Ibid. p. 106.

P 4 AT

AT this key he charged phials, and from electric fire thus obtained, he kindled fpirits, and performed all other electrical experiments which are ufually exhibited by an excited globe or tube.

As every circumftance relating to fo capital a difcovery as this (the greateft, perhaps, that has been made in the whole compafs of philofophy, fince the time of Sir Ifaac Newton) cannot but give pleafure to all my readers, I fhall endeavour to gratify them with the communication of a few particulars which I have from the beft authority.

THE Doctor, after having publifhed his method of verifying his hypothefis concerning the famenefs of electricity with the matter lightning, was waiting for the erection of a fpire in Philadelphia to carry his views into execution; not imagining that a pointed rod, of a moderate height, could anfwer the purpofe; when it occurred to him, that, by means of a common kite, he could have a readier and better accefs to the regions of thunder than by any fpire whatever. Preparing, therefore, a large filk handkerchief, and two crofs flicks, of a proper length, on which to extend it, he took the opportunity of the firft approaching thunder ftorm to take a walk into a field, in which there was a fhed convenient for his purpofe. But dreading the ridicule which too commonly attends unfuccefsful attempts in fcience, he communicated his intended experiment to no body but

but his fon, who affifted him in raifing the kite.

THE kite being raifed, a confiderable time elapfed before there was any appearance of its being electrified. One very promifing cloud had paffed over it without any effect; when, at length, juft as he was beginning to defpair of his contrivance, he obferved fome lofe threads of the hempen ftring to ftand erect, and to avoid one another, juft as if they had been fufpended on a common conductor. Struck with this promifing appearance, he immediately prefented his knucle to the key, and (let the reader judge of the exquifite pleafure he muft have felt at that moment) the difcovery was complete. He perceived a very evident electric fpark. Others fucceeded, even before the ftring was wet, fo as to put the matter paft all difpute, and when the rain had wetted the ftring, he collected electric fire very copioufly. This happened in June 1752, a month after the electricians in France had verified the fame theory, but before he had heard of any thing that they had done.

BESIDES this kite, Dr. Franklin had afterwards an infulated iron rod to draw the lightning into his houfe, in order to make experiments whenever there fhould be a confiderable quantity of it in the atmofphere; and that he might not lofe any opportunity of that nature, he connected two bells with this apparatus, which gave him notice,

6   by

by their ringing, whenever his rod was electrified *.

THE Doctor being able, in this manner, to draw the lightning into his houfe, and make experiments with it at his leifure; and being certain that it was in all refpects of the fame nature with electricity, he was defirous to know if it was of the pofitive or negative kind. The firft time he fucceeded in making an experiment for this purpofe was the 12th of April 1753, when it appeared that the lightning was negative. Having found that the clouds electrified negatively in eight fucceffive thunder gufts, he concluded they were always electrified negatively, and formed a theory to account for it. But he afterwards found he had concluded too foon. For, on the fixth of June following, he met with one cloud which was electrified pofitively; upon which he corrected his former theory, but did not feem able perfectly to fatisfy himfelf with any other. The Doctor fometimes found the clouds would change from pofitive to negative electricity feveral times in the courfe of one thunder guft, and he once obferved the air to be ftrongly electrified during a fall of fnow, when there was no thunder at all †.

* Franklin's Letters, p. 112.   † Ibid. p. 112, &c.

cure

SECTION VIII.

EXPERIMENTS ON ANIMALS.

AS I have conſtructed an electrical bat-tery of conſiderably greater force than any other that I have yet heard of, and as I have ſometimes expoſed animals to the ſhock of it, and have particularly attended to ſeveral circumſtances, which have been overlooked, or miſapprehended by others; it may not be improper to relate a few of the caſes, in which the facts were, in any reſpect, new, or worth notice.

JUNE the 4th. I killed a rat with the diſ-charge of two jars, each containing three ſquare feet of coated glaſs. The animal died immediately, after being univerſally convulſ-ed, at the inſtant of the ſtroke. After ſome time, it was carefully diſſected; but there was no internal injury perceived, particularly no extravaſation, either in the abdomen, thorax, or brain.

JUNE the 19th. I killed a pretty large kitten with the diſcharge of a battery of thirty-three ſquare feet; but no other effect was ob-ſerved, except that a red ſpot was found on the pericranium, where the fire entered. I endeavoured to bring it to life, by diſtending the lungs, blowing with a quill into the

trachea,

trachea, but to no purpofe. The heart beat a fhort time after the ftroke, but refpiration ceafed immediately.

JUNE the 21ft. I killed a fmall field-moufe with the difcharge of a battery of thirty-fix fquare feet, but no other effect was perceived, except that the hair of the forehead was finged, and in part torn off. There was no extravafation any where, though the animal was fo fmall, and the force with which it was killed fo great. This fact, and many others of a fimilar nature, make me fufpect fome miftake, in cafes where larger animals are faid to have had all their blood veffels burft by a much inferior force.

IN all the accounts that I have met with of animals killed by the electric fhock, the victims were either fmall quadrupeds, or fowls; and they are all reprefented as killed fo fuddenly, that it could not be feen how they were affected previous to their expiration. In fome of my experiments, the great force of my battery has afforded me a pretty fair opportunity of obferving in what manner the animal fyftem is affected by the electric fhock, the animals which I have expofed to it being pretty large; fo that a better judgment may be formed of their fenfations, and confequently of the immediate caufe of their death, by external figns. I do not pretend to draw any conclufion myfelf from the following facts. I have only noted them as carefully as I could for the ufe of phyficians and anatomifts.

JUNE.

JUNE the 26th. I difcharged a battery of thirty-eight fquare feet of coated glafs, through the head, and out at the tail of *a full grown cat*, three or four years old. At that inftant, fhe was violently convulfed all over. After a fhort refpite, there came on fmaller convulfions, in various mufcles, particularly on the fides; which terminated in a violent convulfive refpiration, attended with a rattling in the throat. This continued five minutes, without any motion that could be called breathing, but was fucceeded by an exceedingly quick refpiration, which continued near half an hour. Towards the end of this time, fhe was able to move her head, and fore feet, fo as to pufh herfelf backwards on the floor; but fhe was not able to move her hind feet in the leaft, notwithftanding the fhock had not paffed through them. While fhe continued in this condition, I gave her a fecond ftroke, which was attended, as before, with the violent convulfion, the fhort refpite, and the convulfive refpiration; in which, after continuing about a minute, fhe died.

BEING willing to try, for once, the effect of a much greater fhock than that which killed the cat upon a large animal, I gave an explofion of fixty-two fquare feet of coated glafs to a dog of the fize of a common cur. The moment he was ftruck, which was on the head (but, not having a very good light, I could not tell exactly where) all his limbs were extended, he fell backwards, and lay with-

without any motion, or fign of life for about a minute. Then followed convulfions, but not very violent, in all his limbs; and after that a convulfive refpiration, attended with a fmall rattling in the throat. In about four minutes from the time that he was ftruck, he was able to move, though he did not offer to walk till about half an hour after; in all which time, he kept difcharging a great quantity of faliva; and there was alfo a great flux of rheum from his eyes, on which he kept putting his feet; though in other refpects he lay perfectly liftlefs. He never opened his eyes all the evening in which he was ftruck, and the next morning he appeared to be quite blind, though feemingly well in every other refpect.

HAVING difpatched the dog, by fhooting him through the hinder part of his head, I examined one of his eyes (both of which had an uniform blueifh caft, like a film over the pupil) and found all the three humours perfectly tranfparent, and, as far as could be judged, in their right ftate; but the *cornea* was throughout white and opaque, like a bit of griftle, and remarkably thick.

BEFORE this experiment, I had imagined, that animals ftruck blind by lightning had probably a *gutta ferena*, on account of the concuffion which is feemingly given to the nervous fyftem by the electric fhock; whereas this cafe was evidently an inflammation, occafioned by the explofion being made

made ſo near the eyes, terminating in a ſpecies of the *albugo*; but which I ſuppoſe would have been incurable. One of the eyes of this dog was affected a little more than the other; owing, probably, to the ſtroke being made a little nearer to one eye than the other. I intended to give the ſtroke about an inch above the eyes.

IN order to aſcertain the effects of electricity on an animal body, I, after this, began a courſe of experiments on the conducting power of its conſtituent parts; and for ſome time imagined that a piece of ſpinal marrow of an ox-conducted ſenſibly worſe than the muſcular fleſh; but after a great number of trials with pieces of ſpinal marrow from various animals, and pieces of muſcular fleſh, of the ſame ſize and form, and in various ſtates of moiſture and dryneſs, I gave up that opinion as fallacious; but I cannot help wiſhing the experiments were reſumed with ſome more accurate meaſure of conducting power than hath yet been contrived.

BEING willing to obſerve, if poſſible, the immediate effect of the electric ſhock on the heart and lungs of animals, I gave, June the 5th, a ſhock from ſix ſquare feet to a frog, in which the thorax had been previouſly laid open, ſo that the pulſation of the heart might be ſeen. Upon receiving the ſtroke, the lungs were inſtantly inflated; and, together with the other contents of the thorax, thrown

VOL. II.   S   quite

quite out of the body. The heart, however, continued to beat, though very languidly, and there was no other fign of life for about ten minutes. After that, a motion was firft perceived under its jaws; which was propagated, by degrees, to the mufcles of the fides; and at laft the creature feemed as if it would have come to life, if it had not been fo much mangled. The ftroke entered the head, and went out at the hind feet.

June the 6th. I difcharged a battery of thirty-three fquare feet through the head and whole extended body of another frog. Immediately upon receiving the ftroke, there was, as it were, a momentary diftention of all-the mufcles of the body, and it remained fhrivelled up in a moft furprifing manner. For about five minutes there appeared no fign of life, and the pulfation of the heart could not be felt with the finger. But afterwards, there firft appeared a motion under the jaws, then all along the fides, attended with convulfive motions of the other parts, and in about an hour it became, to all appearance, as well as ever.

The fame day, I gave the fame ftroke to two other frogs. They were affected in the fame manner, and perfectly recovered in lefs than three hours.

These facts furprifed me very much. I attribute the recovery of the frogs partly to the moifture, which always feems to cover their

their body, and which might tranfmit a good part of the fhock; and partly to that provifion in their conftitution, whereby they can fubfift a long time without breathing. To afcertain this, I would have given the fhock to toads, ferpents, fifhes, &c. and various other exanguious animals, but I had not an opportunity. Befides, it is paying dear for philofophical difcoveries, to purchafe them at the expence of humanity.

PRIESTLEY:

Natural Philosophy

Joseph Priestley, Vol. I, 'The Preface' *Experiments and Observations Relating to Various Branches of Natural Philosophy,* (London, 1779), pp. v–xiii.

This work is the retitled fourth volume of *Experiments and Observations on Different Kinds of Air* (Vol. 1, 1774; Vol. 2, 1775; Vol. 3, 1777). The title was changed because Priestley's interests were beginning to broaden out from the study of gases. The new title was retained for two further volumes (Vol. 2, 1781; Vol. 3, 1786). The bulk of the work consists of Priestley's reports of his own experiments with gases and, more briefly, other things such as electricity and frost. The volume closes with nine letters to Priestley from various highly qualified correspondents on scientific matters

Priestley is concerned here with arguing for a more central place for natural philosophy in British education. Natural philosophy in its experimental form draws the student into pursuits that are agreeable and physically active, as well as leading them away from dissipation and fruitless pleasure. In following natural philosophy, we choose seriousness, as we, as rational beings, should. He reiterates his favourite theme that the expense of experimentation, among other things, renders such study ideal for those in possession of independent fortunes: that is, the aristocracy. How this sits with Priestley's politics is a difficult matter. He knew the power of élites, and that where the aristocracy went, others would follow in the spirit of emulation. He also knew the value of money; the expense of experiments is a continual concern. If polite society meant the interest of persons of wealth, power and fashion, then Priestley sought to secure such persons both as an audience, and as practitioners.

THE

PREFACE.

AFTER the intimation given in the preface to my third volume of *Observations on different kinds of Air*, publifhed about two years ago, viz. " that " I fhould certainly give myfelf and my " readers fome refpite; forefeeing that my " attention would be fufficiently engaged " by fpeculations of a very different na- " ture ;" fome apology may be expected for obtruding on the public another volume of experiments, and efpecially fo large a one as that which is now before them.

In this cafe, however, it may be fufficient to alledge the inftability of human purpofes and purfuits. But the fpeculations referred to, which were of a metaphyfical nature, did

A 3

not

not happen to engage fo much of my attention as I expected, and did not, at any time,
much interfere with my philofophical purfuits. It is alfo to be obferved, that that
kind of writing is a thing of a very different
nature from this. I can truly fay (nor will
it be thought extraordinary by thofe who
confider the nature of thefe fubjects) that
fingle fections in this work have coft me
more than whole volumes of the other; fo
great is the difference between writing from
the head only, and writing, as it may be
called, from the hands. To the former
little or nothing is requifite but calm reflection; whereas to the latter much *labour*,
and *patience*, and confequently much *time*,
as well as *expence*, are neceffary.

I have, befides, been engaged farther than
I expected in philofophical ftudies by the
profecution of fome inquiries which I had
left unfinifhed before, and efpecially by the
repetition of proceffes the refults of which
had been queftioned by others. Various
other circumftances, of which mention is
made in the courfe of the work, likewife
contributed

contributed to lead me ftill farther in the fame path. And having acquired a fond-nefs for experiments, even flighter inducements than I have had would have been fufficient to determine my conduct.

But in this I would by no means be under-ftood to be making an *apology* for what I have done. I am far from confidering the bufinefs of philofophy as a thing that is cenfureable, or requiring any apology. On the contrary, though I do not confider thefe ftudies as the firft in rank and value, I think their importance is generally much under-rated; and I earneftly wifh that more attention was given to them by thofe who have ability, leifure, and the neceffary means for profecuting them. For it muft be acknowledged that in thefe ftudies mere *genius* can do nothing without the aid of wealth. Indeed, *fpeculation*, without *experiment*, has always been the bane of true philofophy.

I am forry to have occafion to obferve, that natural fcience is very little, if at all,

the

the object of education in this country, in which many individuals have diftinguifhed themfelves fo much by their application to it. And yet fcientifical purfuits have fuch an advantage over moft others, as ought more efpecially to recommend them to perfons of rank and fortune. They never fail to furnifh materials for the moft agreeable and active purfuits, and fuch as are, at the fame time, in the higheft degree, ufeful and honourable, and are, by this means, capable of doing unfpeakably more for them than the largeft fortunes can do without this refource. Were perfons thus engaged, there would be lefs temptation to have recourfe to pleafure and diffipation, for the employment of their vacant time; and fuch purfuits would be particularly valuable to thofe who have no *talent* for politics, or any proper *call*, to occupy themfelves in public affairs. Befides, the laft is a path in which, from the nature of things, only a very few can walk; and the former, *viz.* a courfe of vicious pleafure, it is much to be lamented that any human being fhould tread.

Man

Man is a being endued by his creator with excellent faculties, and not to have *ferious objects of purfuit* is to debafe and degrade himfelf. It is to rank himfelf with beings of a lower order, aiming at nothing that is much higher than the low pleafures they are capable of; at the fame time that, from the remains of nobler powers, of which he cannot wholly diveft himfelf, he is incapable of that unallayed enjoyment of fenfual pleafures that brutes have.

I fhall not repeat, in this place, what I have advanced in favour of fcientifical purfuits, as peculiarly proper for perfons of large fortunes, in the preface to my *Hiftory of Electricity*, and my late *Obfervations on Education*; but would obferve that, if we wifh to lay a good foundation for a philofophical tafte, and philofophical purfuits, perfons fhould be accuftomed to the fight of experiments, and proceffes, in early life. They fhould, more efpecially, be early initiated in the theory and practice of *inveftigation*, by which many of the old difcoveries may

be

be made to be really *their own* ; on which account they will be much more valued by them. And, in a great variety of articles, very young perfons may be made fo far acquainted with every thing neceffary to be previoufly known, as to engage (which they will do with peculiar alacrity) in purfuits truly original.

At all events, however, the curiofity and furprize of young perfons fhould be excited as foon as poffible ; nor fhould it be much regarded whether they properly underftand what they fee, or not. It is enough, at the firft, if ftriking facts make an impreffion on the mind, and be remembered. We are, at all ages, but too much in hafte to *underftand*, as we think, the appearances that prefent themfelves to us. If we could content our-felves with the bare knowledge of new *facts*, and fufpend our judgment with refpect to their *caufes*, till, by their analogy, we were led to the difcovery of more facts, of a fimilar nature, we fhould be in a much

furer

furer way to the attainment of real knowledge.

I do not pretend to be perfectly innocent
in this refpect myfelf; but I think I have as
little to reproach myfelf with on this head
as moft of my brethren; and whenever I
have drawn general conclufions too foon, I
have been very ready to abandon them, as
all my publications, and this volume in particular, will evidence. I have alfo repeatedly
cautioned my readers, and I cannot too much
inculcate the caution, that they are to confider new *facts* only as difcoveries, and mere
deductions from thofe facts, as of no kind of
authority; but to draw all conclufions, and
form all hypothefes, for themfelves.

Having now begun a new work, it may
perhaps be expected, by thofe who are
pleafed to think favourably of my paft
labours, that I fhould proceed with the fame
fuccefs. But nothing can be more uncertain
than this. I before compared philofophizing
to hunting; and though hitherto I have
been

been pretty fortunate, I may hereafter follow the chafe to very little purpofe. All I can fay is, that I fhall think myfelf happy to have *leifure*, and the *means* of profecuting thefe inquiries; and that I fhall certainly, by fome chanel or other, account to the public, in proper time, for whatever fuccefs I may meet with.

I fhall conclude this preface with obferving, that the Abbé Fontana having heard that I had found pure air in water, was fo obliging as to fend me an account of fome experiments of his, made at Paris, above a year ago, in confirmation of the fame thing. He extracted by heat pretty pure air from feveral kinds of water, but efpecially diftilled water; though far fhort of the purity of that which I procured in the circumftances mentioned fect. xxxiii. One meafure of the beft that he procured, mixed with two meafures of nitrous air, occupied the fpace of 2.5 meafures; whereas the fame meafures with mine, as will be

feen,

ſeen, occupied the ſpace of little more than half a meaſure. He alſo does not mention his having obſerved the difference in the quality of air extracted from water in conſequence of expoſure to the air, or the ſun.

London, March 1, 1779.

PRIESTLEY:

Lectures

Joseph Priestley, *Heads of Lectures On A Course of Experimental Philosophy,*
'Lecture XXXIV. Of Electricity', (London, 1794), pp.187–95.

The dedication to this book again returns to the necessity of educating the
young in the study of natural philosophy. The book consists, as its title suggests, of a series of thirty-six lectures on science (notably described here as
'experimental philosophy') with a particular interest in chemistry. Priestley
holds fast to phlogiston, despite the best efforts of the recently executed
Lavoisier; he would stubbornly maintain his belief in this substance for the
rest of his life.

The piece on electricity presented here is the first of three that conclude
the lecture series. This last extract again demonstrates the admirable clarity
of Priestley's writing. The discovery that the muscles are moved by electricity
provided an ideal opportunity for lecturers and public experimenters: natural
philosophers like C. H. Wilkinson, who in 1804 was giving galvanic demonstrations in Soho Square, or John Aldini, who a little earlier in January 1803
was demonstrating the effects of electricity on the body of an executed crimi-
nal at the College of Surgeons. The results of these demonstrations were
clearly dramatic. Moreover, they were to become part of ongoing debates
about the nature of 'life' – whether the causes of life could be traced purely to
a materialist explanation or not.

LECTURE XXXIV.

Of *Electricity.*

ELECTRICITY is a property belonging to, or capable of being communicated to, all substances whatever; and whereas by some of them it is transmitted with great ease, and by others with much difficulty, they have been divided into two classes, and denominated *conductors* or *non-conductors* of electricity. Also the latter receiving this power by friction, and other means, are termed *electrics*, and the former *non-electrics*.

Metals of all kinds, and water, are conductors, though in very different degrees; so also is charcoal. All other substances, and also a perfect vacuum, are non-conductors of electricity. But many of these substances, when they

are

are made very hot, as glaſs, reſin, baked wood, and perhaps all the reſt on which the experiment can be made in this ſtate, are conductors.

It is the property of all kinds of electrics, when they are rubbed by bodies different from themſelves, to attract light ſubſtances of all kinds, to exhibit an appearance of *light*, attended with a particular *ſound*, on the approach of any conductor; and if the noſtrils are preſented, they are affected with a *ſmell* like that of phoſphorus. This attraction is moſt eaſily explained by ſuppoſing that electricity is produced by a fluid exceedingly elaſtic, or repulſive of itſelf, and attracted by all other ſubſtances.

An electric exhibiting the appearances above mentioned, is ſaid to be *excited*, and ſome of them, particularly the *tourmaline*, are excited by heating and cooling, as well as by friction. It appears, however, that excitation conſiſts in the mere transferring of electricity

city from one fubftance to another, and
that the great fource of electricity is in
the earth. On this account it is neceffary to the confiderable excitation of any
electric, that the fubftance againft which
it is rubbed (hence termed *the rubber*)
have a communication with the earth,
by means of conductors: for if the
rubber be *infulated*, that is cut off from
all communication with the earth by
means of electrics, the friction has but
little effect.

When infulated bodies have been attracted by, and brought into contact with, an excited electric, they
begin to be repelled by it, and
alfo to repel one another; nor will they
be attracted again till they have been
brought into contact with fome conductor communicating with the earth;
but after this they will be attracted as at
firft.

If conductors be *infulated*, electric
powers may be communicated to them
by the approach of excited electrics, or
the

the contact of other electrified bodies. They will then attract light bodies, and give sparks, &c. like the excited electrics themselves.

When electricity is strongly communicated to insulated animal bodies, the pulse is quickened, and perspiration increased; and if they receive, or part with, their electricity on a sudden, a painful sensation is felt at the place of communication. But what is more extraordinary, is, that the influence of the brain and nerves upon the muscles seems to be of an electric nature.

This is one of the last and most important of all philosophical discoveries. I shall, therefore, give the result of all the observations that have hitherto been made on the subject, in a *series of propositions,* drawn up by an intelligent friend, who has given much more attention to it than I have done.

1. The nerve of the limb of an animal being laid bare, and surrounded
with

with a piece of sheet lead, or of tinfoil, if a communication be formed between the nerve thus armed and any of the neighbouring muscles, by means of a piece of zinc, strong contractions will be produced in the limb.

2. If a portion of the nerve which has been laid bare be armed as above, contractions will be produced as power-fully, by forming the communication between the armed and bare part of the nerve, as between the armed part and muscle.

3. A similar effect is produced by arming a nerve and simply touching the armed part of the nerve with the me-tallic conductor.

4. Contractions will take place if a muscle be armed, and a communication be formed by means of the conductor between it and a neighbouring nerve. The same effect will be produced if the communication be formed between the
armed

armed mufcle and another mufcle, which is contiguous to it.

5. Contractions may be produced in the limb of an animal by bringing the pieces of metal into contact with each other at fome diftance from the limb, provided the latter make part of a line of communication between the two metallic conductors.

The experiment which proves this is made in the following manner. The amputated limb of an animal being placed upon a table, let the operator hold with one hand the principal nerve, previoufly laid bare, and in the other let him hold a piece of zinc; let a fmall plate of lead or filver be then laid upon the table, at fome diftance from the limb, and a communication be formed, by means of water, between the limb and the part of the table where the metal is lying. If the operator touch the piece of filver with the zinc, contractions will be produced in the limb the moment that the metals come into contact

tact with each other. The same effect will be produced if the two pieces of metal be previoufly placed in contact, and the operator touch one of them with his finger. This fact was difcovered by Mr. William Cruikfhank.

6. Contractions can be produced in the amputated leg of a frog, by putting it into water, and bringing the two metals into contact with each other at a fmall diftance from the limb.

7. The influence which has paffed through, and excited contractions in, one limb, may be made to pafs through, and excite contractions in, another limb. In performing this experiment it is neceffary to attend to the following circumftances: let two amputated limbs of a frog be taken; let one of them be laid upon a table, and its foot be folded in a piece of filver; let a perfon lift up the nerve of this limb with a filver probe, and another perfon hold in his hand a pieee of zinc, with which he is to touch the filver including the foot;

K   let

let the perſon holding the zinc in one
hand catch with the other the nerve of
the ſecond limb, and he who touches
the nerve of the firſt limb is to hold in
his other hand the foot of the ſecond;
let the zinc now be applied to the ſilver
including the foot of the firſt limb, and
contractions will immediately be excited
in both limbs.

8. The heart is the only involuntary
muſcle in which contractions can be excited by theſe experiments.

9. Contractions are produced more
ſtrongly, the, farther the coating is
placed from the origin of the nerve.

10. Animals which were almoſt dead
have been found to be conſiderably revived by exciting this influence.

11. When theſe experiments are repeated upon an animal that has been killed by opium, or by the electric ſhock,
very ſlight contractions are produced;
and no contractions whatever will take
place

place in an animal that has been killed by corrofive fublimate, or that has been ftarved to death.

12. Zinc appears to be the beft exciter when applied to gold, filver, molybdena, fteel, or copper. The latter metals, however, excite but feeble contractions when applied to each other. Next to zinc, in contact with thefe metals, tin and lead, and filver and lead, appear to be the moft powerful exciters.

At leaft two kinds of fifhes, the *torpedo* and the *electrical eel*, have a voluntary power of giving fo ftrong a fhock to the water in which they fwim, as to affect fifhes and other animals which come near them; and by a conducting communication between different parts of thefe fifhes, an electric fhock may be given exactly like that of the Leyden phial, which will be defcribed hereafter; and if the communication be interrupted, a flafh of electric light will be perceived.

The growth of vegetables is alfo quickened by electricity.

MARCET:

Conversations on Natural Philosophy

Jane Marcet, *Conversations on Natural Philosophy in which the Elements of that Science are Familiarly Explained, and Adapted to the Comprehension of Young Pupils*. (London, Longman, Hurst, Rees, Orme, and Brown, 1819), pp. 1–27.

The *Conversations on Natural Philosophy* of Jane Haldimand Marcet (1769–1858) possess the unusual merit of really being good, clear, straightforward guides to the subjects they discuss. As 'conversations', however, they are sad failures: Emily and Mrs B. are hardly characterised at all; and poor Emily becomes a mere provider of prompts and occasional idiocies for her instructress to follow-up or correct. The precise relationship between Mrs B. (that is, Mrs Bryant) and Emily remains intriguingly vague. Clearly, she is not the young girl's mother. Marcet presents natural philosophy as a subject handed down between women; Mrs B. instructs Emily in order for Emily, in her turn, to be able to teach her younger sister. Later in the volume, Mrs B. and Emily are joined by this sister, the livelier Caroline. Although lacking in drama and the glamour of a defined setting, Marcet is admirably homely and simple in her use of metaphor. As a guide to the scientifically perplexed, her book is a welcome relief; she does exactly what she needs to do, clarifying what was unclear before. The influence of her work on the young Michael Faraday (1791–1867), who read the *Conversations on Chemistry*, 2 vols (London, Longman, Hurst, Rees, Orme and Brown, 1806), was profound; the book inspired him to become a chemist. Her primary intended audience, however, were 'particularly the female sex' (*Conversations on Chemistry*, Vol. 1, p. v).

The value of Marcet's work can best be seen by comparing her original book with a near-contemporary reworking of it in the volume on *Natural Philosophy* in the *Library Of Useful Knowledge* (London, Baldwin and Cradock, 1832). This volume offers Marcet minus the dialogue form; instantly the work becomes duller, knottier, and harder to follow. For all her apparent literary ineptness, Marcet had in fact hit upon a form that really would work best for readers who found the material discussed difficult to take in otherwise.

Marcet was a prodigious author of highly popular textbooks for the ignorant but interested, as well as an occasional writer of fiction (such as *Bertha's Visit to Her Uncle In England* (London, John Murray, 1830)). Her most successful book was her *Conversations on Political Economy* (London, Longman,

Hurst, Rees, Orme and Brown, 1816). *Conversations on Natural Philosophy*, although not published until 1819, was written before 1806, and contains Marcet's first attempts at this kind of writing. Her son, Francis Marcet, a Fellow of the Royal Society and a professor at Geneva, revised and edited the fourteenth edition of this work.

Her early life was divided between Switzerland and London (her father was a Swiss merchant). She appears to have had early artistic ambitions, and studied painting with Sir Joshua Reynolds (1723–92) and Sir Thomas Lawrence (1769–1830). She married Alexander Marcet, a physician, in 1799. Alexander Marcet was a keen amateur natural philosopher (he was elected a FRS), and moved in intellectual circles that included Maria Edgeworth (1767–1849) and Thomas Malthus (1766–1834). Among Jane Marcet's friends were Harriet Martineau (1802–76), the naturalist Augustin-Pyramus de Candolle (1778–1841) and Mary Somerville (1780–1872).

Marcet attended Humphry Davy's lectures in 1806:

> On attending for the first time experimental lectures, the Author found it almost impossible to derive any clear satisfactory information from the rapid demonstrations which are usually and perhaps necessarily, crowded into popular courses of this kind. But frequent opportunities having afterwards occurred of conversing with a friend on the subject of chemistry, and repeating a variety of experiments, she became acquainted with the principles of that science, and began to feel highly interested in its pursuit. It was then that she perceived, in attending the excellent lectures delivered at the Royal Institution, by the present Professor of Chemistry [that is, Davy], the great advantage which her previous knowledge of the subject, slight though it was, gave her over others, who had not enjoyed the same means of private instruction. Every fact or experiment attracted her attention, and served to explain some theory to which she was not a total stranger; and she had the gratification to find that the numerous and elegant illustrations, for which that school is so much distinguished, seldom failed to produce on her mind the effect for which they were intended.
>
> Jane Marcet, *Conversations on Chemistry* (Vol. 1, pp. v–vi).

Marcet aims for clarity, rather than elegance. The result is satisfying; even at this distance, it is still easy to see why she became such an influential populariser of science.

CONVERSATION I.

ON GENERAL PROPERTIES OF BODIES.

INTRODUCTION.—GENERAL PROPERTIES OF BODIES.
—IMPENETRABILITY.— EXTENSION.—FIGURE.—
DIVISIBILITY. — INERTIA. — ATTRACTION. — AT-
TRACTION OF COHESION.— DENSITY.— RARITY.
— HEAT. — ATTRACTION OF GRAVITATION.

EMILY.

I MUST request your assistance, my dear Mrs. B.,
in a charge which I have lately undertaken: it is
that of instructing my youngest sister, a task, which I
find proves more difficult than I had at first imagined.
I can teach her the common routine of children's
lessons tolerably well; but she is such an inquisi-
tive little creature, that she is not satisfied without
an explanation of every difficulty that occurs to her,
and frequently asks me questions which I am at a
loss to answer. This morning, for instance, when
I had explained to her that the world was round

like a ball, instead of being flat as she had supposed, and that it was surrounded by the air, she asked me what supported it. I told her that it required no support; she then enquired why it did not fall as every thing else did? This I confess perplexed me; for I had myself been satisfied with learning that the world floated in the air, without considering how unnatural it was that so heavy a body, bearing the weight of all other things, should be able to support itself.

MRS. B.

I make no doubt, my dear. but that I shall be able to explain this difficulty to you; but I believe that it would be almost impossible to render it intelligible to the comprehension of so young a child as your sister Sophia. You, who are now in your thirteenth year, may, I think, with great propriety, learn not only the cause of this particular fact, but acquire a general knowledge of the laws by which the natural world is governed.

EMILY.

Of all things, it is what I should most like to learn; but I was afraid it was too difficult a study even at my age.

MRS. B.

Not when familiarly explained: if you have patience to attend, I will most willingly give you all the information in my power. You may perhaps find the subject rather dry at first; but if I succeed in explaining the laws of nature, so as to make you understand them, I am sure that you will derive not only instruction, but great amusement from that study.

EMILY.

I make no doubt of it, Mrs. B.; and pray begin by explaining why the earth requires no support; for that is the point which just now most strongly excites my curiosity.

MRS. B.

My dear Emily, if I am to attempt to give you a general idea of the laws of nature, which is no less than to introduce you to a knowledge of the science of natural philosophy, it will be necessary for us to proceed with some degree of regularity. I do not wish to confine you to the systematic order of a scientific treatise; but if we were merely to examine every vague question that may chance to occur, our progress would be but very slow. Let us, therefore, begin by taking a short survey of the general properties of bodies, some of which must necessarily be explained before I can attempt to make you understand why the earth requires no support.

When I speak of *bodies*, I mean substances, of whatever nature, whether solid or fluid; and *matter* is the general term used to denote the substance, whatever its nature be, of which the different bodies

B 2

are composed. Thus, wood is the matter of which this table is made; water is the matter with which this glass is filled, &c.

EMILY.

I am very glad you have explained the meaning of the word matter, as it has corrected an erroneous conception I had formed of it: I thought that it was applicable to solid bodies only.

MRS. B.

There are certain properties which appear to be common to all bodies, and are hence called the *essential properties* of bodies; these are, *Impenetrability, Extension, Figure, Divisibility, Inertia,* and *Attraction.* These are called the general properties of bodies, as we do not suppose any body to exist without them.

By impenetrability, is meant the property which bodies have of occupying a certain space, so that, where one body is, another cannot be, without displacing the former; for two bodies cannot exist in the same place at the same time. A liquid may be more easily removed than a solid body; yet it is not the less substantial, since it is as impossible for a liquid and a solid to occupy the same space at the same time, as for two solid bodies to do so. For instance, if you put a spoon into a glass full of water, the water will flow over to make room for the spoon.

EMILY.

I understand this perfectly. Liquids are in reality as substantial or as impenetrable as solid bodies, and they appear less so, only because they are more easily displaced.

MRS. B.

The air is a fluid differing in its nature from liquids, but no less impenetrable. If I endeavour to fill this phial by plunging it into this bason of water, the air, you see, rushes out of the phial in bubbles, in order to make way for the water, for the air and the water cannot exist together in the same space, any more than two hard bodies; and if I reverse this goblet, and plunge it perpendicularly into the water, so that the air will not be able to escape, the water will no longer be able to fill the goblet.

EMILY.

But it rises a considerable way into the glass.

MRS. B.

Because the water compresses or squeezes the air into a small space in the upper part of the glass; but, as long as it remains there, no other body can occupy the same place.

EMILY.

A difficulty has just occurred to me, with regard to the impenetrability of solid bodies; if a nail is driven into a piece of wood, it penetrates it, and both the wood and the nail occupy the same space that the wood alone did before?

MRS. B.

The nail penetrates between the particles of the wood, by forcing them to make way for it; for you know that not a single atom of wood can remain in the space which the nail occupies; and if the wood is not increased in size by the addition of the nail, it is because wood is a porous substance, like sponge, the particles of which may be compressed or squeezed closer together; and it is thus that they make way for the nail.

We may now proceed to the next general property of bodies, *extension*. A body which occupies a certain space must necessarily have extension; that is to say, *length*, *breadth*, and *depth*; these are called the dimensions of extension: can you form an idea of any body without them?

EMILY.

No; certainly I cannot; though these dimensions must, of course, vary extremely in different bodies. The length, breadth, and depth of a box, or of a thimble, are very different from those of a walking-stick, or of a hair.

But is not height also a dimension of extension?

MRS. B.

Height and depth are the same dimension, considered in different points of view; if you measure a body, or a space, from the top to the bottom, you call it depth; if from the bottom upwards, you call it height; thus the depth and height of a box are, in fact, the same thing.

EMILY.

Very true; a moment's consideration would have enabled me to discover that; and breadth and width are also the same dimension.

MRS. B.

Yes; the limits of extension constitute *figure* or shape. You conceive that a body having length, breadth, and depth, cannot be without form, either symmetrical or irregular?

EMILY.

Undoubtedly; and this property admits of almost an infinite variety.

MRS. B.

Nature has assigned regular forms to her productions in general. The natural form of mineral substances is that of crystals, of which there is a great variety. Many of them are very beautiful, and no less remarkable by their transparency, or colour, than by the perfect regularity of their forms,

as may be seen in the various museums and collections of natural history. The vegetable and
animal creation appears less symmetrical, but is
still more diversified in figure than the mineral
kingdom. Manufactured substances assume the
various arbitrary forms which the art of man designs
for them; and an infinite number of irregular forms
are produced by fractures, and by the dismember-
ment of the parts of bodies.

EMILY.

Such as a piece of broken china, or glass?

MRS. B.

Or the fragments of mineral bodies which are
broken in being dug out of the earth, or decayed
by the effect of torrents and other causes. The
picturesque effect of rock-scenery is in a great
measure owing to accidental irregularities of this
kind.

We may now proceed to divisibility; that is to
say, a susceptibility of being divided into an inde-
finite number of parts. Take any small quantity
of matter, a grain of sand for instance, and cut it
into two parts; these two parts might be again
divided, had we instruments sufficiently fine for the
purpose; and if, by means of pounding, grinding,
and other similar methods, we carry this division to
the greatest possible extent, and reduce the body

to its finest imaginable particles, yet not one of the particles will be destroyed, and the body will continue to exist, though in this altered state.

The melting of a solid body in a liquid affords a very striking example of the extreme divisibility of matter; when you sweeten a cup of tea, for instance, with what minuteness the sugar must be divided to be diffused throughout the whole of the liquid.

EMILY.

And if you pour a few drops of red wine into a glass of water, they immediately tinge the whole of the water, and must therefore be diffused throughout it.

MRS. B.

Exactly so; and the perfume of this lavender-water will be almost as instantaneously diffused throughout the room, if I take out the stopper.

EMILY.

But in this case it is only the perfume of the lavender, and not the water itself, that is diffused in the room?

MRS. B.

The odour or smell of a body is part of the body itself, and is produced by very minute. particles or exhalations which escape from odoriferous bodies. It would be impossible that you should smell the lavender-water, if particles of it did not come in actual contact with your nose.

EMILY.

But when I smell a flower, I see no vapour rise from it; and yet I can perceive the smell at a considerable distance.

MRS. B.

You could, I assure you, no more smell a flower, the odoriferous particles of which did not touch your nose, than you could taste a fruit, the flavoured particles of which did not come in contact with your tongue.

EMILY.

That is wonderful indeed; the particles then, which exhale from the flower and from the lavender-water, are, I suppose, too small to be visible?

MRS. B.

Certainly: you may form some idea of their extreme minuteness, from the immense number which must have escaped in order to perfume the whole room; and yet there is no sensible diminution of the liquid in the phial.

EMILY.

But the quantity must really be diminished?

MRS. B.

Undoubtedly; and were you to leave the bottle

open a sufficient length of time, the whole of the water would evaporate and disappear. But though so minutely subdivided as to be imperceptible to any of our senses, each particle would continue to exist; for it is not within the power of man to destroy a single particle of matter; nor is there any reason to suppose that in nature an atom is ever annihilated. ·

EMILY.

Yet, when a body is burnt to ashes, part of it, at least, appears to be effectually destroyed? Look how small is the residue of ashes beneath the grate, from all the coals which have been consumed within it.

MRS. B.

That part of the coals, which you suppose to be destroyed, evaporates in the form of smoke and vapour, whilst the remainder is reduced to ashes. A body, in burning, undergoes no doubt very remarkable changes; it is generally subdivided; its form and colour altered; its extension increased: but the various parts, into which it has been separated by combustion, continue in existence, and retain all the essential properties of bodies.

EMILY.

But that part of a burnt body which evaporates in smoke has no figure; smoke, it is true, ascends

B 6

in columns into the air, but it is soon so much diffused as to lose all form; it becomes indeed invisible.

MRS. B.

Invisible, I allow; but we must not imagine that what we no longer see no longer exists. Were every particle of matter that becomes invisible annihilated, the world itself would in the course of time be destroyed. The particles of smoke, when diffused in the air, continue still to be particles of matter, as well as when more closely united in the form of coals: they are really as substantial in the one state as in the other, and equally so when by their extreme subdivision they become invisible. No particle of matter is ever destroyed: this is a principle you must constantly remember. Every thing in nature decays and corrupts in the lapse of time. We die, and our bodies moulder to dust; but not a single atom of them is lost; they serve to nourish the earth, whence, while living, they drew their support.

The next essential property of matter is called *inertia;* this word expresses the resistance which inactive matter makes to a change of state. Bodies appear to be equally incapable of changing their actual state, whether it be of motion or of rest. You know that it requires force to put a body which is at rest in motion; an exertion of strength is also requisite to stop a body which is already in motion.

The resistance of the body to a change of state, in either case, is called its *inertia*.

EMILY.

In playing at base-ball I am obliged to use all my strength to give a rapid motion to the ball; and when I have to catch it, I am sure I feel the resistance it makes to being stopped. But if I did not catch it, it would soon fall to the ground and stop of itself.

MRS. B.

Inert matter is as incapable of stopping of itself, as it is of putting itself into motion: when the ball ceases to move, therefore, it must be stopped by some other cause or power; but as it is one with which you are yet unacquainted, we cannot at present investigate its effects.

The last property which appears to be common to all bodies is *attraction*. All bodies consist of infinitely small particles of matter, each of which possesses the power of attracting or drawing towards it, and uniting with any other particle sufficiently near to be within the influence of its attraction; but in minute particles this power extends to so very small a distance around them, that its effect is not sensible, unless they are (or at least appear to be) in contact; it then makes them stick or adhere together, and is hence called the *attraction of cohesion*. Without this power, solid bodies would fall in pieces, or rather crumble to atoms.

EMILY.

I am so much accustomed to see bodies firm and solid, that it never occurred to me that any power was requisite to unite the particles of which they are composed. But the attraction of cohesion does not, I suppose, exist in liquids; for the particles of liquids do not remain together so as to form a body, unless confined in a vessel?

MRS. B.

I beg your pardon; it is the attraction of cohesion which holds this drop of water suspended at the end of my finger, and keeps the minute watery particles of which it is composed united. But as this power is stronger in proportion as the particles of bodies are more closely united, the cohesive attraction of solid bodies is much greater than that of fluids.

The thinner and lighter a fluid is, the less is the cohesive attraction of its particles, because they are further apart; and in elastic fluids, such as air, there is no cohesive attraction among the particles.

EMILY.

That is very fortunate; for it would be impossible to breathe the air in a solid mass; or even in a liquid state.

But is the air a body of the same nature as other bodies?

MRS. B.

Undoubtedly, in all essential properties.

EMILY.

Yet you say that it does not possess one of the general properties of bodies — cohesive attraction?

MRS. B.

The particles of air are not destitute of the power of attraction, but they are too far distant from each other to be influenced by it; and the utmost efforts of human art have proved ineffectual in the attempt to compress them, so as to bring them within the sphere of each other's attraction, and make them cohere.

EMILY.

If so, how is it possible to prove that they are endowed with this power?

MRS. B.

The air is formed of particles precisely of the same nature as those which enter into the composition of liquid and solid bodies, in which state we have a proof of their attraction.

EMILY.

It is then, I suppose, owing to the different degrees of attraction of different substances, that they are hard or soft; and that liquids are thick or thin?

MRS. B.

Yes; but you would express your meaning better by the term *density*, which denotes the degree of closeness and compactness of the particles of a body: thus you may say, both of solids, and of liquids, that the stronger the cohesive attraction, the greater is the density of the body. In philosophical language, density is said to be that property of bodies by which they contain a certain quantity of matter, under a certain bulk or magnitude. *Rarity* is the contrary of density; it denotes the thinness and subtlety of bodies: thus you would say that mercury or quicksilver was a very dense fluid; ether, a very rare one, &c.

CAROLINE.

But how are we to judge of the quantity of matter contained in a certain bulk?

MRS. B.

By the weight: under the same bulk bodies are said to be dense in proportion as they are heavy.

EMILY.

Then we may say that metals are dense bodies, wood comparatively a rare one, &c. But, Mrs. B., when the particles of a body are so near as to at-

attract each other, the effect of this power must increase as they are brought by it closer together; so that one would suppose that the body would gradually augment in density, till it was impossible for its particles to be more closely united. Now, we know that this is not the case; for soft bodies, such as cork, sponge, or butter, never become, in consequence of the increasing attraction of their particles, as hard as iron?

MRS. B.

In such bodies as cork and sponge, the particles which come in contact are so few as to produce but a slight degree of cohesion : they are porous bodies, which, owing to the peculiar arrangement of their particles, abound with interstices which separate the particles; and these vacancies are filled with air, the spring or elasticity of which prevents the closer union of the parts. But there is another fluid much more subtle than air, which pervades all bodies, this is *heat*. Heat insinuates itself more or less between the particles of all bodies, and forces them asunder; you may therefore consider heat, and the attraction of cohesion, as constantly acting in opposition to each other.

EMILY.

The one endeavouring to rend a body to pieces, the other to keep its parts firmly united.

MRS. B.

And it is this struggle between the contending forces of heat and attration, which prevents the extreme degree of density which would result from the sole influence of the attraction of cohesion.

EMILY.

'The more a body is heated then, the more its particles will be separated.

MRS. B.

Certainly: we find that bodies swell or dilate by heat: this effect is very sensible in butter, for instance, which expands by the application of heat, till at length the attraction of cohesion is so far diminished that the particles separate, and the butter becomes liquid. A similar effect is produced by heat on metals, and all bodies susceptible of being melted. Liquids, you know, are made to boil by the application of heat; the attraction of cohesion then yields entirely to the expansive power; the particles are totally separated and converted into steam or vapour. But the agency of heat is in no body more sensible than in air, which dilates and contracts by its increase or diminution in a very remarkable degree.

EMILY.

The effects of heat appear to be one of the most interesting parts of natural philosophy.

MRS. B.

That is true; but heat is so intimately connected with chemistry, that you must allow me to defer the investigation of its properties till you become acquainted with that science.

To return to its antagonist, the attraction of cohesion; it is this power which restores to vapour its liquid form, which unites it into drops when it falls to the earth in a shower of rain, which gathers the dew into brilliant gems on the blades of grass.

EMILY.

And I have often observed that after a shower, the water collects into large drops on the leaves of plants; but I cannot say that I perfectly understand how the attraction of cohesion produces this effect.

MRS. B.

Rain does not fall from the clouds in the form of drops, but in that of mist or vapour, which is composed of very small watery particles; these, in their descent, mutually attract each other, and those that are sufficiently near in consequence unite and form a drop, and thus the mist is transformed into a shower. The dew also was originally in a state of vapour, but is, by the mutual attraction of the particles, formed into small globules on the blades of grass: in a similar manner the rain upon the leaf collects into large drops, which when they become too heavy for the leaf to support fall to the ground.

EMILY.

All this is wonderfully curious ! I am almost bewildered with surprise and admiration at the number of new ideas I have already acquired.

MRS. B.

Every step that you advance in the pursuit of natural science, will fill your mind with admiration and gratitude towards its Divine Author. In the study of natural philosophy, we must consider ourselves as reading the book of nature, in which the bountiful goodness and wisdom of God is revealed to all mankind; no study can then tend more to purify the heart, and raise it to a religious contemplation of the Divine perfections.

There is another curious effect of the attraction of cohesion which I must point out to you. It enables liquids to rise above their level in capillary tubes : these are tubes the bores of which are so extremely small that liquids ascend within them, from the cohesive attraction between the particles of the liquid and the interior surface of the tube. Do you perceive the water rising above its level in this small glass tube, which I have immersed in a goblet full of water ?

EMILY.

Oh yes; I see it slowly creeping up the tube, but now it is stationary : will it rise no higher ?

MRS. B.

No; because the cohesive attraction between the water and the internal surface of the tube is now balanced by the weight of the water within it: if the bore of the tube were narrower the water would rise higher; and if you immerse several tubes of bores of different sizes, you will see it rise to different heights in each of them. In making this experiment you should colour the water with a little red wine, in order to render the effect more obvious.

All porous substances, such as sponge, bread, linen, &c., may be considered as collections of capillary tubes: if you dip one end of a lump of sugar into water, the water will rise in it, and wet it considerably above the surface of that into which you dip it.

EMILY.

In making tea I have often observed that effect, without being able to account for it.

MRS. B.

Now that you are acquainted with the attraction of cohesion, I must endeavour to explain to you that of *Gravitation*, which is a modification of the same power; the first is perceptible only in very minute particles, and at very small distances; the other acts on the largest bodies, and extends to immense distances.

EMILY.

You astonish me: surely you do not mean to say, that large bodies attract each other.

MRS. B.

Indeed I do: let us take, for example, one of the largest bodies in nature, and observe whether it does not attract other bodies. What is it that occasions the fall of this book, when I no longer support it?

EMILY.

Can it be the attraction of the earth? I thought that all bodies had a natural tendency to fall.

MRS. B.

They have a natural tendency to fall, it is true; but that tendency is produced entirely by the attraction of the earth: the earth being so much larger than any body on its surface, forces every body, which is not supported, to fall upon it.

EMILY.

If the tendency which bodies have to fall results from the earth's attractive power, the earth itself can have no such tendency, since it cannot attract itself, and therefore it requires no support to prevent it from falling. Yet the idea that bodies do not fall of their own accord, but that they are drawn towards the earth by its attraction, is so new and strange to me, that I know not how to reconcile myself to it.

MRS. B.

When you are accustomed to consider the fall of bodies as depending on this cause, it will appear to you as natural, and surely much more satisfactory, than if the cause of their tendency to fall were totally unknown. Thus you understand, that all matter is attractive, from the smallest particle to the largest mass; and that bodies attract each other with a force proportional to the quantity of matter they contain.

EMILY.

I do not perceive any difference between the attraction of cohesion and that of gravitation: is it not because every particle of matter is endowed with an attractive power, that large bodies, consisting of a great number of particles, are so strongly attractive?

MRS. B.

True. There is, however, this difference between the attraction of particles and that of masses, that the former is stronger than the latter, in proportion to the quantity of matter. Of this you have an instance in the attraction of capillary tubes, in which liquids ascend by the attraction of cohesion, in opposition to that of gravity. It is on this account that it is necessary that the bore of the tube should be extremely small; for if the column of water within the tube is not very minute, the attraction would not be able either to raise or support its weight, in opposition to that of gravity.

You may observe, also, that all solid bodies are enabled by the force of the cohesive attraction of their particles to resist that of gravity, which would otherwise disunite them, and bring them to a level with the ground, as it does in the case of liquids, the cohesive attraction of which is not sufficient to enable it to resist the power of gravity.

EMILY.

And some solid bodies appear to be of this nature, as sand and powder for instance; there is no attraction of cohesion between their particles?

MRS. B.

Every grain of powder or sand is composed of a great number of other more minute particles, firmly united by the attraction of cohesion; but amongst the separate grains there is no sensible attraction, because they are not in sufficiently close contact.

EMILY.

Yet they actually touch each other?

MRS. B.

The surface of bodies is in general so rough and uneven, that when in actual contact, they touch each other only by a few points. Thus, if I lay upon the table this book, the binding of which appears perfectly smooth, yet so few of the particles of its under surface come in contact with the table, that no sensible degree of cohesive attraction takes place; for you see, that it does not stick, or cohere to the table, and I find no difficulty in lifting it off.

It is only when surfaces perfectly flat and well polished are placed in contact, that the particles approach in sufficient number, and closely enough, to produce a sensible degree of cohesive attraction. Here are two hemispheres of polished metal, I press their flat surfaces together, having previously interposed a few drops of oil, to fill up every little porous vacancy. Now try to separate them.

EMILY.

It requires an effort beyond my strength, though there are handles for the purpose of pulling them asunder. Is the firm adhesion of the two hemispheres, merely owing to the attraction of cohesion?

MRS. B.

There is no force more powerful, since it is by this, that the particles of the hardest bodies are

C

held together. It would require a weight of several pounds, to separate these hemispheres.

EMILY.

In making a kaleidoscope, I recollect that the two plates of glass, which were to serve as mirrors, stuck so fast together, that I imagined some of the gum I had been using had by chance been interposed between them; but now I make no doubt but that it was their own natural cohesive attraction which produced this effect.

MRS. B.

Very probably it was so; for plate-glass has an extremely smooth flat surface, admitting of the contact of a great number of particles, between two plates, laid one over the other.

EMILY.

But, Mrs. B., the cohesive attraction of some bodies is much greater than that of others; thus glue, gum, and paste, cohere with singular tenacity.

MRS. B.

That is owing to the peculiar chemical properties of those bodies, independently of their cohesive attraction.

There are some other kinds or modifications of

attraction peculiar to certain bodies; namely, that of magnetism, and of electricity; but we shall confine our attention merely to the attraction of cohesion and of gravity; the examination of the latter we shall resume at our next meeting.

BABBAGE:

Reflections on the Decline of Science in England

Charles Babbage, *Reflections on the Decline of Science in England*, Chap. VI and Conclusion (London, B. Fellowes and J. Booth, 1830), pp. 184–212.

Charles Babbage (1792–1871) was an adolescent prodigy, an omniverous scientist, a man on the make. He was born in Totnes, on Boxing Day, into a wealthy family (his father, Benjamin Babbage was a banker), and grew up to be a delicate and intellectually curious child. While still at Cambridge, he outstripped his professors, and, in an attempt to remedy the parlous state of mathematics in Britain, translated, with George Peacock and John Herschel, Silvestre François Lacroix's *An Elementary Treatise on the Differential and Integral Calculus* (Cambridge, 1816) (*Traité du Calcul différential et du Calcul intégral* (Paris: 1797–1800)), hoping thereby to raise the intellectual standard in his home country.

Babbage's relationship to The Royal Society was a troubled one. He was a man temperamentally inclined to find fault with things as they stood, an irritable, unsatisfied, choleric character. Although he was elected a fellow of The Royal Society in 1816, and received direct help from them in his work on his computational machine, Babbage became critical of the institution that had launched the polite culture of science in England. It is likely some of his ire derived from the two slights he suffered in 1826: firstly, in not being presented with one of the first two Royal Medals of the Royal Society; and secondly, on not being made Junior Secretary of the Society. He was soon to bear other deeper blows. In 1827, Babbage endured the death in quick succession of his father, his wife, and his two children.

Reflections on the Decline of Science in England (published in May 1830) is a little more than just an opportunity for a bereaved and disgruntled man to enact revenge for some unforgiven professional slights. He asserts the necessity for Britain to attain an intellectual power in the abstract sciences commensurate with its pre-eminent success in engineering and industrial expertise. Like Priestley before him, he argues for the reform of educational practice, with a greater emphasis to be placed on science. He declares that those who practice science should enjoy much greater prestige, and that only out of a sense of that prestige would great discoveries be made. However, the main part of the book consists of a detailed assessment of the need for reform in the learned societies formed to encourage the sciences in Britain, most notably the Royal Society itself.

The book inevitably angered the scientific establishment, not least because Babbage had impugned the honesty of the recently deceased Sir Humphry Davy. Although the book proposed some positive changes – the creation of an Order of Merit, the reform of the curriculum in Oxford and Cambridge, the restriction of membership to the Royal Society to natural philosophers of undoubted merit – its guiding spirit was one of needling attack. Some members of the Royal Society flirted with the possibility of expelling Babbage; but to do so would have looked petty and spiteful. The book was politely accepted by the Society's library.

A reply to Babbage was written by Professor G. Moll of Utrecht. Moll affirmed the international reputation of British scientists, most notably Davy and Herschel. He pointed out that it was a universal feature of the European nobility to be uninterested in science; this was not a problem unique to Britain. He disdained the suggestion of an Order of Merit as childish: what man would really be spurred on to greater work by the promise of a few gaudy medals?

Well one such man might be Babbage himself. Perhaps his book serves again as an example of the impoliteness possible in scientific circles: the sad evidence of the influence of personal animus, ambition and spite. While some of what Babbage proposes was clearly a sensible contribution to the prospect of long-term reform, much also is the expression of a personal grudge.

Babbage himself remains an equivocal figure; a pioneer of the computer who none the less failed to produce a working model of his analytical engine; a natural philosopher whose other signficant contribution to science in Britain really resides in his celebration of industrialism and of the mechanical.

If all this sounds mean-spirited, then we should also remember that Babbage ends the main text of his book with a consideration of the respective characters of Sir Humphry Davy and William Hyde Wollaston. Although the way of imagining the difference between the two men was fast becoming a standard of scientific biography, Babbage nonetheless brings to his account a generosity that is strikingly uncharacteristic of his work as a whole. There is a judiciousness and a graciousness in the piece; it is unsurprising to learn that the section was extracted and published as a pamphlet in its own right by R. Clay in London in 1830. For all his pique, Babbage could recognise the quality of greatness.

CHAP. VI.

SUGGESTIONS FOR THE ADVANCEMENT OF SCIENCE
IN ENGLAND.

SECTION 1.

*Of the Necessity that Members of the Royal
Society should express their Opinions.*

ONE of the causes which has contributed to
the success of the *party,* is to be found in the
great reluctance with which many of those whose
names added lustre to the Society expressed their
opinions, and the little firmness with which they
maintained their objections. How many times
have those whose activity was additionally sti-
mulated by their interest, proposed measures
which a few words might have checked; whilst
the names of those whose culpable silence thus
permitted the project to be matured, were immediately afterwards cited by their grateful
coadjutors, as having sanctioned that which
in their hearts they knew to be a job.

Even in the few cases which have passed the limits of such forbearance, when the subject has been debated in the Council, more than one, more than two instances are known, where subsequent circumstances have occurred, which proved, with the most irresistible moral evidence, that members have spoken on one side of the question, and have voted on the contrary.

This reluctance to oppose that which is disapproved, has been too extensively and too fatally prevalent for the interests of the Royal Society. It may partly be attributed to that reserved and retiring disposition, which frequently marks the man of real knowledge, as strongly as an officious interference and flippant manner do the charlatan, or the trader in science. Some portion of it is due to that improper deference which was long paid to every dictum of the President, and much of it to that natural indisposition to take trouble on any point in which a man's own interest is not immediately concerned. It is to be hoped, for the credit of that learned body, that no anticipation of the next feast of St. Andrew* ever influenced the taciturnity of their disposition.

* It may be necessary to inform those who are not members of the Royal Society, that this is the day on which those

SECTION 2.

Of Biennial Presidents.

The days in which the Royal Society can have much influence in science seem long past; nor does it appear a matter of great importance who conduct its mismanaged affairs. Perpetual Presidents have been tried until the Society has become disgusted with dictators. If any reform should be attempted, it might perhaps be deserving consideration whether the practice of several of the younger institutions might not be worthy imitation, and the office of President be

Fellows who choose, meet at Somerset House, to register the names of the Council and Officers the President has been pleased to appoint for the ensuing year; and who afterwards dine together, for the purpose of praising each other over wine, which, until within these few years, was *paid* for out of the *funds* of the *Society*. This abuse was attacked by an enterprising reformer, and of course defended by the *coterie*. It was, however, given up as *too bad*. The public may form some idea of the feeling which prevails in the Council, when they are informed that this practice was defended by one of the officers of the Society, on the ground that, if abolished, *the Assistant Secretary would lose his per centage on the tavern bills.*

continued only during two sessions. There may be some inconveniences attending this arrangement; but the advantages are conspicuous, both in the Astronomical and Geological Societies. Each President is ambitious of rendering the period of his reign remarkable for some improvement in the Society over which he presides; and the sacrifice of time which is made by the officers of those Societies, would become impossible if it were required to be continued for a much longer period. Another circumstance of considerable importance is, that the personal character of the President is less impressed on the Society; and, supposing any injudicious alterations to be made, it is much less difficult to correct them.

SECTION 3.

Of the Influence of the Colleges of Physicians and Surgeons in the Royal Society.

The honour of belonging to the Royal Society is much sought after by medical men, as contributing to the success of their professional efforts, and two consequences result from it. In the first place, the pages of the Transactions of the Royal Society occasionally contain medical papers of very moderate merit; and, in the second, the preponderance of the medical interest introduces into the Society some of the jealousies of that profession. On the other hand, medicine is intimately connected with many sciences, and its professors are usually too much occupied in their practice to exert themselves, except upon great occasions.

SECTION 4.

Of the Influence of the Royal Institution on the Royal Society.

The Royal Institution was founded for the cultivation of the more popular and elementary branches of scientific knowledge, and has risen, partly from the splendid discoveries of Davy, and partly from the decline of the Royal Society, to a more prominent station than it would otherwise have occupied in the science of England. Its general effects in diffusing knowledge among the more educated classes of the metropolis, have been, and continue to be, valuable. Its influence, however, in the government of the Royal Society, is by no means attended with similar advantages, and has justly been viewed with considerable jealousy by many of the Fellows of that body. It may be stated, without disparagement to the Royal Institution, that the scientific qualifications necessary for its officers, however respectable, are not quite of that high order which ought to be required for those of the Royal Society, if the latter body were in a state of vigour.

The Royal Institution interest has always been sufficient to appoint one of the Secretaries of the Royal Society; and at the present moment they have appointed two. In a short time, unless some effectual check is put to this, we shall find them nominating the President and the rest of the officers. It is certainly not consistent with the dignity of the Royal Society thus to allow its offices to be given away as the rewards of services rendered to other institutions. The only effectual way to put a stop to this increasing interest would be, to declare that no manager or officer of the Royal Institution should ever, at the *same time,* hold office in the Royal Society.

The use the Members of the Royal Institution endeavour to make of their power in the

Council of the Royal Society, is exemplified in the minutes of the Council of March 11, 1830, which may be consulted with advantage by those who doubt.

SECTION 5.

Of the Transactions of the Royal Society.

The Transactions of the Royal Society, unlike those of most foreign academies, contain nothing relating to the history of the Society. The volumes contain merely those papers .communicated to the Society in the preceding year which the Council have selected for printing, a meteorological register, and a notice of the award of the annual medals, without any list of the Council and officers of the Society, by whom that selection and that award have been made.

Before I proceed to criticise this state of things, I will mention one point on which I am glad to be able to bestow on the Royal Society the highest praise. I refer to the extreme regularity with which the volumes of the Transactions are published. The appearance of the half-volumes at intervals of six months, insures for any communication almost immediate publicity; whilst the shortness of the time between its reception and publication, is a guarantee to the public that the whole of the paper was really communicated at the time it bears date. To this may also be added, the rarity of any alterations made previously to the printing, a circumstance which ought to be imitated, as well as admired, by other societies. There may, indeed, be some, perhaps the Geological, in which the task is more difficult, from the nature of the subject. The sooner, however, all societies can reduce themselves to this rule, of rarely allowing any thing but a few verbal corrections to papers that are placed in their hands, the better it will be for their own reputation, and for the interests of science.

It has been, and continues to be, a subject of deep regret, that the first scientific academy in Europe, the Institute of France, should be thus negligent in the regularity of its publications; and it is the more to be regretted, that it should be years in arrear, from the circumstance, that the memoirs admitted into their collection are usually of the highest merit. I know some of their most active members have wished it were otherwise; I would urge them to put a stop to a practice, which, whilst it has no advantages to recommend it, is unjust to those who contribute, and is only calculated to produce conflicting claims, equally injurious to science, and to the reputation of that body, whose negligence may have given rise to them.*

One of the inconveniences arising from having no historical portion in the volumes of the Royal Society is, that not only the public, but our own members are almost entirely ignorant of all its affairs. With a means of giving considerable publicity (by the circulation of above 800 copies of the Transactions) to whatever we wish to have made known to our members or to the world, will it be credited, that no notice was taken in our volume for 1826, of the foundation of two Royal medals, nor of the conditions under which they were to be distributed?† That in 1828, when

---

* Mr. Herschel, speaking of a paper of Fresnel's, observes—"This memoir was read to the Institute, 7th of October, 1816; a supplement was received, 19th of January, 1818; M. Arago's report on it was read, 4th of June, 1821: and while every optical philosopher in Europe has been impatiently expecting its appearance for seven years, it lies as yet unpublished, and is only known to us by meagre notices in a periodical journal." *Mr. Herschel's Treatise on Light*, p. 533.—*Encyclopædia Metropolitana.*

† That the Council refrained from having their first

a new fund, called the donation fund, was established, and through the liberality of Dr. Wollaston and Mr. Davies Gilbert, it was endowed by them with the respective sums of 2,000*l*. and 1,000*l*. 3 per cents ; no notice of such fact appears in our Transactions for 1829. Other gentlemen have contributed ; and if it is desirable to possess such a fund, it is surely of importance to inform the non-attending, which is by far the largest part of the Society, that it exists ; and that we are grateful to those by whom it has been founded and augmented. Neither did the Philosophical Transactions inform our absent members, that they could purchase the President's Discourses at the trade-price.

The list of the Officers, Council, and Members of the Royal Society is printed annually ; yet, who ever saw it bound up with the Philosophical Transactions, to which it is intended to be attached ? I never met with a single copy of that work so completed, not even the one in our own library. It is extremely desirable that the Society should know the names of their Council; and whilst it would in some measure contribute

award of those medals thus communicated, is rather creditable to them, and proves that they had a becoming feeling respecting their former errors.

O

to prevent the President from placing incompetent persons upon it, it would also afford some check, although perhaps but a slight one, on the distribution of the medals. When I have urged the expediency of the practice, I have been answered by excuses, that the list could not be made up in time for the volume. If this is true of the first part, they might appear with the second; and even if this were impracticable, the plan of prefixing them to the volume of the succeeding year, would be preferable to that of omitting them altogether. The true reason, however, appeared at last. It was objected to the plan, that by the present arrangement, the porter of the Royal Society took round the list to those members resident in London, and got from some of them a remuneration, in the shape of a Christmas-box;* and this would be lost, if the time of printing were changed. Such are the paltry interests to which those of the Royal Society are made to bow.

Another point on which information ought to be given in each volume, is the conditions on which the distribution of the Society's medals

---

* During the printing of this chapter, a friend, on whom I had called, complained that the porter of the Royal Society had demanded half-a-crown for leaving the list.

are made. It is true that these are, or ought to be, printed with the Statutes of the Society; but that volume is only in the hands of members, and it is for the credit of the medals themselves, that the laws which regulate their award should be widely known, in order that persons, not members of the Society, might enter into competition for them.

Information relative to the admissions and deaths amongst the Society would also be interesting; a list of the names of those whom the Society had lost, and of those members who had been added to its ranks each year, would find a proper place in the historical pages which ought to be given with each volume of our Transactions.

The want of a distinction between the working members of the Society, and those who merely honour it with their patronage, renders many arrangements, which would be advantageous to science, in some cases, injudicious, and in other instances, almost impossible.

Collections of Observations which are from time to time given to the Society, may be of such a nature, that but few of the members are interested in them. In such cases, the expense of printing above 800 copies may reasonably induce the Council to decline printing them altogether; whereas, if they had any means of discrimination for distributing them, they might be quite willing to incur the expense of printing 250. Other cases may occur, in which great advantage would accrue, if the principle were once admitted. Government, the Universities, public bodies, and even individuals might, in some cases, be disposed to present to the Royal Society a limited number of copies of their works, if they knew that they were likely to be placed in the hands of persons who would use them. Fifty or a hundred additional copies might, in some cases, not be objected to on the ground of expense, when seven or eight hundred would be quite out of the question.

Let us suppose twenty copies of a description of some new chemical process to be placed at the disposal of the Royal Society by any public body; it will not surely be contended that they ought all to remain on the Society's shelves. Yet, with our present rules, that would be the case. If, however, the list of the Members of the Society were read over to the Council, and the names of those gentlemen known to be conversant with chemical science were written down; then, if nineteen copies of the work were given to those nineteen persons on this list, who had contributed most to the Transactions of the Society, they would in all probability be placed in the fittest hands.

Complete sets of the Philosophical Transactions have now become extremely bulky; it might be well worth our consideration, whether the knowledge of the many valuable papers they contain would not be much spread, by publishing the abstracts of them which have been read at the ordinary meetings of the Society. Perhaps two or three volumes octavo, would contain all that has been done in this way during the last century.

Another circumstance, which would contribute much to the order of the proceedings of the Council, would be to have a distinct list made out of all the statutes and orders of the Council relating to each particular subject.

Thus the President, by having at one view before him all that had ever been decreed on the question under consideration, would be much better able to prevent inconsistent resolutions, and to save the time of the Council from being wasted by unnecessary discussions.

SECTION 6.

Order of Merit.

Amongst the various proposals for encouraging science, the institution of an order of merit has been suggested. It is somewhat singular, that whilst in most of the other kingdoms * of Europe, such orders exist for the purpose of rewarding, by honorary distinctions, the improvers of the arts of life, or successful discoverers in science, nothing of the kind has been established in England.

Our orders of knighthood are favourable only to military distinction. It has been urged, as an argument for such institutions, that they are a cheap mode of rewarding science, whilst, on the

* At the great meeting of the philosophers at Berlin, in 1828, of which an account. is given in the Appendix; the respect in which Berzelius, Oersted, Gauss, and Humboldt were held in their respective countries was apparent in the orders bestowed on them by the Sovereigns of Sweden, of Denmark, of Hanover, and of Prussia; and there were present many other philosophers, whose decorations sufficiently attested the respect in which science was held in the countries from which they came.

other hand, it has been objected, that they would diminish the value of such honorary distinctions by making them common. The latter objection is of little weight, because the numbers who pursue science are few, and, probably, will long continue so. It would also be easily avoided, by restricting the number of the order or of the class, if it were to form a peculiar class of another order. Another objection, however, appears to me to possess far greater weight; and, however strong the disposition of the Government might be (if such an order existed) to fill it properly, I do not believe that, in the present state of public opinion respecting science, it could be done, and, in all probability, it would be filled up through the channels of patronage, and by mere jobbers in science.

Another proposal, of a similar kind, has also been talked of, one which it may appear almost ridiculous to suggest in England, but which would be considered so in no other country. It is, to ennoble some of the greatest scientific benefactors of their country. Not to mention political causes, the ranks of the nobility are constantly recruited from the army, the navy, and the bar; why should not the family of that man, whose name is imperishably connected with the steam-engine, be enrolled amongst the nobility of his country? In utility and profit, not merely to that country, but to the human race, his deeds may proudly claim comparison even with the most splendid of those achieved by classes so rich in glorious recollections. An objection, in most cases fatal to such a course, arises from the impolicy of conferring a title, unless a considerable fortune exists to support it; a circumstance very rarely occurring to the philosopher. It might in some measure be removed, by creating such titles only for life. But here, again, until there existed some knowledge of science amongst the higher classes, and a sound state of public opinion relative to science, the execution of the plan could only be injurious.

Section 7.

Of the Union of Scientific Societies.

This idea has occurred to several persons, as likely to lead to considerable advantages to science. If the various scientific societies could unite in the occupation of one large building, considerable economy would result from the union. By properly arranging their evenings of meeting, one meeting-room only need be required. The libraries might either be united, or arranged in adjoining rooms; and such a system would greatly facilitate the inquiries of scientific persons.

Whether it would be possible to reunite in any way the different societies to the Royal Society, might be a delicate question; but although, on some accounts, desirable, that event is not necessary for the purpose of their having a common residence.

The Medico-Botanical Society might, perhaps, from sympathy, be the first to which the Royal Society would apply; and by a proper interchange of diplomas,* the two societies might be inoculated with each other. But even here some tact would be required; the Medico-Botanical is a little particular about the purity of its written documents, and lately attributed blame to one of its officers for some slight tampering with them, a degree of illiberality which the Council of the Royal Society are far from imitating.

* A thing well understood by the *initiated*, both at *home* and *abroad*.

The Geological and the Astronomical Societies nourish no feelings of resentment to the parent institution for their early persecution; and though they have no inducement to seek, would scarcely refuse any union which might be generally advantageous to science.

CONCLUSION.

IN a work on the Decline of Science, at a period when England has so recently lost two of its brightest ornaments, I should hardly be excused if I omitted to devote a few words to the names of Wollaston and of Davy. Until the warm feelings of surviving kindred and admiring friends shall be cold as the grave from which remembrance vainly recalls their cherished forms, invested with all the life and energy of recent existence, the volumes of their biography must be sealed. Their contemporaries can expect only to read their éloge.

In habits of intercourse with both those distinguished individuals, sufficiently frequent to mark the curiously different structure of their minds, I was yet not on such terms even with him I most esteemed, as to view his great qualities through that medium which is rarely penetrated by the eyes of long and very intimate friendship.

Caution and precision were the predominant

features of the character of Wollaston, and those who are disposed to reduce the number of principles, would perhaps justly trace the precision which adorned his philosophical, to the extreme caution which pervaded his moral character. It may indeed be questioned whether the latter quality will not in all persons of great abilities produce the former.

Ambition constituted a far larger ingredient in the character of Davy, and with the daring hand of genius he grasped even the remotest conclusions to which a theory led him. He seemed to think invention a more common attribute than it really is, and hastened, as soon as he was in possession of a new fact or a new principle, to communicate it to the world, doubtful perhaps lest he might not be anticipated; but, confident in his own powers, he was content to give to others a chance of reaping some part of that harvest, the largest portion of which he knew must still fall to his own share.

Dr. Wollaston, on the other hand, appreciated more truly the rarity of the inventive faculty; and, undeterred by the fear of being anticipated, when he had contrived a new instrument, or detected a new principle, he brought all the information that he could collect from others, or which arose from his own reflection, to bear upon it for years, before he delivered it to the world.

The most singular characteristic of Wollaston's mind was the plain and distinct line which separated what he knew from what he did not know; and this again, arising from his precision, might be traced to caution.

It would, however, have been visible to such an extent in few except himself, for there were very few so perfectly free from vanity and affectation. To this circumstance may be attributed a peculiarity of manner in the mode in which he communicated information to those who sought it from him, which was to many extremely disagreeable. He usually, by a few questions, ascertained precisely how much the inquirer knew upon the subject, or the exact point at which his ignorance commenced, a process not very agreeable to the vanity of mankind; taking up the subject at this point, he would then very clearly and shortly explain it.

His acquaintance with mathematics was very limited. Many years since, when I was an unsuccessful candidate for a professorship of mathematics, I applied to Dr. W. for a recommendation; he declined it, on the ground of its not being his pursuit. I told him I asked it, because I thought it would have weight, to which he replied, that it ought to have none whatever. There is no doubt his view was the just one. Yet such is the state of ignorance which exists on these subjects, that I have several times heard him mentioned as one of the greatest mathematicians of the age.* But in this as in all other points, the precision with which he comprehended and retained all he had ever learned, especially of the elementary applications of mathematics to physics, was such, that he possessed greater command over those subjects than many of far more extensive knowledge.

In associating with Wollaston, you perceived that the predominant principle was to avoid error ; in the society of Davy, you saw that it was the desire to see and make known truth. Wollaston never could have been a poet ; Davy might have been a great one.

A question which I put, successively, to each of these distinguished philosophers, will show how very differently a subject may be viewed by minds even of the highest order.

About the time Mr. Perkins was making his experiments on the compression of water, I was

* This of course could only have happened in England.

much struck with the mechanical means he had brought to bear on the subject, and was speculating on other applications of it, which I will presently mention.

Meeting Dr. Wollaston one morning in the shop of a bookseller, I proposed this question: If two volumes of hydrogen and one of oxygen are mixed together in a vessel, and if by mechanical pressure they can be so condensed as to become of the same specific gravity as water, will the gases under these circumstances unite and form water? " What do you think they will do?" said Dr. W. I replied, that I should rather expect they would unite. " I see no reason to suppose it," said he. I then inquired whether he thought the experiment worth making. He answered, that he did not, for that he should think it would certainly *not* succeed.

A few days after, I proposed the same question to Sir Humphry Davy. He at once said, " they will become water, of course ;" and on my inquiring whether he thought the experiment worth making, he observed that it was a good experiment, but one which it was hardly necessary to make, as it must succeed.

These were off-hand answers, which it might perhaps be hardly fair to have recorded, had they been of persons of less eminent talent; and it adds to the curiosity of the circumstance to mention, that I believe Dr. Wollaston's reason for supposing no union would take place, arose from the nature of the electrical relations of the two gases remaining unchanged, an objection which did not weigh with the philosopher whose discoveries had given birth to it.

[The result of the experiment appeared, and still appears to me, to be of the highest importance; and I will shortly state the views with which it was connected. The next great discovery in chemistry to definite proportions, will be to find means of forming all the simple unions of one atom with one, with two, or with more of any other substance: and it occurred to me that the gaseous bodies presented the fairest chance of success; and that if wishing, for instance, to unite four atoms of one substance with one of another, we could, by mechanical means, reduce the mixed gases to the same specific gravity as the substance would possess which resulted from their union, then either that such union would actually take place, or the particles of the two substances would be most favourably situated for the action of caloric, electricity, or other causes, to produce the combination. It would indeed seem to follow, that if combination should take place under such circumstances, then the most probable proportion in which the atoms would unite, should be that which furnished a fluid of the least specific gravity : but until the experiments are made, it is by no means certain that other combinations might not be produced.]

The singular minuteness of the particles of bodies submitted by Dr. Wollaston to chemical analysis, has excited the admiration of all those who have had the good fortune to witness his experiments; and the methods he employed deserve to be much more widely known.

It appears to me that a great mistake exists on the subject. It has been adduced as one of those facts which prove the extraordinary acuteness of the bodily senses of the individual,—a circumstance which, if it were true, would add but little to his philosophical character; I am, however, inclined to view it in a far different light, and to see in it one of the natural results of the admirable precision of his knowledge.

During the many opportunities I have enjoyed of seeing his minute experiments, I remember but one* instance in which I noticed any

* This was at Mr. South's observatory, and the object

remarkable difference in the acuteness of his bodily faculties, either of his hearing, his sight, or of his sense of smell, from those of other persons who possessed them in a good degree. He never showed me an almost microscopic wire, which was visible to his, and invisible to my own eye : even in the beautiful experiments he made relative to sounds inaudible to certain ears, he never produced a tone which was unheard by mine, although sensible to his ear; and I believe this will be found to have been the case by most of those whose minds had been much accustomed to experimental inquiries, and who possessed their faculties unimpaired by illness or by age.

It was a much more valuable property on which the success of such inquiries depended. It arose from the perfect attention which he could command, and the minute precision with which he examined every object. A striking illustration of the fact that an object is frequently not seen, *from not knowing how to see it*, rather than from any defect in the organ of vision, occurred to me some years since, when on a visit at Slough. Conversing with Mr. Herschel on

was, the dots on the declination circle of his equatorial; but, in this instance, Dr. Wollaston did not attempt to *teach me how to see them.*

the dark lines seen in the solar spectrum by Fraunhofer, he inquired whether I had seen them; and on my replying in the negative, and expressing a great desire to see them, he mentioned the extreme difficulty he had had, even with Fraunhofer's description in his hand and the long time which it had cost him in detecting them. My friend then added, " I will prepare the apparatus, and put you in such a position that they shall be visible, and yet you shall look for them and not find them : after which, while you remain in the same position, I will instruct you *how to see them,* and you shall see them, and not merely wonder you did not see them before, but you shall find it impossible to look at the spectrum without seeing them."

On looking as I was directed, notwithstanding the previous warning, I did *not* see them ; and after some time I inquired how they might be seen, when the prediction of Mr. Herschel was completely fulfilled.

It was this attention to minute phenomena which Dr. Wollaston applied with such powerful effect to chemistry. In the ordinary cases of precipitation the cloudiness is visible in a single drop as well as in a gallon of a solution ; and in those cases where the cloudiness is so slight, as to require a mass of fluid to render it visible, previous evaporation, quickly performed on slips of window glass, rendered the solution more concentrated.

The true value of this minute chemistry arises from its cheapness and the extreme rapidity with which it can be accomplished: it may, in hands like those of Wollaston, be used for discovery, but not for measure. I have thought it more necessary to place this subject on what I consider its true grounds, for two reasons. In the first place, I feel that injustice has been done to a distinguished philosopher in attributing to some of his bodily senses that excellence which I think is proved to have depended on the admirable training of his intellectual faculties. And, in the next place, if I have established the fact, whilst it affords us better means of judging of such observations as lay claim to an accuracy *" more than human,"* it also opens, to the patient inquirer into truth, a path by which he may acquire powers that he would otherwise have thought were only the gift of nature to a favoured few.

PARIS:

The Life of Sir Humphry Davy

John Ayrton Paris, *The Life of Sir Humphry Davy, Bart. LL.D. Late President of the Royal Society, Foreign Associate of the Royal Institute of France &c. &c. &c.* (London, Henry Coburn and Richard Bentley, 1831), Chap. III, pp. 87–99.

Sir Humphry Davy (1778–1829) remains, with Newton and Priestley, arguably one of the three great public figureheads of science in the long eighteenth century. If Newton was the unparallelled genius, and Priestley the quintessential radical philosopher, then Davy was the mercurial man who once again made chemistry and natural philosophy a fashion. An inspiring lecturer, Davy was, like Priestley, both populariser and practitioner. He helped to effect a bringing together of science and poetry that had an enormous impact on the character of literature from William Wordsworth to Mary Shelley. He was more than a chemist, he was someone who seemed to be creating a view of the world seen through science. He united an audience for natural philosophy – one that his biographer points out brought together men and women, the literary and the scientific, the serious and the fashionable. Although it is far from telling the whole story, Coleridge's comment extracted here on why he attended Davy's Royal Institution lectures goes to the heart of the poets' interest in natural philosophy.

As a subject for a biography, Davy was ideally heroic material. His very flaws rendered him interesting to a society inspired by the eccentric and the idiosyncratic. Davy's rise from very modest circumstances in provincial Cornwall to the heights of success in cosmopolitan London was the kind of rags-to-riches tale beloved by nineteenth-century readers. The biography excerpted here plays up this aspect of Davy's life, seeking to portray him as a flawed and somewhat clumsy parvenu, as well as a fascinating firebrand of a man, a truly startling intellect. In this case, as in many others, the shadow of Bonaparte lingers behind our hero's story, being the ultimate model for the early nineteenth-century celebration of the provincial hero.

John Ayrton Paris (1785–1856) was Davy's first biographer. In some ways, Paris was a suitable person to be the first in the field. Though Cambridge-born and educated, he had strong Cornish connections; moreover he was a physician with deep interests in natural philosophy. He wrote many other works, including: *A Memoir on the Physiology of the Egg* (London, W. Glindon, 1810); an earlier biography of a Cornish mineralogist, *Memoir of the Life and Scientific Labours of the Late Rev. Wm. Gregor, A.M.* (London, William Phillips, 1818); the very popular and often reprinted *Pharmacologia; or the History of Medicinal Substances* (Third Edition) (London, W. Phillips, 1820); and the anonymously published (the author is simply called 'A Physician'), *A Guide to the Mount's Bay and the Land's End* (London, W. Phillips, 1824). Much of the information that Paris relied upon in his biography of Sir Humphry Davy derived from the great man's affectionately estranged wife, Jane Davy. He received a thousand guineas for writing this biography – a measure of the public interest in the famous natural philosopher's life.

The Life of Sir Humphry Davy was published in two forms: a large folio one-volume edition and a two-volume edition (London, Henry Coburn and Richard Bentley, 1831). The extract that follows is reproduced from the one-volume edition.

Paris's interest in Davy's literary and lecturing style is a key feature in the extract that follows. Behind the praise for Davy's 'ethereal clearness of style' lies the ongoing debate regarding the best language for the communication of difficult scientific subjects for the audience of polite society.

Although during 1801 Davy had given some desultory Lectures, his splendid career cannot be said to have commenced until the following year, when on the 21st of January he delivered his Introductory Lecture, to a crowded and enlightened audience in the Theatre of the Royal Institution ; which was afterwards printed at the request of a respectable proportion of the Society.

It contains a masterly view of the benefits to be derived from the various branches of science. He represents the Chemist as the Ruler of all the elements that surround us, and which he employs either for the satisfaction of his wants, or the gratification of his wishes. Not contented with what is to be found on the surface of the earth, he describes him as penetrating into her bosom, and even of searching the depths of the ocean, for the purpose of allaying the restlessness of his desires, or of extending and increasing the boundaries of his power.

In examining the science of Chemistry, with regard to its great agency in the improvement of society, he offers the following almost prophetic remarks. " Unless any great physical changes should take place upon the globe, the permanency of the Arts and Sciences is rendered certain, in consequence of the diffusion of knowledge, by means of the invention of Printing ; and by which those words which are the immutable instruments of thought, are become the constant and widely diffused nourishment of the mind, and the preservers of its health and energy."

"Individuals influenced by interested motives or false views, may check for a time the progress of knowledge ;—moral causes may produce a momentary slumber of the public spirit ;—the adoption of wild and dangerous theories, by ambitious or deluded men, may throw a temporary opprobrium on literature ; but the influence of true philosophy will never be despised ; the germs of improvement are sown in minds, even where they are not perceived ; and sooner or later, the spring-time of their growth must arrive.

" In reasoning concerning the future hopes of the human species, we may look forward with confidence to a state of society, in which the different orders and classes of men will contribute more effectually to the support of each other than they have hitherto done. This state, indeed, seems to be approaching fast; for, in consequence of the multiplication of the means of instruction, the man of science and the manufacturer are daily becoming more assimilated to each other. The artist, who formerly affected to despise scientific principles, because he was incapable of perceiving the advantages of them, is now so far enlightened as to favour the adoption of new processes in his art, whenever they are evidently connected with a diminution of labour ; and the increase of projectors, even to too great an extent, demonstrates the enthusiasm of the public mind in its search after improvement.

" The arts and sciences, also, are in a high degree cultivated and patronized by the rich and privileged orders. The guardians of civilization and of refinement,. the most powerful and respected part of society, are daily growing more attentive to the realities of life ; and giving up many of their unnecessary enjoyments, in consequence of the desire to be useful, are becoming the friends and protectors of the labouring part of the community.

" The unequal division of property and of labour, the differences of rank and condition amongst mankind, are the sources of power in civilized life—its moving causes, and even its very soul. In considering and hoping that the human species is capable of becoming more enlightened and more happy, we can only expect that the different parts of the great whole of society should be intimately united together, by means of knowledge and the useful arts; that they should act as the children of one great parent, with one determinate end, so that no power may be rendered useless—no exertions thrown away.

" In this view, we do not look to distant ages, or amuse ourselves with brilliant though delusive dreams, concerning the infinite improveability of man, the annihilation of labour, disease, and even death, but we reason by analogy from simple facts, we consider only a state of human progression arising out of its present condition,—we look for a time that we may reasonably expect — FOR A BRIGHT DAY, OF WHICH WE ALREADY BEHOLD THE DAWN."

The extraordinary sensation produced amongst the members of the Institution by this first course of lectures, has been vividly described by various persons who had the good fortune to be his auditors; and foreigners have recorded in their travels the enthusiasm with which the great English chemist had inspired his countrymen.

The members of the Tepidarian Society, sanguine in the success of their child,—for so they considered Davy,—purposely appointed their anniversary festival on the day of his anticipated triumph. They were not disappointed in their hopes; and their dinner was marked by every demonstration of hilarity. In the evening, Davy accompanied by a few friends, attended, for the first time in his life, a masquerade which was given at Ranelagh.

On the following day, he dined with Sir Harry Englefield. I have a copy of the invitation, addressed to Mr. Underwood, now before me.

DEAR UNDERWOOD,

DAVY, covered with glory, dines with me to-day at five. If you could meet him it would give me great pleasure.

Yours truly,
H. C. ENGLEFIELD.

Tilney Street, Friday.

At this dinner, Sir Harry wrote a request to Davy to print his Lecture, which was signed by every one present, except Mr. Underwood, who declined,

N

from the apprehension that the signature of so intimate a friend might give to that which was a spontaneous homage to talent, the appearance of a previously concerted scheme.

I shall here weave into my narrative some extracts from several letters, with which Mr. Purkis, one of the earliest friends of Davy, has lately favoured me.

" On his first appointment at the Royal Institution, I was specially intro-duced to him by a common friend, Thomas Poole, Esq. of Nether Stowey in Somersetshire ; and I continued in habits of friendship with him during a great portion of his life, though somewhat less intimately during the last few years. I loved him living—I lament his early death : I shall ever honour his memory.

" The sensation created by his first course of Lectures at the Institution, and the enthusiastic admiration which they obtained, is at this period scarcely to be imagined. Men of the first rank and talent,—the literary and the scien-tific, the practical and the theoretical, blue-stockings, and women of fashion, the old and the young, all crowded—eagerly crowded the lecture-room. His youth, his simplicity, his natural eloquence, his chemical knowledge, his happy illustrations and well-conducted experiments, excited universal attention and unbounded applause. Compliments, invitations, and presents, were showered upon him in abundance from all quarters ; his society was courted by all, and all appeared proud of his acquaintance.

" One instance of attention is particularly recalled to my memory. A talented lady, since well known in the literary world, addressed him anony-mously in a poem of considerable length, replete with delicate panegyric and genuine feeling. It displayed much originality, learning, and taste ; the lan-guage was elegant, the versification harmonious, the sentiments just, and the imagery highly poetical. It was accompanied with a handsome ornamental appendage for the watch, which he was requested to wear when he delivered his next lecture, as a token of having received the poem, and pardoned the freedom of the writer. It was long before the fair authoress was known to him, but they afterwards became well acquainted with each other."

I should not redeem the pledge given to my readers, nor fulfil the duties of an impartial biographer, were I to omit acknowledging that the manners and habits of Davy very shortly underwent a considerable change. Let those who have vainly sought to disparage his excellence, enjoy the triumph of knowing that he was not perfect ; but it may be asked in candour, where is the man of twenty-two years of age, unless the temperature of his blood were below zero, and his temperament as dull and passionless as the fabled god of the Brahmins, who could remain uninfluenced by such an elevation ? Look at Davy in the laboratory at Bristol, pursuing with eager industry various abstract points of research ; mixing only with a few philosophers, sanguine like himself in the investigation of chemical phenomena, but whose sphere of observation must have been confined to themselves, and whose worldly knowledge could scarcely have extended beyond the precincts of the Institution in which they were engaged. Shift the scene—behold him in the Theatre of the Royal Institution, surrounded by an aristocracy of intellect as well as of rank ; by the flowers of genius, the *élite* of fashion, and the beauty of England, whose very respirations were suspended in eager expectation to catch his novel and satisfactory elucidations of the mysteries of Nature. Could the author of the Rambler have revisited us, he would certainly have rescinded the passage in which he says—" All appearance of science is hateful to women ; and he who desires to be well received by them, must qualify himself by a total rejection of all that is rational and important ; must consider learning as perpetually interdicted, and devote all his attention to trifle, and all his eloquence to compliment."

It is admitted that his vanity was excited, and his ambition raised, by such extraordinary demonstrations of devotion ; that the bloom of his simplicity was dulled by the breath of adulation ; and that, losing much of the native frankness which constituted the great charm of his character, he unfortunately assumed the garb and airs of a man of fashion ; let us not wonder if, under such circumstances, the inappropriate robe should not always have fallen in graceful draperies.

At length, so popular did he become, under the auspices of the Duchess of Gordon and other leaders of high fashion, that even their *soirées* were considered incomplete without his presence ; and yet these fascinations, strong as they must have been, never tempted him from his allegiance to Science ; never did the charms of the saloon allure him from the pursuits of the laboratory, or distract him from the duties of the lecture-room. The crowds that repaired to the Institution in the morning were, day after day, gratified by newly devised and highly illustrative experiments, conducted with the utmost address, and explained in language at once perspicuous and eloquent.

He brought down Science from those heights which were before accessible only to a few, and placed her within the reach of all; he divested the goddess of all severity of aspect, and represented her as attired by the Graces.

It is perhaps not possible to convey a better idea of the fascination of his style, than by the relation of the following anecdote. A person having observed the constancy with which Mr. Coleridge attended these lectures, was induced to ask the poet what attractions he could find in a study so unconnected with his known pursuits. "I attend Davy's lectures," he replied, "to increase my stock of metaphors."

But, as Johnson says, in the most general applause some discordant voices will always be heard; and so was it upon the present occasion. It was urged by several modern *Zoili*, that the style was far too florid and imaginative for communicating the plain lessons of truth; that he described objects of Natural History by inappropriate imagery, and that violent conceits frequently usurped the place of philosophical definitions. This was Bœotian criticism; the Attic spirits selected other points of attack; they rallied him on the ground of affectation, and whimsically represented him as swayed by a mawkish sensibility, which constantly betrayed him into absurdity. There might be some shew of justice in this accusation: The world was not large enough to satisfy the vulgar ambition of the conqueror, but the minutest production of nature afforded ample range for the scrutinising intelligence of the philosopher; and he would consider a particle of crystal with so delicate a regard for its minute beauties, and expatiate with so tender a tone of interest on its fair proportions, as almost to convey an idea that he bewailed the condition of necessity which for ever allotted it so slender a place in the vast scheme of creation.

After the observations which have been offered with regard to the injurious tendency of metaphors in all matters relating to science, I may probably be charged with inconsistency in defending Davy from the attacks thus levelled against his style. We need not the critic to remind us that the statue of a Lysippus may be spoiled by gilding; but I would observe that the style which cannot be tolerated in a philosophical essay, may under peculiar circumstances be not only admissible, but even expedient, in a popular lecture. "*Neque ideo minus efficaces sunt orationes nostræ quia ad aures judicantium cum voluptate perveniunt. Quid enim si infirmiora horum temporum templa credas, quia non rudi cæmento, et informibus tegulis exstruuntur; sed marmore nitent et auro radiantur?*"

Let us consider, for a moment, the class of persons to whom Davy addressed himself. Were they students prepared to toil with systematic precision, in order to obtain knowledge as a matter of necessity?—No—they were composed of the gay and the idle, who could only be tempted to admit instruction by the prospect of receiving pleasure,—they were children, who could only be induced to swallow the salutary draught by the honey around the rim of the cup.

It has been well observed, that necessity alone can urge the traveller over barren heaths and snow-topped mountains, while he treads with rapture along the fertile vales of those happier climes where every breeze is perfume, and every scene a picture.

If Science can be promoted by increasing the number of its votaries, and by enlisting into its service those whom wealth and power may render valuable as examples or patrons, there does not exist a class of philosophers to which we are more largely indebted than to popular lecturers, or to those whose eloquence has clothed with interest, subjects otherwise severe and uninviting. How many disciples did Mineralogy acquire through the lectures of Dr. Clarke at Cambridge, who may truly be said to have covered a desert with verdure, and to have raised from barren rocks, flowers of every hue and fragrance! In the sister university, what an accession of strength and spirit have the animated discourses of Dr. Buckland brought to the ranks of Geologists! To judge fairly of the influence of a popular style, we should acquaint ourselves with the effects of an opposite method; and if an appeal be made to experience, I may very safely abide the issue. Dr. Young, whose profound knowledge of the subjects he taught, no one will venture to question, lectured in the same theatre, and to an audience similarly constituted as that which was attracted by Davy, but he found the number of his attendants to diminish daily, and for no other reason than that he adopted too severe and didactic a style. *

In speaking of Davy's lectures as mere specimens of happy oratory, we do injustice to the philosopher; had he merely added the Corinthian foliage to a temple built by other hands, we might have commended his taste, and admired his talent of adaptation; and there our eulogium must have ended; but the edifice itself was his own, he dug the materials from the quarry, formed them

* From the following minute it would appear, that Dr. Young's connection with the Royal Institution was but of short duration. It will be remembered that his appointment took place on July 6, 1801.

"Resolved—That Dr. Young be paid the balance of two years' complete salary, and that his engagement with the Institution terminate from this time—July 4, 1803."

into a regular pile, and then with his masterly touch added to its strength beauty, and to its utility grace.

In addition to these morning lectures, we find that he was also engaged in delivering a course in the evening; of which the following notice is extracted from one of the scientific journals of the time.—" On the 25th, Mr. Davy commenced a course of lectures on Galvanic phenomena. Sir Joseph Banks, Count Rumford, and other distinguished philosophers, were present. The audience were highly gratified, and testified their satisfaction by general and repeated applause.

" Mr. Davy, who appears to be very young, acquitted himself admirably. From the sparkling intelligence of his eye, his animated manner, and the *tout ensemble*, we have no doubt of his attaining a very distinguished eminence."

From a Minute entered on the Records of the Institution, it appears that, at a meeting of Managers held on the 31st of May 1802, it was moved by Sir Joseph Banks, and seconded by Mr. Sullivan,—

" That Mr. Humphry Davy be for the future styled *Professor of Chemistry* to the Royal Institution."

A sufficient proof of the universal feeling of admiration which his lectures had excited.

The success of his exertions is communicated by him to his early friend, in the following letter.

TO DAVIES GIDDY, ESQ.

DEAR FRIEND,

SINCE the commencement of the Session at the Institution, I have had but few moments of leisure. The composition of a first course of lectures, and the preparation for experiments, have fully occupied my time; and the anxieties and hopes connected with a new occupation have prevented me from paying sufficient attention even to the common duties and affections of life. Under such circumstances, I trust you will pardon me for having suffered your letters to remain so long unanswered. In human affairs, anticipation often constitutes happiness; your correspondence is to me a real source of pleasure, and believe me, I would suffer no opportunity to escape of making it more frequent and regular.

My labours in the theatre of the Royal Institution have been more successful than I could have hoped from the nature of them. In lectures, the effect produced upon the mind is generally transitory; for the most part, they amuse rather than instruct, and stimulate to inquiry rather than give information. My audience has often amounted to four and five hundred, and upwards; and amongst them some promise to become permanently attached to Chemistry. This science is much the fashion of the day.

Amongst the latest scientific novelties, the two new planets occupy the attention of Astronomers, while Natural Philosophers and Chemists are still employed upon Galvanism.

In a paper lately read before the Royal Society, Dr. Herschel examines the magnitudes of the bodies discovered by Mr. Piazzi and Dr. Olbers. He supposes the apparent diameter of Ceres to be about 22″, and that of Pallas, 17″ or 13″, so that their real diameters are 163, and 95 or 71 English miles —How small! The Doctor thinks that they differ from planets in their general character, as to their diminutive size, the great inclination of their orbits, the coma surrounding them, and as to the proximity of their orbits.— From comets, in their want of their eccentricity, and any considerable nebulosity. He proposes to call them *Asteroids*.

I mentioned to you in a former letter the great powers of Galvanism in effecting the combustion of metals. I have lately had constructed for the laboratory of the Institution, a battery of immense size; it consists of four hundred plates of five inches in diameter, and forty, of a foot in diameter. By means of it, I have been enabled to inflame cotton, sulphur, resin, oil, and ether; it fuses platina wire, and makes red hot and burns several inches of iron wire of 1-300th of an inch in diameter; it easily causes fluid substances, such as oil and water, to boil, decompounds them, and converts them into gases. I am now examining the agencies of it upon certain substances that have not as yet been decomposed, and in my next letter I hope to be able to give you an account of my experiments.

I shall hope soon to hear that the roads of England are the haunts of Captain Trevitheck's dragons. You have given them a characteristic name.

I wish any thing would happen to tempt you to visit London. You would find a number of persons very glad to see you, with whose attentions you could not be displeased. With unfeigned respect,

Yours sincerely,

H. DAVY.

It is perhaps not possible to imagine a greater contrast, than between the elegant manner in which Davy conducted his experiments in the theatre, and the apparently careless and slovenly style of his manipulations in the laboratory; but in the one case he was communicating knowledge, in the other, obtaining it. Mr. Purkis relates an anecdote very characteristic of this want of refinement in his working habits. " On one occasion, while reading over to me an introductory lecture, and wishing to expunge a needless epithet, instead of taking up the pen, he dipped his forefinger into the ink bottle, and thus blotted out the unmeaning expletive."

It was his habit in the laboratory, to carry on several unconnected experiments at the same time, and he would pass from one to the other without any obvious design or order; upon these occasions he was perfectly reckless of his apparatus, breaking and destroying a part, in order to meet some want of the moment. So rapid were all his movements, that, while a spectator imagined he was merely making preparations for an experiment, he was actually obtaining the results, which were just as accurate as if a much longer time had been expended. With Davy, rapidity was power.

The rapid performance of intellectual operations was a talent which displayed itself at every period of his life. We have heard with what extraordinary rapidity he read at the age of five years ; and we now learn that his chemical enquiries were conducted with similar facility and quickness.

His early friend Mr. Poole bears his testimony to the existence of the same quality in the following passage, extracted from a letter I had lately the favour of receiving from him. " From my earliest knowledge of my admirable friend, I consider his most striking characteristic to have been the quickness and truth of his apprehension. It was a power of reasoning so rapid, when applied to any subject, that he could hardly be himself conscious of the process ; and it must, I think, have been felt by him, as it appeared to me, pure intuition. I used to say to him, ' You understand me before I half understand myself ?'

" I recollect on our first acquaintance, he knew but little of the practice of agriculture. I was at that time a considerable farmer, and very fond of the occupation. During his visits in those days, I was at first something like his teacher, but my pupil soon became my master both in theory and practice."

The chemical manipulations of Wollaston and Davy offered a singular contrast to each other, and might be considered as highly characteristic of the temperaments and intellectual qualities of these remarkable men. Every process of the former was regulated with the most scrupulous regard to microscopic accuracy, and conducted with the utmost neatness of detail. It has been already stated with what turbulence and apparent confusion the experiments of the latter were conducted; and yet each was equally excellent in his own style; and, as artists, they have not unaptly been compared to Teniers and Michael Angelo. By long discipline, Wollaston had acquired such power in commanding and fixing his attention upon minute objects, that he was able to recognise resemblances, and to distinguish differences, between precipitates produced by re-agents which were invisible to ordinary observers, and which enabled him to submit to analysis the minutest particle of matter with success. Davy, on the other hand, obtained his results by an intellectual process, which may be said to have consisted in the extreme rapidity with which he seized upon, and applied, appropriate means at appropriate moments.

Many anecdotes might be related, in illustration of the curiously different structure of the minds of these two ornaments of British Science. The reader will, in the course of these memoirs, be furnished with sufficient evidence of the existence of those qualities which I have assigned to Davy; another biographer will no doubt ably illustrate those of Dr. Wollaston.

I shall only observe, that to this faculty of minute observation, which Dr. Wollaston applied with so much advantage, the chemical world is indebted for the introduction of more simple methods of experimenting,—for the substitution of a few glass tubes, and plates of glass, for capacious retorts and receivers, and for the art of making grains give the results which previously required pounds. A foreign philosopher once called upon Dr. Wollaston with letters of introduction, and expressed an anxious desire to see his laboratory. "Certainly," he replied; and immediately produced a small tray containing some glass tubes, a blow-pipe, two or three watch-glasses, a slip of platinum, and a few test bottles.

Wollaston appeared to take great delight in shewing by what small means he could produce great results. Shortly after he had inspected the grand galvanic battery constructed by Mr. Children, and had witnessed some of those brilliant phenomena of combustion which its powers produced, he accidentally met a brother chemist in the street, and seizing his button, (his constant habit when speaking on any subject of interest,) he led him into a secluded corner; when taking from his waistcoat pocket a tailor's thimble,

o

which contained a galvanic arrangement, and pouring into it the contents of a small phial, he instantly heated a platinum wire to a white heat.

There was another peculiarity connected with Wollaston's habit of minute observation; it enabled him to press into his service, at the moment, such ordinary and familiar materials as would never have occurred to less observing chemists. Mr. Brande relates an anecdote admirably calculated to exemplify this habit. He had called upon Dr. Wollaston to consult him upon the subject of a calculus;—it will be remembered that neither phosphate of lime, constituting the '*bone earth*' species, nor the ammoniaco-magnesian phosphate, commonly called the '*triple phosphate*,' is *per se* fusible; but that when mixed, these constitute the '*fusible calculus*' which readily melts before the blow-pipe.—Dr. Wollaston, on finding the substance under examination refractory, took up his paper folder, and scraping off a fragment of the ivory, placed it on the specimen, when it instantly fused.

Having contrasted the manipulations of Davy, as exhibited in the theatre, with those performed by him in the laboratory, it may, in this place, be interesting to offer a few remarks upon the difference of his style as a lecturer and as a writer. Whatever diversity of opinion may have been entertained as to the former, I believe there never was but one sentiment with respect to the latter. There is an ethereal clearness of style, a simplicity of language, and, above all, a freedom from technical expression, which render his philosophical memoirs fit studies and models for all future chemists. Mr. Brande, in a late lecture delivered before the members of the Royal Institution, very justly alluded to this latter quality of his writings, and forcibly contrasted it with the system of Berzelius, of whom it is painful to speak but in terms of the most profound respect, and yet it is impossible not to express a deep regret at this distinguished chemist's introduction of a system of technical expressions, which from its obscurity is calculated to multiply rather than to correct error, and from its complications, to require more labour than the science to which it administers: to apply the quaint metaphor of Locke, " it is no more suited to improve the understanding than the move of a jack is to fill our bellies."

From the readiness with which some continental chemists have adopted such terms, and from the spirit in which they have defended them, one might almost be led to suspect that they believed them, like the words used by the Magi of Persia, to possess a cabalistic power. Davy foresaw the injury which science must sustain from such a practice, and endeavoured, both by precept and example, to discountenance it.

With regard to the introduction of a figurative and ornamental style into memoirs purely scientific, no one could entertain a more decided objection ; and in his " last days," he warns us against the practice.

" In detailing the results of experiments, and in giving them to the world, the chemical philosopher should adopt the simplest style and manner ; he will avoid all ornaments, as something injurious to his subject, and should bear in mind the saying of the first king of Great Britain, respecting a sermon which was excellent in doctrine, but overcharged with poetical allusions and figurative language,—" that the tropes and metaphors of the speaker were like the brilliant wild flowers in a field of corn, very pretty, but which did very much hurt the corn."

WHEWELL:

On the Connexion of the Physical Sciences

William Whewell, Review of 'On the Connexion of the Physical Sciences by Mrs. Somerville', Quarterly Review, 51 (1834) (London, John Murray, 1834), pp. 54–68.

William Whewell's review of Mary Somerville's On the Connexion of the Physical Sciences (London, John Murray, 1834) is chiefly remembered for being the place where, for the first time, the word 'scientist' appeared in print. The moment might act as a suitable finale for this selective journey through the polite culture of science – revealing, in a word, the moment of self-consciousness in which the subjectivity of the natural philosopher finds its own linguistic identity. It is only right that the word should be coined in the midst of discussion of increasing professionalisation, diffusion and specialisation, combined with the sense that all the separate fields of science none the less add up to one field, and one kind of person, one endlessly varied and yet fundamentally similar way of enacting a 'scientific subjectivity'.

The piece is also remarkable for its praise of a woman scientist and for the place of women in the history of science. Mary Fairfax Somerville (1780–1872) was chiefly an expositor and populariser of other people's work. Born in Scotland (as Whewell points out), at the age of fourteen she began a life-long passion for algebra. Her chief works are the one here reviewed by Whewell, and her exposition of Laplace, The Mechanism of the Heavens (London, John Murray, 1831), written on the encouragement of Henry Brougham (1778–1868). Her most successful work was Physical Geography (London, 1848), which went into four editions and was still being printed in 1878. Somerville College, Oxford, is named after her.

It seems that Whewell (like Babbage, Faraday, Herschel and others) corresponded with Somerville during her writing of her On the Connexion of the Physical Sciences. Somerville was writing as an expert among experts, a member of a predominantly male group of natural philosophers.

William Whewell (1794–1866) was keenly concerned with creating a usable vocabulary for science: he also coined the words 'ion', 'anode', 'cathode', 'Eocene', "Miocene', 'Pliocene', as well as introducing the term, 'physicist'. Whewell brought to natural philosophy (as this review shows) a classical education, and a range of literary knowledge: he was also known as a competent translator of German poetry. Whewell was predominantly an historian and a gifted philosopher of science; although his contribution to the study of tides is outstripped only by Sir Isaac Newton. It is worth bearing in mind when reading his account of Hypatia and Agnesi, that Whewell was a Christian and an Anglican, a faith that eventually led him to deny the possibility of life on other planets.

ART. III.—*On the Connexion of the Physical Sciences.* By
Mrs. Somerville.

THERE are two different ways in which *Physical Science* may be
made popularly intelligible and interesting: by putting forward the things of which it treats, or their relations;—by dwelling
on the substance of discoveries, or on their history and bearing ;—
by calling up definite images and trains of reasoning ; or by taking
these for granted, and telling what can be told in general terms
concerning such matters. Popular knowledge of the former kind
ought to be conveyed by the public lecturer, when, by means of his
models, his machines, his diagrams, he exhibits to the senses com-
plexities of form and position which it would baffle us to conceive
without such sensible representations. Popular knowledge of the
latter kind may be conveyed by the same lecturer, when, turning
from his apparatus, he explains to his audience the progress and
prospects of his science, the relation of what is now doing to that
which has already been done, the bearing of new facts in one subject upon theory in another. Each of these two methods has its
appropriate place and its peculiar advantages. The former excites
notions perfectly distinct as far as they go, but is necessarily very
limited in extent, because such notions cannot be caught and held
without close attention and considerable effort ; the latter method
presents to us rapid views of connexion, dependence, and promise,
which reach far and include much, but which are on that account
necessarily incomplete and somewhat vague.

This

This latter course is, however, by no means without its use and value : for, strange as it may seem, it is undoubtedly true, that such general aspects of the processes with which science is concerned may be apprehended by those who comprehend very dimly and obscurely the nature of the processes themselves. Words can call up thought as well as things; and, in spite of the philosophers of Laputa, with their *real* vocabulary, the trains of reflection suggested in the former way are often more to our purpose, because more rapid and comprehensive, than those we arrive at in the latter mode. The office of language is to produce a picture in the mind; and it may easily happen in this instance, as it happens in the pictures of some of our un-Pindaric artists, that we are struck by the profound thought and unity displayed in the colouring, while there is hardly a single object outlined with any tolerable fidelity and distinctness. The long-drawn vista, the level sunbeams, the shining ocean, spreading among ships and palaces, woods and mountains, may make the painting offer to the eye a noble expanse magnificently occupied; while, even in the foreground, we cannot distinguish whether it is a broken column or a sleeping shepherd which lies on the earth, and at a little distance we may mistake the flowing sleeve of a wood-nymph for an arm of the sea. In like manner, language may be so employed that it shall present to us science as an extensive and splendid prospect, in which we see the relative positions and bearings of many parts, though we do not trace any portion into exact detail—though we do not obtain from it precise notions of optical phenomena, or molecular actions.

Mrs. Somerville's work is, and is obviously intended to be, a popular view of the present state of science, of the kind we have thus attempted to describe. In her simple and brief dedication to the Queen, she says, ' If I have succeeded in my endeavour to make the laws by which the material world is governed, more familiar to my countrywomen, I shall have the gratification of thinking, that the gracious permission to dedicate my book to your Majesty has not been misplaced.' And if her ' countrywomen ' have already become tolerably familiar with the technical terms which the history of the progress of human speculations necessarily contains; if they have learned, as we trust a large portion of them have, to look with dry eyes upon oxygen and hydrogen, to hear with tranquil minds of perturbations and excentricities, to think with toleration that the light of their eyes may be sometimes polarized, and the crimson of their cheeks capable of being resolved into *complementary colours ;*—if they have advanced so far in philosophy, they will certainly receive with gratitude Mrs. Somerville's able and *masterly* (if she will excuse this word) exposition

of

of the present state of the leading branches of the physical sciences. For our own parts, however, we beg leave to enter a protest, in the name of that sex to which all critics (so far as we have ever heard) belong, against the appropriation of this volume to the sole use of the author's country*women*. We believe that there are few individuals of that gender which plumes itself upon the exclusive possession of exact science, who may not learn much that is both novel and curious in the recent progress of physics from this little volume. Even those who have most sedulously followed the track of modern discoveries cannot but be struck with admiration at the way in which the survey is brought up to the present day. The writer ' has read up to Saturday night,' as was said of the late Sir Samuel Romilly; and the latest experiments, and speculations in every part of Europe are referred to, rapidly indeed, but appropriately and distinctly.

We will give one or two extracts. We take one concerning Halley's comet; the more especially as this, remarkable visiter, is expected to reappear next year.

' Halley computed the elements of the orbit of a comet that appeared in the year 1682, which agreed so nearly with those of the comets of 1607 and 1531, that he concluded it to be the same body returning to the sun, at intervals of about seventy-five years. He consequently predicted its reappearance in the year 1758, or in the beginning of 1759. Science was not sufficiently advanced in the time of Halley to enable him to determine the perturbations this comet might experience; but Clairaut computed that it would be retarded in its motion a hundred days by the attraction of Saturn, and 518 by that of Jupiter, and consequently, that it would pass its perihelion about the middle of April, 1759, requiring 618 days more to arrive at that point than in its preceding revolution. This, however, he considered only to be an approximation, and that it might be thirty days more or less: the return of the comet on the 12th of March, 1759, proved the truth of the prediction. MM. Damoiseau and Pontécoulant have ascertained that this comet will return either on the 4th or the 7th of November, 1835; the difference of three days in their computations arises from their having employed different values for the masses of the planets. This is the first comet whose periodicity has been established; it is also the first whose elements have been determined from observations made in Europe; for although the comets which appeared in the years 240, 539, 565, and 837, are the most ancient whose orbits have been traced, their elements were computed from Chinese observations.'—pp. 364-5.

We may add to what is here said, that Mr. Lubbock has also investigated the course of this body, and has come to a conclusion somewhat different from both these above-mentioned astronomers. The ' Nautical Almanac ' for 1835, just published, contains a representation

representation of the path of the comet among the stars, according to each of these three mathematicians, its places being marked from Aug. 7, 1835, to Feb. 7, 1836. The positions, according to the different computations, though not very far asunder, are sufficiently distinct to make the separation, at a certain period, very wide. M. Pontécoulant, M. Damoiseau, and Mr. Lubbock, start their comets close together in August; but by the 4th of October, Pontécoulant is a whole length behind Damoiseau, (except these ' fiery steeds ' have bodies and tails of portentous prolixity,) and Lubbock decidedly shoots a-head of both. It will be extremely interesting, when the period arrives, to observe which of the three lines Comet himself will select. We recommend this subject to those of our friends who have taken an interest in our recent philosophical disquisitions concerning the Turf, and especially if their ' adverse stars ' prohibit a visit to Newmarket: for the stars, in this case, offer them a very sufficient compensation; and our amateurs, by backing one of the three calculated paths of this ' courser of celestial race,' as the true one, ' to be decided' by the comet himself when he makes his appearance, may have the luxury of *higher* play than has yet been known.

But we must return to Mrs. Somerville's chapter on Comets, and quote the account of another of these curious bodies. After speaking of Encke's comet, which has a period of 1207 days, she says—

' The other comet belonging to our system, which returns to its perihelion after a period of $6\frac{3}{4}$ years, has been accelerated in its motion by a whole day during its last revolution, which puts the existence of ether beyond a doubt, and forms a strong presumption in corroboration of the undulating theory of light. The comet in question was discovered by M. Biela at Johannisberg on the 27th of February, 1826, and ten days afterwards it was seen by M. Gambart at Marseilles, who computed its parabolic elements, and found that they agreed with those of the comets which had appeared in the years 1789 and 1795, whence he concluded them to be the same body moving in an ellipse, and accomplishing its revolution in 2460 days. The perturbations of this comet were computed by M. Damoiseau, who predicted that it would cross the plane of the ecliptic on the 29th of October, 1832, a little before midnight, at a point nearly 18484 miles within the earth's orbit; and as M. Olbers, of Bremen, in 1805, had determined the radius of the comet's head to be about 21136 miles, it was evident that its nebulosity would envelop a portion of the earth's orbit—a circumstance which caused great alarm in France, and not altogether without reason, for if any disturbing cause had delayed the arrival of the comet for one month, the earth must have through passed its head. M. Arago dispelled their fears by the excellent treatise on comets which appeared in the Annuaire of 1832, where

where he proves that, as the earth would never be nearer the comet than 24800000 British leagues, there could be no danger of collision.' —pp. 369-70.

We may observe that the alarm of which Mrs. Somerville here speaks, affords an example of the confusion of ideas, which popular views of scientific matters often involve; and thus shows us how valuable a boon it is to the mass of readers, when persons of real science, like Mrs. Somerville, condescend to write for the wider public, as in this work she does. The apprehensions with regard to Biela's (or, as it ought rather to be called, Gambart's) comet, which were entertained by our worthy neighbours, *tout le monde* of Paris, were of a kind somewhat peculiar. The expected arrival of this visiter, with his fiery train, produced a commotion scarcely inferior to that which was excited among the good people of Strasburg by the stranger in the red-plush inexpressibles. That his head or his tail would do us irreparable harm—that he would burn us with his nucleus—or drown or poison us with his atmosphere—were slight terrors compared with those excited by the combination of terms '*perturbations*' and '*orbite de la terre*.' It appeared that the comet would cross the earth's orbit; what mischief might not come of this? It was true that the earth would not be near the crossing at that time; but then, might not the orbit itself be seriously injured? Instead of an imaginary line in the trackless ocean of space, the fears of our friends appear to have represented to them the earth's orbit as a sort of railroad, which might be so damaged by what Mr. Campbell calls the ' bickering wheels and adamantine car' of the ' fiery giant,' that the earth must stick or run off, the next time the revolving seasons brought her to the fatal place. In M. Arago's agreeable and instructive article in the ' *Annuaire du Bureau des Longitudes*,' written in order to calm the panic arising from these ' horrible imaginings,' he says,—

' Shall I be so fortunate as to do this? I hope so; yet without being very confident. Have I not seen persons who, while they acknowledged that the earth would not receive, in 1832, any *direct blow* from the comet, still believed that this body could not go through our orbit without *altering its form*; as if this orbit was a material thing; as if the parabolic path which a bomb is just going to describe, could be affected by passing through the space which other bombs had traversed before!!'

But we must not dwell too long on one part of Mrs. Somerville's work; we must recollect that her professed object is to illustrate ' The *Connexion* of the Physical Sciences.' This is a noble object; and to succeed in it would be to render a most important service to science. The tendency of the sciences has

long

long been an increasing proclivity to separation and dismember-
ment. Formerly, the 'learned' embraced in their wide grasp all
the branches of the tree of knowledge; the Scaligers and Vossiuses
of former days were mathematicians as well as philologers, physical as well as antiquarian speculators. But these days are past;
the students of books and of things are estranged from each other
in habit and feeling. If a moralist, like Hobbes, ventures into
the domain of mathematics, or a poet, like Goethe, wanders into
the fields of experimental science, he is received with contradiction
and contempt; and, in truth, he generally makes his incursions
with small advantage, for the separation of sympathies and intellectual habits has ended in a destruction, on each side, of that
mental discipline which leads to success in the other province.
But the disintegration goes on, like that of a great empire falling
to pieces; physical science itself is endlessly subdivided, and the
subdivisions insulated. We adopt the maxim 'one science only
can one genius fit.' The mathematician turns away from the
chemist; the chemist from the naturalist; the mathematician, left
to himself, divides himself into a pure mathematician and a mixed
mathematician, who soon part company; the chemist is perhaps
a chemist of electro-chemistry; if so, he leaves common chemical
analysis to others; between the mathematician and the chemist
is to be interpolated a '*physicien*' (we have no English name for
him), who studies heat, moisture, and the like. And thus science,
even mere physical science, loses all traces of unity. A curious
illustration of this result may be observed in the want of any name
by which we can designate the students of the knowledge of the
material world collectively. We are informed that this difficulty
was felt very oppressively by the members of the British Association for the Advancement of Science, at their meetings at York,
Oxford, and Cambridge, in the last three summers. There was
no general term by which these gentlemen could describe themselves with reference to their pursuits. *Philosophers* was felt to
be too wide and too lofty a term, and was very properly forbidden them by Mr. Coleridge, both in his capacity of philologer
and metaphysician; *savans* was rather assuming, besides being
French instead of English; some ingenious gentleman proposed
that, by analogy with *artist*, they might form *scientist*, and added
that there could be no scruple in making free with this termination
when we have such words as *sciolist*, *economist*, and *atheist*—but
this was not generally palatable; others attempted to translate the
term by which the members of similar associations in Germany
have described themselves, but it was not found easy to discover
an English equivalent for *natur-forscher*. The process of examination which it implies might suggest such undignified compounds

as

as *nature-poker* *, or *nature-peeper*, for these *naturæ curiosi*; but these were indignantly rejected.

The inconveniences of this division of the soil of science into infinitely small allotments have been often felt and complained of. It was one object, we believe, of the British Association, to remedy these inconveniences by bringing together the cultivators of different departments. To remove the evil in another way is one object of Mrs. Somerville's book. If we apprehend her purpose rightly, this is to be done by showing how detached branches have, in the history of science, united by the discovery of general principles.

' In some cases identity has been proved where there appeared to be nothing in common, as in the electric and magnetic influences ; in others, as that of light and heat, such analogies have been pointed out as to justify the expectation that they will ultimately be referred to the same agent ; and in all there exists such a bond of union, that proficiency cannot be attained in any one without a knowledge of others.'—*Preface*.

We may add, that in the same way in which a kindred language proves the common stock and relationship of nations, the connexion of all the sciences which are treated of in the work now before us is indicated by the community of that *mathematical* language which they all employ. Our space does not allow us to dwell on the illustration of this point, but we may select a passage or two. We cannot even refer to the curious sections on the properties of light; on the fringes of shadows, the colours of thin plates, the results of polarization, and of the analysis of polarized light after passing through crystals; on the evidence and proofs of the undulatory theory ; which last great question our author, rightly, as we conceive, judges to be now nearly settled in favour of the undulationists. But we may quote what she says on one of the analogies which we have already noticed :—

' It has been observed that heat, like light and sound, probably consists in the undulations of an elastic medium. All the principal phenomena of heat may actually be illustrated by a comparison with those of sound. The excitation of heat and sound are not only similar, but often identical, as in friction and percussion ; they are both communicated by contact and radiation ; and Dr. Young observes, that the effect of radiant heat in raising the temperature of a body upon which it falls resembles the sympathetic agitation of a string, when the sound of another string, which is in unison with it, is transmitted

---

* When the German association met at Berlin, a caricature was circulated there, representing the ' collective wisdom' employed in the discussion of their mid-day meal with extraordinary zeal of mastication, and dexterity in the use of the requisite implements, to which was affixed the legend—' Wie die natur-forscher natur-forschen,' which we venture to translate ' *the poking of the nature-pokers*.'

to it through the air. Light, heat, sound, and the waves of fluids, are all subject to the same laws of reflection, and, indeed, their undulatory theories are perfectly similar. If, therefore, we may judge from analogy, the undulations of some of the heat-producing rays must be less frequent than those of the extreme red of the solar spectrum ; but if the analogy were perfect, the interference of two hot rays ought to produce cold, since darkness results from the interference of two undulations of light—silence ensues from the interference of two undulations of sound—and still water, or no tide, is the consequence of the interference of two tides. The propagation of sound, however, requires a much denser medium than that either of light or heat ; its intensity diminishes as the rarity of the air increases ; so that at a very small height above the surface of the earth the noise of the tempest ceases, and the thunder is heard no more in those boundless regions where the heavenly bodies accomplish their periods in eternal and sublime silence.'—pp. 250, 251.

We refer to the following on account of the novelty of the subject :—

' After Mr. Faraday had proved the identity of the magnetic and electric fluids by producing the spark, heating metallic wires, and accomplishing chemical decomposition, it was easy to increase these effects by more powerful magnets and other arrangements. The following apparatus is now in use, which is in effect a battery, where the agent is the magnetic instead of the voltaic fluid, or, in other words, electricity.

' A very powerful horse-shoe magnet, formed of twelve steel plates in close approximation, is placed in a horizontal position. An armature consisting of a bar of the purest soft iron has each of its ends bent at right angles, so that the faces of those ends may be brought directly opposite and close to the poles of the magnet when required. Two series of copper wires—covered with silk, in order to insulate them—are wound round the bar of soft iron as compound helices. The extremities of these wires, having the same direction, are in metallic connexion with a circular disc, which dips into a cup of mercury, while the ends of the wires in the opposite direction are soldered to a projecting screw-piece, which carries a slip of copper with two opposite points. The steel magnet is stationary ; but when the armature, together with its appendages, is made to rotate horizontally, the edge of the disc always remains immersed in the mercury, while the points of the copper slip alternately dip in it and rise above it. By the ordinary laws of induction, the armature becomes a temporary magnet while its bent ends are opposite the poles of the steel magnet, and ceases to be magnetic when they are at right angles to them. It imparts its temporary magnetism to the helices which concentrate it ; and while one set conveys a current to the disc, the other set conducts the opposite current to the copper slip. But as the edge of the revolving disc is always immersed in the mercury, one set of wires is constantly

constantly maintained in contact with it, and the circuit is only completed when a point of the copper slip dips in the mercury also ; but the circuit is broken the moment that point rises above it. Thus, by the rotation of the ,armature, the circuit is alternately broken and renewed ; and as it is only at these moments that electric action is manifested, a brilliant spark takes place every time the copper point touches the surface of the mercury. Platina wire is ignited, shocks smart enough to be disagreeable are given, and water is decomposed with astonishing rapidity, by the same means, which proves beyond a doubt the identity of the magnetic and electric agencies, and places Mr. Faraday, whose experiments established the principle, in the first rank of experimental philosophers.'—pp. 339, 340.

The following speculations are somewhat insecure, but they are proposed as conjectures rather than assertions, and are well worth notice :—

' From the experiments of Mr. Faraday, and also from theory, it is possible that the rotation of the earth may produce electric currents in its own mass. In that case, they would flow superficially in the meridians, and if collectors could be applied at the equator and poles, as in the revolving plate, negative electricity would be collected at the equator, and positive at the poles ; but without something equivalent to conductors to complete the circuit, these currents could not exist.

' Since the motion, not only of metals but even of fluids, when under the influence of powerful magnets, evolves electricity, it is probable that the gulf stream may exert a sensible influence upon the forms of the lines of magnetic variation, in consequence of electric currents moving across it, by the electro-magnetic induction of the earth. Even a ship passing over the surface of the water, in northern or southern latitudes, ought to have electric currents running directly across the line of her motion. Mr. Faraday observes, that such is the facility with which electricity is evolved by the earth's magnetism, that scarcely any piece of metal can be moved in contact with others without a development of it, and that consequently, among the arrangements of steam engines and metallic machinery, curious electro-magnetic combinations probably exist, which have never yet been noticed.

' What magnetic properties the sun and planets may have it is impossible to conjecture, although their rotation might lead us to infer that they are similar to the earth in this respect. According to the observations of MM. Biot and Gay-Lussac, during their aërostatic expedition, the magnetic action is not confined to the surface of the earth, but extends into space. A decrease in its intensity was perceptible; and as it most likely follows the ratio of the inverse square of the distance, it must extend indefinitely. It is probable that the moon has become highly magnetic by induction, in consequence of her proximity to the earth, and because her greatest diameter always points towards it. Should the magnetic, like the gravitating force,

extend

extend through space, the induction of the sun, moon, and planets must occasion perpetual variations in the intensity of terrestrial magnetism, by the continual changes in their relative positions.

' In the brief sketch that has been given of the five kinds of electricity, those points of resemblance have been pointed out which are characteristic of one individual power; but as many anomalies have been lately removed, and the identity of the different kinds placed beyond a doubt by Mr. Faraday, it may be satisfactory to take a summary view of the various coincidences in their modes of action on which their identity has been so ably and completely established by that great electrician.'—pp. 352-354.

We shall not here pursue this subject, as the examination of it at suitable length would lead us too far. We add some examples of the information contained in this work :—

' M. Melloni, observing that the maximum point of heat is transferred farther and farther towards the red end of the spectrum, according as the substance of the prism is more and more permeable to heat, inferred that a prism of rock-salt, which possesses a greater power of transmitting the calorific rays than any other known body, ought to throw the point of greatest heat to a considerable distance beyond the visible part of the spectrum—an anticipation which experiment fully confirmed, by placing it as much beyond the dark limit of the red rays as the red part is distant from the bluish-green band of the spectrum.'—p. 237.

The establishment of the identity of charcoal and diamond led sanguine persons to anticipate the time when our home-manufactures should rival the produce of Golconda. In such speculations it is but reasonable to take into account the reflection with which Mrs. S. closes the following passage:—

' It had been observed that, when metallic solutions are subjected to galvanic action, a deposition of metal, generally in the form of minute crystals, takes place on the negative wire: by extending this principle, and employing a very feeble voltaic action, M. Becquerel has succeeded in forming crystals of a great proportion of the mineral substances precisely similar to those produced by nature. The electric state of metallic veins makes it possible that many natural crystals may have taken their form from the action of electricity bringing their ultimate particles, when in solution, within the narrow sphere of molecular attraction already mentioned as the great agent in the formation of solids. Both light and motion favour crystallization. Crystals which form in different liquids are generally more abundant on the side of the jar exposed to the light; and it is a well-known fact that still water, cooled below thirty-two degrees, starts into crystals of ice the instant it is agitated. Light and motion are intimately connected with electricity, which may, therefore, have some influence on the laws of aggregation; this is the more likely, as a feeble action is alone necessary, provided it be continued for a sufficient time. Crystals

tals formed rapidly are generally imperfect and soft, and M. Becquerel found that even years of constant voltaic action were necessary for the crystallization of some of the hard substances. 'If this law be general, how many ages may be required for the formation of a diamond!'—pp. 307, 308.

The following is the history of the successive approximations to the place of the magnetic pole:—

' In the year 1819, Sir Edward Parry, in his voyage to discover the north-west passage round America, sailed near the magnetic pole; and in 1824, Captain Lyon, on an expedition for the same purpose, found that the magnetic pole was then situated in 63° 26' 51" north latitude, and in 80° 51' 25" west longitude. It appears, from later researches, that the law of terrestrial magnetism is of considerable complexity, and the existence of more than one magnetic pole in either hemisphere has been rendered highly probable; that there is one in Siberia seems to be decided by the recent observations of M. Hansteen,—it is in longitude 102° east of Greenwich, and a little to the north of the 60th degree of latitude: so that, by these data, the two magnetic poles in the northern hemisphere are about 180° distant from each other: but Captain Ross, who is just returned from a voyage in the polar seas, has ascertained that the American magnetic pole is in 70° 14' north latitude, and 96° 40' west longitude. The magnetic equator does not exactly coincide with the terrestrial equator; it appears to be an irregular curve, inclined to the earth's equator at an angle of about 12°, and crossing it in at least three points in longitude 113° 14' west, and 66° 46' east of the meridian of Greenwich, and again somewhere between 156° 30' of west longitude, and 116° east.'—pp. 310, 311.

We may add that the place thus determined by Captain Ross agrees with that collected from considerations, which we conceive to be more trustworthy than observations made at one place, with so imperfect an instrument as a dipping needle is for such purposes. In Mr. Barlow's Memoir ' On the present situation of the Magnetic Lines of Equal Variation,' just published in the Philosophical Transactions, he says, ' The pole itself'—(as deter mined by Captain Ross and his nephew)—' is precisely that point on my globe and chart, in which, by supposing all the lines to meet, the separate curves would best preserve their unity of character, both separately and as a system.'

Our readers cannot have accompanied us so far without repeatedly feeling some admiration rising in their minds, that the work of which we have thus to speak is that of a woman. There are various prevalent opinions concerning the grace and fitness of the usual female attempts at proficiency in learning and science; and it would probably puzzle our most subtle analysts of common sense or common prejudice to trace the thread of rationality or irrationality
which

which runs through such popular judgments. But there is this remarkable circumstance in the case,—that where we find a real and thorough acquaintance with these branches of human knowledge, acquired with comparative ease, and possessed with unobtrusive simplicity, all our prejudices against such female acquirements vanish. Indeed, there can hardly fail, in such cases, to be something peculiar in the kind, as well as degree, of the intellectual character. Notwithstanding all the dreams of theorists, there is a sex in minds. One of the characteristics of the female intellect is a clearness of perception, as far as it goes : with them, action is the result of feeling ; thought, of seeing ; their practica emotions do not wait for instruction from speculation ; their reasoning is undisturbed by the prospect of its practical consequences. If they theorize, they do so

> ' In regions mild, of calm and serene air,
> Above the smoke and stir of this dim spot
> Which men call earth.'

Their course of action is not perturbed by the powers of philosophic thought, even when the latter are strongest. The heart goes on with its own concerns, asking no counsel of the head ; and, in return, the working of the head (if it does work) is not impeded by its having to solve questions of casuistry for the heart. In men, on the other hand, practical instincts and theoretical views are perpetually disturbing and perplexing each other. Action must be conformable to rule ; theory must be capable of application to action. The heart and the head are in perpetual negotiation, trying in vain to bring about a treaty of alliance, offensive and defensive. The end of this is, as in many similar cases, inextricable confusion—an endless seesaw of demand and evasion. In the course of this business, the man is mystified ; he is involved in a cloud of words, and cannot see beyond it. He does not know whether his opinions are founded on feeling or on reasoning, on words or on things. He learns to talk of matters of speculation without clear notions ; to combine one phrase with another at a venture ; to deal in generalities ; to guess at relations and bearings ; to try to steer himself by antitheses and assumed maxims. Women never do this : what they understand, they understand clearly ; what they see at all, they see in sunshine. It may be, that in many or in most cases, this brightness belongs to a narrow Goshen ; that the heart is stronger than the head ; that the powers of thought are less developed than the instincts of action. It certainly is to be hoped that it is so. But, from the peculiar mental character to which we have referred, it follows, that when women are philosophers, they are likely to be lucid ones ; that when they extend the range of their speculative views, there will be a peculiar illumination thrown over the prospect. If they attain to the merit of being profound, they will add to this the great excellence of being also clear.

We conceive that this might be shown to be the case in such women of philosophical talent as have written in our own time. But we must observe, that none of these appear to have had possession of the most profound and abstruse province of human knowledge, mathematics, except the lady now under review. Indeed, the instances of eminent female mathematicians who have appeared in the history of the world are very rare. There are only two others who occur to us as worthy of entirely honourable notice—Hypatia and Agnesi ; and both these were very extraordinary persons. It is, indeed, a remarkable circumstance, that the ' Principia' of Newton were in the last century translated and commented on by a French lady ; as the great French work on the same subject, in our own time, the ' Mécanique Céleste' of Laplace, has been by a lady of this country. But Madame de Chastelet's whole character and conduct have not attracted to her the interest which belongs to the other two. The story of Hypatia is unhappily as melancholy as it is well known. She was the daughter of Theon, the celebrated Platonist and mathematician of Alexandria, and lived at the time when the struggle between Christianity and Paganism was at its height in that city. Hypatia was educated in the doctrines of the heathen philosophy, and in the more abstruse sciences ; and made a progress of which contemporary historians speak with admiration and enthusiasm. Synesius, bishop of Ptolemais, sends most fervent salutations ' to her, the philosopher, and that happy society which enjoys the blessings of her divine voice.' She succeeded her father in the government of the Platonic school, where she had a crowded and delighted audience. She was admired and consulted by Orestes, the governor of the city, and this distinction unhappily led to her destruction. In a popular tumult she was attacked, on a rumour that she was the only obstacle to the reconciliation of the governor and of Cyril the archbishop. ' On a fatal day,' says Gibbon, ' in the holy season of Lent, Hypatia was torn from her chariot, stripped naked, dragged to the church, and inhumanly butchered by the hands of Peter the reader and a troop of savage and merciless fanatics : her flesh was scraped from her bones with oyster-shells, and her quivering limbs were delivered to the flames.'

From this strange and revolting story, we turn to the other name which we have mentioned, Madame Agnesi, who flourished during the last century at Bologna, where her father was professor ; and when the infirmity of his health interfered with his discharge

of

óf this duty, the filial feelings óf the daughter were gratified by a pérmission froni Pope Benedict XIV. to fill the professorial chair, which she did with distinguished credit.   Befóre this, at the. age of nineteen (in 1738), she had published ' Propositioues Phisophicæ;' and, along with a profound knowledge of analysis, she possessed a complete acquaintance with the Latin, Greek, Hebrew, French, Germah, and Spanish lánguages.   Her ' Instituzioni Analitiche' weie translated by Colson, the Lucasiau professor of mathematics at Cambridge ; and this version was at one time a book in familiar use at that university.   The end of her history, though not of the terrible nature of that of Hypatia, is perhaps what an Englishwoman would look upon as rather characteristic thari happy.   She relinquished the studies of her early life, and went into the monastery of the *Blue* Nuns, at Milan, where she died January 9, 1799.*

We must leave it to some future reviewers to tell of the rapid acquisitions and extensive accomplishments of Mrs. Somerville ; which, indeed, will bear confronting with those of Hypatia and Agnesi.   Her profound mathematical work on the ' Mechanism of the Heavens' has already been treated of in this Journal ; the germ of the present treatise was the preliminary dissertation to that work ;. and what opinion this development of that sketch is likely to give the world at large of her talents as a philosopher and writer, we hope we have enabled our readers to determine.

The reader of ancient folios (if any such persons remain in the land) will easily imagine how, a few centuries ago, such works as these would have come forth preluded by ' commendatorie verses,' in which the author would have been compared to Minerva and to Urania, or probably (very reasonably) preferred to all the nine Muses and the goddess to boot.   In a case so fitted to excite untisual admiratión, we are not at all surprised that thè ancient usage should have been thought of ; and though neither Mrs. Somérville's modesty nor the fashion of the day would authorize thé insertion of such effusions in her pages, we happen to be ablé to lay before our readeis one or two of these productions : we présume they áre ihtended to be valued (like coronation medals strück in base metal) rather for the rarity of the occasion than the ex-

---

* We have not met with any account of this sisterhood ; but we conceive that when Protestaut nunneries are establıshed ın this country, (as we have occasionally recommended,) it would be desirable to have one foundation, åt least; of this colour.   We presume that they would substitute a review for the breviary, and a confidential critic or professor for the father confessor.   We do not pretend to suggest any rule for the *dress* of the order; but their prıncıpal daıly meetıng would probably be a repast upon bread and water—(*toasted* bread and *warm* water ın thıs severe clımate could not be considered blameable ındulgences ;) and ıt mıght correspond with the *lauds* of Catholic ihstitütions—' *Lauds,*—the last portion of *nocturns—officium matutinum—vespertınum.'*

cellence

cellence of the article; and with that view we shall insert two specimens from the mint of Cambridge. The first is a sonnet:—

' Lady, it was the wont in earlier time,
When some fair volume from a valued pen,
Long looked for, came at last, that grateful men
Hailed its forthcoming in complacent lays;
As if the Muse would gladly haste to praise
That which her mother, Memory, long should keep
Among her treasures. Shall such custom sleep
With us, who feel too slight the common phrase
For our pleased thoughts of you: when thus we find
That dark to you seems bright, perplexed seems plain,
Seen in the depths of a pellucid mind,
Full of clear thought; free from the ill and vain
That cloud our inward light? An honoured name
Be yours, and peace of heart grow with your growing fame.'

Another of these versifiers proceeds thus, after a well-known model :—

' Three women, in three different ages born,
Greece, Italy, and England did adorn;
Rare as poetic minds of master flights,
Three only rose to science' loftiest heights.
The first a brutal crowd in pieces tore,
Envious of fame, bewildered at her lore;
The next through tints of darkening shadow passed,
Lost in the azure sisterhood at last;
Equal to these, the third, and happier far,
Cheerful though wise, though learned, popular,
Liked by the many, valued by the few,
Instructs the world, yet dubbed by none a Blue.'

We are not going to draw our critical knife upon these *nugæ academicæ;* but we may observe, that we believe our own country-woman does not claim to have been born in a different century from Madame Agnesi; and that, though Hypatia talked Greek, as Mrs. Somerville does English, the former was an Egyptian, and the latter, we are obliged to confess, is Scotch by her birth, though we are very happy to claim her as one of the brightest ornaments of England.

BIBLIOGRAPHY

Full Titles

Sprat, Thomas, *The History of the Royal Society of London for the Improving of Natural Knowledge* (London, J. Martyn, 1667).

Hooke, Robert, *The Posthumous Works of Robert Hooke* (London, R. Waller, 1705).

Fontenelle, Bernard le Bovier de, *Conversations with a Lady, on the Plurality of Worlds, translated by Mr Glanvill*, 4th edition (London, M. Wellington, 1719).

Desaguliers, John Theophilus, *The Newtonian System of the World, the Best Model of Government: An Allegorical Poem. With a Plain and Intelligible Account of the System of the World, by Way of Annotations: With Copper Plates: To which is Added, Cambria's Complaint Against the Intercalary Day in the Leap-Year* (Westminster, J. Roberts, 1728).

Voltaire (François-Marie Arouet), *The Elements of Sir Isaac Newton's Philosophy … Translated from the French. Revised and corrected by J. Hanna … With explication of some words in alphabetical order* (London, Stephen Austen, 1738).

Algarotti, Francesco, *Sir Isaac Newton's Philosophy. Explain'd for the Use of the Ladies in Six Dialogues on Light and Colours*, trans. Elizabeth Carter, 2 vols (London, E. Cave, 1739).

Jones, Henry, *Philosophy, A Poem, Addressed to the Young Ladies who Attended Mr. Booth's Lectures in Dublin* (Dublin, S. Powell, 1746).

Martin, Benjamin, *Biographia Philosophica. Being an Account of the Lives, Writings, and Inventions, of the Most Eminent Philosophers and Mathematicians Who Have Flourished from the earliest Ages of the World to the Present Time* (London, W. Owen, 1764).

Priestley, Joseph, *The History of Electricity*, 3rd edn (London, C. Bathurst and T. Lowndes, 1775).

——, *Experiments and Observations Relating to Various Branches of Natural Philosophy* (London, 1779).

——, *Heads of Lectures On A Course of Experimental Philosophy* (London, J. Johnson, 1794).

Marcet, Jane, *Conversations on Natural Philosophy in which the Elements of that Science are Familiarly Explained, and Adapted to the Comprehension of Young Pupils.* (London, Longman, Hurst, Rees, Orme, and Brown, 1819).

Babbage, Charles, *Reflections on the Decline of Science in England* (London, B. Fellowes and J. Booth, 1830).

Paris, John Ayrton, *The Life of Sir Humphry Davy, Bart. LL.D. Late President of the Royal Society, Foreign Associate of the Royal Institute of France &c. &c. &c.* (London, Henry Coburn and Richard Bentley, 1831).

Whewell, William, Review of '*On the Connexion of the Physical Sciences* by Mrs. Somerville', *Quarterly Review*, 51 (1834) (London, John Murray, 1834), pp. 54–68.

Literary Parallels

The following list presents some of the many examples of literary works that either represent or form a part of the polite culture of science in the long eighteenth century. A full list would include every literary representation, popularisation and popular work of natural philosophy from the period. As that clearly would be impossible, the following list is merely indicative, and mostly consists of selected key works that are conventionally 'literary', such as periodical essays, poems, plays, and prose fictions. However, it is one contention of this volume, even of this series, that distinctions between the 'literary' and the scientific are not tenable.

Adams, George, *Essays for the Microscope* (London, W. and S. Jones, 1798).

Addison, Joseph, *The Spectator*, no. 420, (London, S. Buckley and J. Tonson, 1712–15).

Akenside, Mark, 'Hymn to Science' (1739).

Anon., *A Letter from a Hutchinsonian to his Friend, Relating to a Prophecy Lately Fulfilled* (Oxford, J. Barrett, 1752).

Anon., *The Newtonian System of Philosophy Adapted to the Capacities of Young Ladies and Gentlemen, Being the Substance of Six Lectures by Tom Telescope* (London, J. Newbery, 1761).

Berkeley, George, *The Analyst* (Dublin, S. Fuller and J. Leathly, 1734).

Baker, Henry, *The Microscope Made Easy* (London, R. Dodsley, 1742).

Blake, William, *An Island in the Moon* (1787).

——, 'Annotations to Swedenborg' (1789).

——, *The Laocoön* (1820) in *William Blake's Laocoön: a Last Testament, with Related Works* (London, Trianon Press for William Blake Trust, 1976).

——, MS annotations to *The Works of Sir Joshua Reynolds*, Edward Malone (ed.), (London, T. Cadell and W. Davies, 1798).

——, 'Mock on, mock on, Voltaire, Rousseau' (c. 1800).

——, 'You Don't Believe' (1807).

Boyle, Robert, *The Christian Virtuoso* (London, John Taylor, 1690).

——, *Some Considerations Touching the Usefulness of Experimental Natural Philosophy* (Oxford, Henry Hall for Richard Davis, 1664).

——, *The Sceptical Chymist* (London, J. Crooke, 1661).

Brown, Tom, *Amusements Serious and Comical* (London, John Nutt, 1700).

Butler, Samuel, 'Occasional Reflections on Dr Charleton's Feeling a Dog's Pulse at Gresham College. By R.B. Esq.'; *Hudibras* (Part II, Canto III) (London, J. Martyn and J. Allestry, 1664).

Campbell, Thomas, *The Pleasures of Hope* (Edinburgh, Mundell, 1799).

Cavendish, Margaret, Duchess of Newcastle, *Poems and Fancies* (London, J. Martin and J. Allestrye, 1653).

Centlivre, Susan, *The Basset-Table* (London, J. Nutt, 1706).

Coleridge, Samuel Taylor, *Biographia Literaria* (chapter XII) (London, R. Fenner, 1817).

——, 'A Mathematical Problem' (1791).

——, *Religious Musings* (1794–6).

——, *The Notebooks of Samuel Taylor Coleridge*, ed. Katherine Coburn, etc. (London, Routledge & Kegan Paul, 1957–).

—, *Collected Letters of Samuel Taylor Coleridge, 1772–1834*, Earl Leslie Griggs (ed.), 6 vols (Oxford, Oxford University Press, 2000).

Defoe, Daniel, *An Essay on Projects* (London, Tho. Cockerill, 1697).

——, *The Complete English Tradesman* (London, Charles Rivington, 1727).

Derham, William, *Physico-Theology* (London, W. Innys, 1713).

Desaguliers, John Theophilus, *A Course of Experimental Philosophy*, 2 vols (London, J. Senex, W. Innys, T. Longman etc., 1734, 1744).

——, *A Course of Mechanical and Experimental Philosophy* (London, T. Longman, 1725).

——, *Fires Improv'd … written in French, by Monsieur Gauger, made English and improved by J. T. Desaguliers* (London, J. Senex, E. Curll, 1715).

——, *Lectures of Experimental Philosophy* (London, W. Mears, 1717).

——, *Physico-Mechanical Lectures* (London, Printed for the Author, 1717)

Evelyn, John, *Sylva, or A Discourse of Forest-trees, and the Propagation of Timber* (London, Jo. Martyn and Ja. Allestry, 1664).

Ferguson, James, *An Easy Introduction to Astronomy for Young Gentlemen and Ladies* (London, T. Cadell, 1769).

Fielding, Henry, 'Philosophical Transactions for the Year 1742–3: Several Papers relating to the Terrestrial Chrysipus, Golden-Foot or Guinea' (1743).

Glanvil, Joseph, *Scepsis Scientifica* (London, Thomas White (called Thomas Blacklow), 1665).

——, *Plus Ultra* (London, J. Collins, 1688).

Glover, Richard, 'A Poem on Sir Isaac Newton' in Henry Pemberton, *A View of Sir Isaac Newton's Philosophy* (London, S. Palmer, 1728).

Harris, John, *Astronomical Dialogues Between a Gentleman and a Lady* (London, B. Cowes, 1719).

Haywood, Eliza, *The Female Spectator. Being Selections from Miss Eliza Heywood's Periodical, 1744–6*, Mary Priestley (ed.) (London, John Lane, 1929).

Hill, Aaron, 'Epitaph on Sir Isaac Newton' (1727).

Hooke, Robert, *An Attempt to Prove the Motion of the Earth from Observations* (London, J. Martyn, 1674).

——, *Micrographia* (London, I. Martin and J. Allestry, 1665).

——, *The Posthumous Works of Robert Hooke*, Richard Waller (ed.) (London, R. Waller, 1705).

Horsley, John, *A Short and General Account of the most Necessary and Fundamental Principles of Natural Philosophy. Containing Mechanics, Hydrostatics, Pneumatics, Optics and Astronomy. Revised, Corrected, and Adapted to a Course of Experiments, Perform'd in Glasgow by John Booth* (Glasgow, Andrew Stalker, 1743).

Jones, Henry, *The Earl of Essex* (London, 1753).

King, William, *Dialogues of the Dead Relating to the Present Controversy Concerning the Epistles of Phalaris* (9th dialogue) (London, A. Baldwin, 1699).

——, *Useful Transactions in Philosophy* (London, Bernard Lintot, 1709).

Martin, Benjamin, *The Philosophical Grammar; Being a View of the Present State of Experimental Physiology, or Natural Philosophy* (London, J. Noon, 1735).

——, *The Young Gentleman and Lady's Philosophy* (London, W. Owen, 1759).

Miller, James, *Humours of Oxford* (London, J. Watts, 1730).

Molyneux, William, Preface to *Dioptrica Nova* (London, B. Tooke, 1692, 1709).

Newton, Isaac, *Opticks* (London, Sam Smith and Benj. Walford, 1704).

——, *Philosophiae Naturalis Principia Mathematica* (London, J. Streater for the Royal Society, 1687).

Pemberton, Henry, *A View of Sir Isaac Newton's Philosophy* (London, S. Palmer, 1728).

Pope, Alexander, *The Rape of the Lock* (London, Bernard Lintot, 1714).

——, *An Essay on Man* (London, 1733–4).

——, 'Epitaph on Sir Isaac Newton' (1727).

——, *The New Dunciad* (London, T. Cooper, 1742).

Prior, Matthew, *Alma: or the Progress of the Mind* (1718).

Puff-Indorst, Fartinando, *The Benefit of Farting Explain'd* (London, A. Moore, 1722).

Shadwell, Thomas, *The Sullen Lovers* (London, Henry Herringman, 1668).

——, *The Virtuoso* (London, Henry Herringman, 1676).

Shelley, Percy Bysshe, *Queen Mab* (London, Printed by P. B. Shelley, 1813).

——, *The Daemon of the World* (1816; London, Privately printed by H. Buxton Forman, 1896).

——, 'Hymn to Intellectual Beauty', 'Mont Blanc' (1818) in *Poems* (London, Folio Press, 1973).

Shelley, Mary Wollstonecraft, *Frankenstein, or the Modern Prometheus* (London, Lackington, Hughes, Harding, etc., 1818).

Sprat, Thomas, *Observations on Monsieur de Sorbier's Voyage into England* (London, 1665).

Steele, Richard, 'Essay on the Orrery', in *The Englishman* no. 11, 1713 (London, Sam. Buckley, 1714).

Stubbe, Henry, *Legends No Histories* (London, 1670).

Swift, Jonathan, 'A Meditation Upon a Broom-Stick' (London, 1710).

——, *Travels into Several Parts of the World* (London, Benj. Motte, 1726).

——, *A Tale of a Tub* (London, John Nutt, 1704).

——, *Gulliver's Travels* (London, Henry Curll, 1726).

Thomson, James, *A Poem Sacred to the Memory of Sir Isaac Newton* (London, J. Millan, 1727).

——, 'Summer', lines 287–317, from *The Seasons* (London, A. Millar, 1744).

Toland, John, *Letters to Serena* (London, B. Lintot, 1704; reprint edn Stuttgart, 1964).

Voltaire (François-Marie Arouet), *Discours en Vers sur l'Homme* (Amsterdam, 1738).

——, *Eléments de la Philosophie de Neuton* (Amsterdam and Paris, 1738).

——, *The Elements of Sir Isaac Newton's Philosophy*. By Mr. Voltaire. Translated from the French. Revised and Corrected by John Hanna (London, Stephen Austen, 1738).

——, *Letters Concerning the English Nation* (London, C. Davis and A. Lyon, 1733).

Ward, Ned, *London Spy* (London, J. Nutt, 1698).

'Will of a Virtuoso', *The Tatler*, 26 Aug. 1710 (London, Charles Lillie, John Morphew, 1710).

Whiston, William, *An Account of a Surprizing Meteor Seen in the Air* ... (London, J. Senex and W. Taylor, 1716).

Wordsworth, William, and Samuel Taylor Coleridge, *Lyrical Ballads* (London, J. and A. Arch, 1798).

——, 'Preface' to *Lyrical Ballads* (London, Longman and Rees, 1800).

——, 'On the Power of Sound' (1835).

Young, Edward, *The Complaint; or Night Thoughts*, e.g. IX, lines 1575 ff., and 2196 ff. (London, G. Hawkins, 1744).

Suggestions for Further Reading

Arato, Franco, *Il Secolo delle Cose. Scienza e Storia in Francesco Algarotti* (Genova, Marietti, 1991).

Aubrey, John, *Aubrey's 'Brief Lives'*, Oliver Lawson Dick (ed.), 3rd edn (London, Secker and Warburg, 1958).

Barthes, Roland, *Mythologies*, trans. Annette Lavers (New York, Hill and Wang, 1972).

Besterman, Theodore, *Voltaire*, 3rd edn (Oxford, Basil Blackwell, 1976).

——(ed.), *Voltaire: Correspondance*, 13 vols (Paris, Gallimard, 1977–93).

Biagioli, Mario, *Galileo, Courtier: the Practice of Science in the Culture of Absolutism* (Chicago, University of Chicago Press, 1993).

Boyle, Robert, *The Works of the Honourable Robert Boyle*, Thomas Birch (ed.), 6 vols (London, 1772).

——, *The Works of Robert Boyle*, Michael Hunter and Edward B Davis (eds), 14 vols (London, Pickering & Chatto, 1999–2000).

Burwick, Frederick, *The Damnation of Newton: Goethe's Color Theory and Romantic Perception* (Berlin, de Gruyter, 1986).

Cook, Alan, *Edmond Halley. Charting the Heavens and the Seas* (Oxford, Clarendon Press, 1998).

Cope, Jackson I., *Joseph Glanvill, Anglican Apologist* (St Louis, Washington University Press, 1956).

Elias, Norbert, *The Civilizing Process: the History of Manners and State Formation and Civilization* (Oxford, Blackwell, 1994).

Frank, Thomas, *The Conquest of Cool: Business Culture, Counterculture, and the Rise of Hip Consumerism* (Chicago, University of Chicago Press, 1997).

Fullmer, June Z., *Young Humphry Davy: The Making of an Experimental Chemist* (Philadelphia, American Philosophical Society, 2000).

Galison, Peter and Bruce Hevly, *Big Science: the Growth of Large-scale Research* (Stanford, CA., Stanford University Press, 1992).

Galison, Peter and Lorraine Daston, *Images of Objectivity* (in preparation).

Golinski, Jan, *Science as Public Culture: Chemistry and Enlightenment in Britain 1760–1820* (Cambridge, Cambridge University Press, 1992).

Gross, Alan G., *The Rhetoric of Science* (Cambridge, Mass. and London, Harvard University Press, 1990).

Grundy, Isobel, *Lady Mary Wortley Montagu* (Oxford, Oxford University Press, 1999).

Harwood, John T., 'Rhetoric and Graphics in *Micrographia*' in Michael Hunter and Simon Schaffer (eds), pp. 119–47.

Hesse, M. B., 'Hooke's Philosophical Algebra', *Isis*, 57 (1966), pp. 67–83.

Hunter, Michael, *Science and Society in Restoration England* (Cambridge, Cambridge University Press, 1981).

——, *The Royal Society and its Fellows 1660–1700. The Morphology of an Early Scientific Institution*, 2nd edn (Oxford, British Society for the History of Science, 1994).

——, *Establishing the New Science. The Experience of the Royal Society* (Woodbridge, Boydell Press, 1989).

Hunter, Michael, and Simon Schaffer (eds), *Robert Hooke. New Studies* (Woodbridge, Boydell Press, 1989).

Hyman, Anthony, *Charles Babbage: Pioneer of the Computer* (Princeton, Princeton University Press, 1982).

Jacob, Margaret C., *The Newtonians and the English Revolution 1689–1720* (Sussex, The Harvester Press, 1976).

——, *Scientific Culture and the Making of the Industrial West* (Oxford, Oxford University Press, 1997).

Jardine, Lisa, *Ingenious Pursuits. Building the Scientific Revolution* (London, Little, Brown and Co., 1999).

Johnson, Samuel, *The Rambler*, Donald D. Eddy (ed.), 2 vols (New York & London, Garland Publishing, Inc., 1978).

Jordanova, Ludmilla, 'Nature Unveiling Before Science', in *Sexual Visions. Images of Gender in Science and Medicine between the Eighteenth and Twentieth Centuries* (Madison, University of Wisconsin Press, 1989), Ch. 5.

Knight, David, *Science in the Romantic Era* (Aldershot, Ashgate, 1998).

——, *Humphry Davy: Science and Power* (Cambridge, Cambridge University Press, 1996).

Knowlson, James, *Universal Language Schemes in England and France 1600–1800* (Toronto, University of Toronto Press, 1975).

Lindgren, Michael, *Glory and Failure: the Difference Engines of Johann Müller, Charles Babbage and Georg and Edvard Scheutz* (Cambridge, Mass., MIT Press, 1990).

Lyons, Sir Henry, *The Royal Society 1660–1940* (Cambridge, Cambridge University Press, 1944).

McCalman, Ian, John Mee, Gillian Russell, Clara Tuite, Kate Fullagar, and Patsy Hardy (eds), *An Oxford Companion to the Romantic Age: British Culture 1776–1832* (Oxford, Oxford University Press, 1999).

Mason, Haydn, *Voltaire. A Biography* (London, Granada Publishing in Paul Elek, 1981).

Merchant, Carolyn, *The Death of Nature. Women, Ecology and the Scientific Revolution* (London, Wildwood House, 1982).

Meyer, Gerard Dennis, *The Scientific Lady in England 1650–1760* (Berkeley and Los Angeles, University of California Press, 1955).

Mullan, John, 'Gendered Knowledge, Gendered Minds: Women and Newtonianism, 1690–1760' in Marina Benjamin (ed.), *A Question of Identity. Women, Science, and Literature* (New Brunswick, New Jersey, Rutgers University Press, 1993), pp. 41–56.

Nicolson, Marjorie Hope, *Science and Imagination* (Ithaca, New York, Great Seal Books, 1956).

——, *Newton Demands the Muse* (Princeton, Princeton University Press, 1968).

Nicolson, Marjorie Hope and Nora M. Mohler, 'The Scientific Background to Swift's *Voyage to Laputa*' in Nicolson, *Science and Imagination*.

Phillips, Patricia, *The Scientific Lady. A Social History of Women's Scientific Interests 1520–1918* (London, Weidenfeld and Nicolson, 1990).

Poggi, Stefano and Maurizio Bossi, *Romanticism in Science: Science in Europe 1790–1840* (Dordrecht, Kluwer, 1994).

Porter, Roy, *Enlightenment: Britain and the Creation of the Modern World* (London, Allen Lane, 2000).

Purver, Margery, *The Royal Society. Concept and Creation* (London, Routledge & Kegan Paul, 1967).

Rauch, Alan, *Useful Knowledge: Morality and 'The March of Intellect' in the Victorian Novel* (Durham, NC., Duke University Press, 2001).

Schiebinger, Londa, *Nature's Body: Gender in the Making of Modern Science* (Boston, MA., Beacon, 1993).

Schlereth, Thomas J., *The Cosmopolitan Ideal in Enlightenment Thought: its Form and Function in the Ideas of Franklin, Hume and Voltaire 1694–1970* (Notre Dame, University of Notre Dame Press, 1977).

Schofield, Robert E., *The Enlightenment of Joseph Priestley: a Study of his Life and Work from 1733–1773* (University Park, Pennsylvania State University Press, 1997).

Sennett, Richard, *The Fall of Public Man* (New York, Knopf, 1977).

Shapin, Steven, 'Who was Robert Hooke?' in Hunter and Schaffer, pp. 253–83.

——, *A Social History of Truth: Civility and Science in Seventeenth-century England* (Chicago, Chicago University Press, 1994).

Shapin, Steven, and Simon Schaffer, *Leviathan and the Air-Pump: Hobbes, Boyle, and the Experimental Life* (Princeton, NJ., Princeton University Press, 1985).

Slaughter, M. M., *Universal Languages and Scientific Taxonomy in the Seventeenth Century* (Cambridge, Cambridge University Press, 1982).

Sprat, Thomas, *The History of the Royal Society*, Jackson I. Cope and Harold W. Jones (eds) (St Louis, Washington University Studies; London, Routledge & Kegan Paul, 1958).

Stewart, Larry, *The Rise of Public Science: Rhetoric, Technology, and Natural Philosophy in Newtonian Britain; 1660–1750* (Cambridge, Cambridge University Press, 1992).

Stimson, Dorothy, *Scientists and Amateurs. A History of the Royal Society* (New York, Henry Schuman, 1948).

Thomson, James, *The Complete Poetical Works of James Thomson*, J. Logie Robertson (ed.) (London, Oxford University Press, 1908; reprint edn 1951).

Uglow, Jenny, *The Lunar Men: The Friends Who Made the Future* (London, Faber and Faber, 2002).

Voltaire (François-Marie Arouet), *Letters Concerning the English Nation*, Nicholas Cronk (ed.) (Oxford, Oxford University Press, 1994).

Webster, Charles (ed.), *The Intellectual Revolution of the Seventeenth Century* (London & Boston, Routledge & Kegan Paul, 1974).

Weld, C. R., *A History of the Royal Society* (London, Parker, 1848).

Westfall, Richard S., *The Construction of Modern Science. Mechanisms and Mechanics* (New York, Wiley, 1971; Cambridge, Cambridge University Press, 1977).

——, *Never at Rest. A Biography of Isaac Newton* (Cambridge, Cambridge University Press, 1980).

White, Paul, 'Science at Home', in *Thomas Huxley: Making the 'Man of Science'* (New York, Cambridge University Press, 2002), Ch. 1.

Yeo, Richard, *Defining Science: William Whewell, Natural Knowledge, and Public Debate in Early Victorian Britain* (Cambridge, Cambridge University Press, 1993).

NOTES

Sprat: *The History of the Royal Society*

p. 6, l. 13: 'an *Elegant Book*': *Histoire de l'Académie Françoise* (1653) by Paul Péllisson-Fontanier.

p. 7, l. 24: 'the *Academy* lately begun at *Paris*': the Académie Royale des Sciences, established in 1666 by Colbert.

p. 9, l. 3: 'the fate of *Archimedes*': While tracing a mathematical figure in the sand, Archimedes was killed by a Roman soldier at the massacre of Syracuse (212 BC).

Hooke: 'The Present State of Natural Philosophy'

p. 22, l. 13: '*Nihil esse in intellectu quod non fuit prius in sensu*': 'Nothing to be in the understanding which was not first in the sense'.

p. 24, l. 57: 'the incomparable *Verulam*': Francis Bacon, Baron Verulam of Verulam.

Fontenelle: *Conversations with a Lady on the Plurality of Worlds*

p. 42, ll. 24–5: 'all the Philosophers of Gresham': Gresham College was the Royal Society's headquarters.

p. 45, l. 26: Mr Flamsted: John Flamsteed (1646–1719), Astronomer Royal, who founded the Greenwich Observatory.

p. 46, ll. 4–5: 'one of the agreeable Follies of Ariosto': *Orlando Furioso*, published in 1516.

p. 48, ll. 6–8: 'a Donation which the Emperor Constantine made Sylvester': a deed made by the Emperor to Pope Sylvester I (314–35), which appointed the Popes rulers of Rome and Italy. In 1440 Lorenzo Valla proved it to be a forgery.

p. 50, ll. 9–10: 'like so much Queen of Hungary's Water': Queen of Hungary's water was a fashionable inhaler, a mixture of alcohol and rosemary, which was supposed to relieve the symptoms of rheumatism and gout.

Desaguliers: *Newtonian System of the World*

p. 66, l. 2 Earl of Ilay: Archibald Campbell, Earl of Islay (1682–1761), 3rd Duke of Argyll.

p. 85, l. 28: King *Alphonsus*: Alfonso X, King of Castile and León (1221–84).

p. 87, l. 13 (n.): 'Jam patet, horrificis quâ sit via flexa Cometis … Phœnomena Astri': 'Along what paths the fearsome Comets swerve, / Without alarm or terror we observe' (all references are to Halley's 'Ode to Newton', translated by Dr N. E. Emerton in Alan Cook, *Edmond Halley. Charting the Heavens and the Seas* (Oxford, Clarendon Press, 1998), pp. 163–4.

p. 89, l. 2: 'golden Dreams': the South Sea Bubble.

p. 92, l. 19 (n.): 'Quæ toties animos veterum torsere sophorum / Obvia conspicimus …'. These lines refer to 'Quæ toties animos veterum torsere sophorum … Obvia conspicimus nubem pellente Mathesi': 'The minds of ancient Sages were perplexed … Such things we can discern with ease today – / Astronomy has cleared the clouds away'.

p. 93, continuation of l. 19 (n.): 'Talia monstrantem celebrate … / NEWTONUM clausi referantem serinia veri. ' These lines refer to 'Talia monstrantem celebrate Camaenis, / Vos qui coelesti gaudetis nectare vesci, / Newtonum clausi reserantem scrinia Veri / Newtonum Musis charum': 'Ye Muses, fed on nectar from above, / Join me in praising Newton, whom ye love; Newton, who opened Truth's sealed casket wide'.

'Intima panduntur victi penetralia Cæli': 'To us the secret depth of heaven's revealed'; 'Quæ Superum penetrare domos, atque ardua cæli, / Scandere sublimis genii concessit acumem': 'For now the Genius of Newton's mind / Allows us to ascend towards the Sky / And penetrate the regions up on high'; 'Sol solio residens ad se jubet omnia prono / Tendere descensu, nec recto tramite currus/ Sidereos patitur vastum per inane moveri; / Sed rapit immotis, se centro, singula gyris': 'The Sun commands to bow before his throne / The planets circling through the void alone; / He from the centre holds each one in place / By strong attraction from the depths of space'.

p. 99, l. 18 (n.): 'Discimus hinc tandem, qua causa argentea Phoebe, / Passibus haud æquis graditur, cur subdita nulli / Hactenus Astronomo numerorum frœna recuset': 'We learn the silver Moon's uneven gait, / Unreckoned by Astronomers of late'.

Voltaire: *Introduction to the Philosophy of Newton*

p. 109: 'The Marchioness du CH**': Emilie du Châtelet (1706–49), Voltaire's lover and the wife of the Marquis du Châtelet.

p. 110 l. 3: 'Pedant *Zoilus*': the grammarian and critic of Homer: an envious critic (*OED*).

p. 111, l. 5: 'that all-moving Spring': Voltaire's favourite metaphor for Newton's theory of gravitation. There are several versions of this metaphor in his *Elements of Sir Isaac Newton's Philosophy*. In his *Letters Concerning the English Nation,* Voltaire describes attraction as 'the great Spring by which all Nature is mov'd' (Cronk, *Letters Concerning the English Nation*, p. 73).

p. 112, l. 2: 'that wond'rous Man' : see James Thomson, 'To the Memory of Sir Isaac Newton': 'the wondrous man', l. 148 (J. Logie Robertson (ed.), *The Complete Poetical Works of James Thomson* (London: Oxford University Press, 1908; reprint edn 1951), p. 440).

Algarotti: *Sir Isaac Newton's Philosophy Explained*

p. 124, l. 9: '*Malebranche*': Nicolas Malebranche (1638–1715), French philosopher and theologian .

p. 150, l. 15: '*Pemberton, Gravesand*': Henry Pemberton, Professor of Physics at Gresham College, was Newton's editor. Pemberton's popularization of Newtonian physics, *A View of Sir Isaac Newton's Philosophy*, was published in 1728. Willem Gravesande was a Dutch proponent of Newtonianism.

p. 151, ll. 23–4: 'the most polite Philosopher in *France*': Fontenelle.

p. 167, l. 9: 'the famous Clock of *Strasbourg*': the great clock of Strasbourg cathedral with its crowing cock (1352).

p. 175, ll. 2–3: 'the most philosophical Satyr upon Mankind': Swift's *Gulliver's Travels*, published in 1726.

p. 177, ll. 15–17: 'an Angel in *Milton*, who assures us, that the Sun draws his Aliment from humid Exhalations …': 'The sun that light imparts to all, receives / From all his alimental recompense / In humid exhalations, and at even / Sups with the ocean', *Paradise Lost*, Book V, ll. 423–6.

Jones: 'Philosophy, A Poem'

p. 185, l. 5: 'THRICE happy few': See Thomson's allusion to Shakespeare's *Henry V,* IV. iii, in 'To the Memory of Sir Isaac Newton', where he describes Newton's inner circle as 'ye happy few', l. 144 (Logie, *Complete Poetical Works of James Thomson*, p. 440). Jones uses the heroic phrase to refer to the ladies who attended Mr Booth's lectures. The phrase 'thrice happy' appears in formulaic praise in two other poems in Jones's *Poems on Several Occasions*.

Martin: 'The Life of Newton'

p. 191, l. 18: '*Isaac Barrow*': Barrow (1630–77) was a professor of geometry at Gresham College, and the first Lucasian Professor of Mathematics at Cambridge.

In 1669, he resigned his chair at Cambridge in favour of Newton. A supporter of the Royalist cause, he took Anglican orders on the restoration of Charles II. Newton most probably attended Barrow's mathematical lectures in 1664 (few others did), and the older man almost certainly also influenced his work on optics.

p. 191, l. 22–3: '*Des Cartes's* Geometry, with *Oughtred's* Clavis, *Kepler's* Optics, and *Schooten's* Miscellanies': All standard works of the period: William Oughtred's (1574–1660) *Clavis Mathematica* (London, 1631) was a key mathematical textbook – Oughtred invented the slide-rule; Franz van Schooten (1615–60) was a Dutch mathematician. René Descartes (1596–1650) is the French mathematician and philosopher; Johannes Kepler (1571–1630) is the German astronomer.

p. 192, l. 12: 'discovered by *Grimaldi*': Francesco Maria Grimaldi (1618–63) discovered the diffraction of light, after making experiments with a beam of sunlight let into a darkened room, and also refracting a beam of light off the surface of a deep container of water. He recorded his experiments in *Physico-mathesis de lumine, coloribus, et iride* (Physicomathematical Thesis of Light, Colours and the Rainbow) (Bononiae, 1665).

p. 194, l. 6: '*Nicholas Mercator*': Nicholas Mercator (1620–87), born in Holstein in Denmark, became a Fellow of the Royal Society.

p. 194, l. 8: '*Logarithmotechnia*': published in September 1668, the work offers a simplified method of calculating logarithms. On seeing Mercator's book, Barrow wrote to John Collins of The Royal Society:

A friend of mine here, that hath a very excellent genius to these things, brought me the other day some paper, wherein he hath sett downe methods of calculating the dimensions of magnitudes like that of Mr Mercator concerning the hyperbola, but very generall (Quoted in Gale E. Christianson, *In the Presence of the Creator: Isaac Newton and His Times* (London, The Free Press, 1984), p. 122).

p. 194, l. 24: '*Monsieur Fontenelle*': Martin derives all his information concerning Newton and Mercator from Fontenelle's *Eloge de M. Neuton* in *Histoire et Mémoires* (Paris, Académie Royale des Sciences, 1727), pp. 151–72, translated as *The Life of Sir Isaac Newton* (London, J. Woodman and D. Lyon, 1728).

p. 194, l. 35: '*Commercium Epistolicum*': *Commercium Episolicum D. Johannis Collins et aliorum de analysi promota* [The Correspondence of John Collins and others Relating to the Progress of Analysis] (London, Pearson, 1712) in which Newton, through his friends, covertly attacked Leibniz, effectively branding him a plagiarist. William Whiston wrote of how Newton believed that this rebuttal broke Leibniz's heart (William Whiston, *Historical Memoirs of the Life of Dr Samuel Clarke* (London, 1730), p. 132.

p. 194, l. 39: '*Mr. John Collins, F.R.S.* ': Collins (1624–83) was a non-conformist mathematician, and great accountant; he reportedly died as a consequence of drinking cider that was too warm.

p. 195, l. 1: '*Brounker*': Lord Brouncker (1620–84) was born in Munster in Ireland, studied at Oxford, and was elected President of the Royal Society in 1662.

p. 195, l. 23: '*Catadioptrical Telescope*': that is, a reflecting telescope, rather than the refracting telescopes currently used at the time. The refracting telescope forms the image of the object through the use of lenses. Using a parabolic mirror from which all light is reflected at the same angle, the reflector creates a much clearer image free of chromatic aberration.

p. 195, l. 24: '*Monsieur Gallois*': Jean Gallois, editor of the *Journal des Savants*, the journal of the Académie Royal des Sciences.

p. 195, l. 25: '*Monsieur Huygens*': Christian Huygens (1629–95), the Dutch physicist and astronomer, is now remembered for his invention of the pendulum clock in 1657, and for the first exposition of the wave theory of light in 1678, a theory developed after much experimentation with telescopes of his own making. Regarding astronomy, Huygens discovered the rings of Saturn and its moon, Titan. While visiting London, on 12 June 1689, Huygens met Newton, amicably enough, at the Royal Society.

p. 195, ll. 27–8: 'Mr. *Henry Oldenburg*': Oldenburg (1626–78) was born in Bremen and came to London as a consul during the Protectorate. He stayed on in England as the tutor of an Irish nobleman, and then enrolled as a student himself at Oxford. While there, he fell in with the members of the embryonic Royal Society, and ended up as its Secretary.

p. 195, ll. 28–9: 'Mr. *John Flamstead*': Flamsteed (1646–1719), from 1675, was the first Astronomer Royal based at Greenwich Observatory. His most famous achievement is his cataloguing of the stars, a work which still forms the basis of contemporary star catalogues. Newton and Flamsteed were to fall out bitterly over Flamsteed's reluctance to publish his own work, recording his observations of the motions of the stars and planets.

p. 195, l. 29: 'Dr. *Edmund Halley*': Halley (1656–1742), the notable mathematician and enthusiastic astronomer, was a great friend of Newton's. Elected to the Royal Society in 1678, he became Astronomer Royal in 1720. Most famous for his work on comets, and for successfully predicting the return in 1758 of the comet that came to be named after him.

p. 196, l. 1: 'Mr. *Jones*': I presume this refers to William Jones (1675–1749), a teacher of mathematics in London, who came in on Newton's side against Leibniz.

p. 196, ll. 8–9: 'the Comet': not 'Halley's Comet', which appeared in 1682. Martin's account is very unclear. In November 1680, Halley, Flamsteed and Newton observed a comet moving towards the sun. Shortly afterwards, in December 1680, they observed a comet coming from the sun. The question was had they seen two comets, or the same comet twice. The answer to the question (it was indeed one comet) had implications for the study of gravity and the motion of the planets around the sun.

p. 196, l. 12: 'Mr. *Hooke*': At the end of 1679, Robert Hooke had been engaged in an awkward scientific correspondence with an increasingly testy Newton.

p. 196, ll. 16–17: '*Picart* had not long before, *viz.* in 1679': Jean Picard (1620–82), French priest and astronomer.

p. 196, l. 25: '*Kepler*': Johannes Kepler (1571–1630) asserted that the planets moved around the sun in elliptical rather than circular or epicyclic orbits, speeding up when nearest to the sun.

p. 196, ll. 30–1: '*Philosophiæ naturalis principia Mathematica*': This work ('Mathematical Principles of Natural Philosophy) appeared in 1687, publication being paid for by Edmund Halley.

p. 197, l. 13: 'Mr *Roger Cotes*': In 1706, Cotes (1682–1716), a handsome twenty-four year-old mathematician, was elected Professor of Astronomy and Experimental Philosophy at Cambridge, mainly due to Newton's influence.

p. 197, l. 24: 'Marquis *de l'Hospital*': Guillaume de L'Hôpital (1661–1704), noted French mathematician, a teenage prodigy. The Marquis experienced an interesting contradiction between his mathematical enthusiasm and his belief that such interests did not fit the dignity of a nobleman.

p. 197, l. 25–6: 'some *English* Gentleman': the English gentleman was actually that Scottish gentleman, Dr John Arbuthnot (1667–1735).

p. 197, l. 33: '*Tycho Brahe*': Brahe (1546–1601), the Danish astronomer, made many of these observations at an observatory built for him by King Frederick II on the island of Hven.

p. 198, l. 7: 'Earl of *Hallifax*': Charles Montagu, Lord Halifax, (1661–1715) was a favourite student of Newton's while he attended Cambridge.

p. 198, l. 15: 'Dr. *Arbuthnot*'s Book': this can only be John Arbuthnot, *Tables of the Grecian, Roman and Jewish Measures, Weights and Coins; Reduc'd to the English Standard* (London, Ralph Smith, 1705). However, it seems unlikely that Martin is correct.

p. 198, l. 16: 'Mr. *William Whiston*': Whiston (1667–1752) became Lucasian Professor following Newton's resignation. Eventually he was expelled from Cambridge, after coming out as an Arian.

p. 198, ll. 25–6: 'Treatise of the *Reflections, Refractions, Inflections, and Colours of Light*': Isaac Newton, *Opticks: of, A Treatise of the Reflexions, Refractions, Inflexions, and Colours of Light* (London: Sam. Smith & Benj. Walford, 1704).

p. 199, l. 23: 'Corpuscularian Philosophy': i.e. that light consists of corpuscles or particles. Opposed at the time to the wave theory of light, as first developed by Huygens.

p. 200, ll. 5–7: '*Arithmetica Universalis, sive de Compositione et Resolutione Arithemeticæ Liber*': published by 'Typis Academicis' (Academic Press) at Cambridge in 1707, and translated as *Universal Arithmetick: or, A Treatise of Arithmetical Composition and Resolution*, trans. Mr Raphson (London, J. Senex, W. Taylor, T. Warner, J. Osborn, 1720).

p. 200, ll. 7–8: '*Analysis per Quantitatum Series, Fluxiones, & Differentias, cum Enumeratione Linearum tertii Ordinis*': a collection of previously unpublished papers presented to the Royal Society on 31 January 1711. Translated as *The Method of Fluxions and Infinite Series; with its Application to the Geomety of Curved-Lines*, trans. with a commentary by John Colson (London, J. Nourse, 1736).

p. 200, l. 9: '*William Jones*, Esq': see above.

p. 200, l. 18: '*Ditton*': Thomas Ditton (1675–1715), mathematician. With William Whiston, he came up with the plan to determine longitude by having ships anchored across the Atlantic, firing cannon. The DNB declares that 'his energy injured his health'.

p. 200, l. 36: 'The Princess of *Wales*': Caroline, Princess of Wales (1683–1737), was a noted collector of intellectuals, including Leibniz.

p. 201, l. 11: 'Abbé *Conti*': During a visit to London in 1714, Antonio-Schinella Conti (1679–1755), a high-born Italian cleric and a supporter of Leibniz, was charmed into becoming a friend of Newton's. Newton came to dislike him, and consider him a traitor to the cause.

p. 201, l. 15: 'Father *Souciet*': Etienne Souciet, a Jesuit, soon dropped his 'attack' on Newton's chronology.

p. 202, l. 36–p. 203, l. 14: Newton's Latin epitaph: Fatio de Dullier's epitaph is translated in *The Universal Magazine of Knowledge and Pleasure* (London, 1734), Vol. 84, pp. 241–2.

'Here lies intombed Sir ISAAC NEWTON, Knight, / Who, by a Spirit nearly Divine, / Was the First that solv'd, / With the Light of his Mathematical Principles, / The Motion and Figure of the Planets, / The Paths of the Comets, / And the Ebbing and Flowing of the Sea, / By the most exact Researches, / He discovered the Dissimilarity of the rays of Light, / And the Properties of Colours from thence arising, / Which none but himself had ever thought of. /

He was a diligent, wise and faithful Interpretor / Of Nature, Antiquity, and the Holy Scriptures: / By his Philosophy / He asserted the Majesty of the Supreme Being; / By the Purity of his Life / He expressed the Simplicity of the Gospel. / Let Mortals pride themselves / In the existence of so great an Ornament / To the HUMAN RACE! / He was born Dec. 25, 1642; and died March 20, 1726. /'

p. 203, l. 16: 'Dr. *Pemberton*': see Thomas Pemberton's *A View of Sir Isaac Newton's Philosophy* (London, 1728).

p. 204, l. 35: '*Slusius*': Renatus Franciscus Sluvius, *Mesolabum* (Leodij Eburonum, Typis I. F. va Milst, 1659).

p. 204, l. 37–8: '*Hugh de Omerique*': Hugo de Omerique (1634–?), Spanish mathematician.

p. 204, l. 39: '*Apollonius's Book de Sectione Rationis*': Classical Greek geometrician.

p. 206, l. 7: 'Mr. *Hume* in his History of *England*': Quoted from David Hume, *The History of England, from the Invasion of Julius Cæsar to the Revolution in 1688* (London, A. Millar, 1763), Vol. 8, pp. 322–3. Hume has just been writing of Robert Boyle, whom he describes as 'a great partizan of the mechanical philosophy; a theory, which, by discovering some of the secrets of nature, and allowing us to imagine the rest, is so agreeable to the natural vanity and curiosity of men' (ibid., 322).

p. 206, l. 26: 'And another ingenious Author': I have been unable to trace this author, but suspect that it might be Martin himself, the author of *A Panegyrick on the Newtonian Philosophy. Shewing the Nature and Dignity of the Science* (London, W. Owen, 1749).

Priestley: *The History of Electricity*

p. 217, l. 18: 'Dr. Watson': William Watson (1715–87), M.D. , F.R.S., author of *Observations upon the Effects of Electricity, Applied to a Tetanus, or Muscular Rigidity, of Four Months Contiuance* (London, W. Richardson and S. Clark, 1763). In 1747, Watson astonished the general public by passing an electric current through the River Thames.

p. 217, l. 18: 'Dr. Franklin': John Canton (see below) introduced Priestley to Benjamin Franklin (1706–90) soon after Priestley's arrival in London in December 1765. Franklin was a largley self-taught American writer, natural philosopher and printer. He was currently living in London as the agent of the Pennsylvanian government. Franklin's friendship with Priestley was a key event in the Englishman's life, and Franklin's *Experiments and Observations on Electricity, Made at Philadelphia in America* (London, E. Cave, 1751) became a central text in his intellectual history.

p. 217, l. 19: 'Mr. Canton': John Canton (1718–72) was an English physicist and F.R.S., and one of the first to study electromagnetic induction. Priestley met the London-based Canton through John Seddon, the rector at Warrington's Dissenting Academy. Canton then introduced Priestley to his many friends in London's scientific world. Canton acted as one of Priestley's mentors during the writing of the *The History and Present State of Electricity*.

p. 217, l. 29: 'Rev. Dr. Price': Richard Price (1723–91) was a dissenting minister, a moralist, and a writer on politics. Price was a good friend of Priestley's, though on matters of metaphysics the two men were opposed: unlike Priestley, Price held to the belief in the immateriality of the soul. Price introduced Priestley to William Petty, Lord Shelburne, who became Priestley's patron. Price's sermon, 'On the Love of Our Country' was the spark for Edmund Burke's *Reflections on the Revolution in France* (London, J. Dodsley, 1791). Canton, Price, Watson and Franklin (and Samuel Chandler) nominated Priestley for The Royal Society.

p. 217, l. 30: 'Rev. Mr. Holt': John Holt of Kirkdale, the tutor in Mathematics and Natural Philosophy at Warrington.

p. 217, l. 31: 'Warrington': The Dissenting Academy where Priestley taught for six years from September 1761 to September 1767, and where he married Mary Wilkinson, daughter of Isaac Wilkinson, the ironmaster at Bersham, and sister to John Wilkinson, the industrialist.

p. 223, l. 8: 'Sir Isaac Newton': Newton remains for Priestley the archetypal natural philosopher.

p. 223, l. 14: 'Roger Bacon, or Sir Francis': Roger Bacon (1214–92) was a medieval scholar, alchemist, astronomer, and mathematician. For a long time, he was popularly considered to be a practitioner of magic. Sir Francis Bacon (1561–1626) was a writer of essays, statesman, and a natural philosopher. Priestley follows an English genealogy of natural philosophy.

p. 232, ll. 16–17: 'Dr. Hartley': David Hartley (1705–57) was a physician and philosopher, most noted for his *Observations on Man, His Frame, His Duty and His Expectations* (London, S. Richardson, 1749). In this work, Hartley argues that our moral sense is born from the association of ideas, and suggests that the process by which these associations work on us is a physical one occasioned by 'vibrations' in the brain. Hartley was one of the great intellectual inspirations of Priestley's life. He read Hartley while studying at the dissenting academy in Daventry from 1752–5. Shortly afterwards, Priestley corresponded with Hartley regarding the practical application of his ideas in a system of education, but the idea came to nothing due to Hartley's death. Priestley's *A Course of Lectures on Oratory and Criticism* (London, J. Johnson, 1777) was one of the means by which Hartleian ideas of the imagination impacted upon the thinking of William Wordsworth (1770–1850) and Samuel Taylor Coleridge (1772–1834). Although not printed until 1777, these lectures were first given in the Academy at Warrington in 1762.

p. 235, l. 33, Priestley's third footnote: 'Franklin's Letters': Priestley uses two different editions of Franklin's *Experiments and Observations on Electricity, Made at Philadelphia in America*, moving between the 1751 (London, E. Cave) and 1774 (London, F. Newbery) editions.

p. 237, l. 18: 'Mr. Wilson': Benjamin Wilson (1721–88) was another pioneer in the study of electricity. Wilson struggled against poverty and want to become one of the authorities on the subject, writing among many other books, *A Treatise on Electricity* (London, C. Davis, 1750). He published *Observations on a Series of Electrical Experiments* (London, T. Payne, 1756), written with Benjamin Hoadly, a physician. Franklin quotes from the second edition of this work, published in 1769. This book aims to show that the electrical fluid and Isaac Newton's 'æther' are one and the same. Wilson and Franklin engaged in a long-running dispute over whether lightning conductors should be round or pointed at their tip.

Priestley drew upon the electrical researches of a number of other natural philosophers, including: Abbé Jean Antoine Nollet (1700–70), a Fellow of the Royal Society and member of the Académie des Sciences; Johann Heinrich Winckler (1703–70) of Erfurt, and Professor at Leipzig who, among other things, worked on the development of the Leyden Jar; the so-called 'Dantzick Memoirs', that is, Naturforschende Gesellschaft, *Versuche und Abhandlungen der Naturforschenden Gesellschaft in Danzig*, 3 vols (Danzig, 1747; Danzig and Leipzig, 1754, 1756); and Jean Jallabert (1712–68), Professor of Philosophy and Mathematics, and the author of *Experiences sur l'Électricité avec quelques conjectures sur la cause de ses effets* (Geneva, Barrillot & Fils, 1748).

p. 238, ll. 19–20: 'thunder storm at Stretham, described by Dr. Miles': Dr Miles is Dr Hales in the 1751 edition, though this was changed to Dr Miles by the edition of 1769 (London, David Henry). Dr Miles is, of course, Henry Miles (1698–1763), Doctor of Divinity, F.R.S., and writer on natural philosophy. Another dissenter, Miles was particularly interested in natural history, metereology and electricity.

p. 244, l. 24: 'pericranium': the mebrane that envelops the skull.

p. 247, l. 28: '*gutta serena*': otherwise known as an amaurosis, the partial or total loss of sight due to damage or disease in the optic nerve, but with no visible change in the external eye.

Priestley: *Natural Philosophy*

p. 253, ll. 2–3: '*Observations on different kinds of air*': a three volume work, *Experiments and Observations on Different Kinds of Air* (London, Vol. I, 1774, Vol. 2, 1775, Vol. 3, 1777). Priestley, of course, discovered oxygen, and equally famously would never agree that this is what he had done. Instead, he declared that he had made dephlogisticated air: that is, air from which Georg Ernst Stahl's (1660–1734) flammable 'phlogiston' had been removed.

p. 253, ll. 8–9: 'speculations of a very different nature': Priestley's interests were becoming increasingly theological and philosophical at this point; though it would be perhaps wrong to consider any of Priestley's sets of ideas in isolation.

p. 257, ll. 16–17: '*Observations on Education*': *Miscellaneous Observations relating to Education* (Bath, J. Johnson, 1778).

p. 260, ll. 10: 'Abbé Fontana': Felice Fontana (1730–1805) was an Italian natural philsopher, naturalist and physiologist. While Court Physician in Florence, he ordered the construction of a unique set of anatomical models made from coloured wax. As well as anatomical work on the eye, Fontana had a keen interest, like Priestley, in 'kinds of air': that is, gases. Although he wore ecclesiastical dress, Fontana never actually took Holy orders.

Priestley: *Lectures*

p. 268, ll. 20–1: 'an intelligent friend': I have not been able to identify this friend.

p. 271, l. 6: 'Mr. William Cruikshank': William Cumberland Cruikshank (1745–1800) was a Scottish anatomist, best known for his study of reproduction in rabbits and for his work, *The Anatomy of the Absorbing Vessels of the Human Body* (London, G. Nichol, 1786).

Babbage: *Reflections on the Decline of Science in England*

p. 307, l. 4: 'the *party*': it was one of Babbage's chief complaints that The Royal Society was run by a coterie who looked after their own interests and gave out honours chiefly on the principle of cronyism.

p. 311, l. 11: '*the Royal Institution*': founded by the American physicist, Benjamin Thompson, Count Rumford (1753–1814) and Sir Joseph Banks (1743–1820), the English botanist. The Royal Institution was intended to diffuse scientific knowledge and present scientific research to the public. It was also the possessor of one of the very best laboratories in Britain.

p. 315, l. 19: 'Mr. Herschel': the English astronomer, Sir John Frederick William Herschel (1792–1871) was Babbage's contemporary at Cambridge and one of his best friends.

p. 315, l. 19: 'Fresnel's': Augustin Jean Fresnel (1788–1827) was a French physicist, and the man who established, in 1821, the transverse-wave theory of light.

p. 315, l. 22: 'M. Arago's report': Dominique François Arago (1786–1853), French physicist and astronomer, was a supporter of Fresnel in the latter's work on the nature of light, the two men collaborating on the study of polarization.

p. 315, ll. 26–7: '*Mr. Herschel's Treatise on Light*, p. 533. - *Encyclopædia Metropolitana*': that is, the entry entitled 'Light' (dated Slough, 12 Dec. 1827) published in Edward Smedley (ed.), *Encyclopædia Metropolitana* (London, 1817–45).

p. 321, l. 14: 'the great meeting of the philosophers at Berlin': an account of the Congress of Philosophers held at Berlin on 18 September 1828.

p. 321, l. 16: 'Berzelius, Oersted, Gauss, and Humboldt': Jöns Jacob Berzelius (1779–1848), Swedish chemist; Hans Christian Oersted (1777–1851), Danish natural philosopher; Karl Friedrich Gauss (1777–1855), German mathematician born in Brunswick, astronomer, and physicist; Friedrich Heinrich Alexander, Baron von Humboldt (1769–1859), Berlin-born traveller and natural historian.

p. 325, l. 5: 'Wollaston and of Davy': Babbage pre-empts John Paris' distinction between the character of the two most famous British natural philosophers of the day; the comparison became a commonplace. (Davy actually was an amateur poet). William Hyde Wollaston (1766–1828) was considered at the time to be one of England's greatest chemists, opticians, and physiologists.

p. 329, l. 24: 'Mr. Perkins': Angier March Perkins (1799–1881), was an engineer and inventor, and an important figure in the history of plumbing: he introduced a system for warming buildings by means of hot water circulating through pipes. This system was not always successful, as John Davies, *On the System of Warming Buildings By Hot Water. A Reply to Mr. Perkins's 'Answer'* (Manchester, Love and Barton, 1841).

p. 332, l. 26: 'Mr South's observatory': the astronomer James South (1785–1867) was also a friend of John Herschel's.

p. 334, l. 2: 'Fraunhofer': the Bavarian Josef von Fraunhofer (1787–1826), the son of a glazier, and once an impoverished apprentice mirror-maker and glass polisher, investigated the dark lines in the solar spectrum, and developed the spectroscope.

Paris: *The Life of Sir Humphry Davy*

p. 339, l. 4: 'Theatre of the Royal Institution': on Albemarle Street in London.

p. 341, l. 20: 'Trepidarian Society': according to David Knight, *Humphry Davy, Science and Power* (Cambridge, Cambridge University Press, 1996): 'They were apparently a group of "twenty-five of the most violent republicans of the day", who met to drink tea at Old Slaughter's Coffee House in St. Martin's Lane' (45).

p. 341, l. 25: 'Ranelagh': London pleasure gardens.

p. 341, l. 26: 'Sir Harry Englefield': Sir Henry Charles Englefield (1752–1822) was an antiquary and writer on natural philosophy. He was elected a Fellow of the Royal Society in 1778. By all accounts, he was a jolly and high-spirited dining companion.

p. 341, l. 27: 'Mr. Underwood': Thomas Underwood was, according to David Knight, a radical and a member of Coleridge's circle.

p. 342, l. 5: 'Mr. Purkis': Samuel Purkis: I have been unable to locate any other information on this friend of Davy's.

p. 342, l. 8: 'Thomas Poole, Esq. of Nether Stowey': Thomas Poole (1765–1837) was the close friend of Wordsworth, Coleridge and Davy. Poole was thereby one of the conduits by which these poets and natural philosophers befriended and influenced each other. A farmer and tanner by trade, Poole was a generous and amiable man.

p. 342, ll. 23–4: 'A talented lady': the only female poet to mention Davy listed in the English Poetry Database is Joanna Baillie (1762–1851), who refers to him, in passing, in her poem 'An Address to a Steam Vessel'. The context makes it unlikely that Baillie is the poet that Paris mentions.

p. 343, l. 14: 'the author of the Rambler': that is, of course, Samuel Johnson (1709–84).

p. 343, ll. 27–8: 'the Duchess of Gordon': the energetic and vivacious Jane, Duchess of Gordon (1749?–1812) was both an arbitress of fashion in Edinburgh, and a centre for Tory social life in London. Paris is interested to note that Davy was moving from the radical circles of Poole and Coleridge into the highest social echelons of Pall Mall.

p. 344, l. 5: 'Mr. Coleridge': Samuel Taylor Coleridge's (1772–1834) friendship with Davy is one of the key symbolic meeting points between literature and science in the 1790s and 1800s. They sampled nitrous oxide together; Coleridge introduced Davy to Wordsworth, with direct effects on the latter's critical ideas.

p. 344, l. 11: 'Zoili': after Zoilus, the harsh fourth century BC critic of Homer, a name for any unnecessarily severe and envious critic.

p. 344, ll. 14–15: 'This was Bœotian criticism; the Attic spirits': that is, dull, rustic and uninformed criticism; the Attic spirits are altogether more elegant and intellectual.

p. 344, l. 29: 'Lysippus': Greek sculptor from the fourth century BC, known for introducing naturalistic proportion into Greek sculpture.

p. 344, ll. 31–5: '*Neque ideo minus efficaces sunt orationes nostræ quia ad aures judicantium cum voluptate perveniunt. Quid enim si infirmiora horum temporum templa credas, quia non rudi cæmento, et informibus tegulis exstruuntur; sed marmore nitent et auro radiantur?*': 'Nor are our speeches therefore any less effective because they reach with pleasure the ears of those who judge. So why are you inclined to believe that the temples of these lesser times are weaker structures, since they are not built with elementary blocks and weak roofs, but shine with marble and glow with gold?' I have been unable to trace the source of this quotation.

p. 345, l. 15: 'Dr. Clarke': Edward Daniel Clarke (1769–1822) was a notable mineralogist and geologist. Although a fellow and bursar of Jesus College, Cambridge, college life did not suit him, and he preferred gathering mineral specimens in the field, including a tour of Scandinavia, Russia and the Middle East. He was a friend of Davy's.

p. 345, l. 19: 'Dr. Buckland': William Buckland (1784–1856) was the author of numerous religious geological works, mainly concerned to show the compatability of geology with The Bible. He was, in a long career, both Professor of Geology at Oxford and the Dean of Westminster.

p. 345, l. 22: 'Dr. Young': Thomas Young (1773–1829) also lectured (unsuccessfully) at The Royal Institution, and worked on the decipherment of the Rosetta Stone, optics, and physiology.

p. 345, l. 28: 'Corinthian foliage': that is, structurally unnecessary but attractive architectural decoration. The Hellenic bias in Paris's metaphors is striking.

p. 346, l. 6: 'Galvanic phenomena': Davy was responding enthusiastically to Alessandro Volta's (1745–1827) critique of Luigi Galvani (1737–98). Galvani had thought that because the muscles of a dead frog contract when brought into contact with two dissimilar metals (brass and iron), this suggested that electricity was somehow inherent in the animal's body. Repeating Galvani's experiments, Volta realised that the source of the electrical current was in the two metals and not in the animal's body fluids, as Galvani had supposed.

p. 346, l. 6: 'Sir Joseph Banks': Sir Joseph Banks (1743–1820), the English botanist, was the power behind the Royal Institution at the time of its inception.

p. 346, l. 7: 'Count Rumford': Benjamin Thompson (1753–1814), co-founder of the Royal Institution, was made Count Rumford after moving to Bavaria following the American Declaration of Independence.

p. 346, l. 15: 'Mr. Sullivan': I have been unable to identify this man.

p. 346, l. 22: 'TO DAVIES GIDDY, ESQ. ': the Cornish MP Davies Gilbert (formerly Giddy) (1767–1839), Davy's early educational patron, eventually succeeded Davy as President of the Royal Society, following the younger man's resignation in 1827.

p. 347, l. 9: 'Dr. Herschel': Frederick William Herschel (1738–1822), born in Hanover, became one of the greatest English astronomers: his most famous achievement was the discovery of Uranus in 1781 (though Herschel's preferred name for the new planet was Georgium Sidum, or 'George's Star'). In 1782, he was appointed court astronomer.

p. 347, l. 10: 'Mr. Piazzi': Giuseppe Piazzi (1746–1826) was an Italian astronomer; he discovered Ceres, the first minor planet, in January 1801. The little planet was temporarily lost until relocated by Baron von Zach (1754–1832).

p. 347, l. 10: 'Dr. Olbers': Heinrich Wilhelm Matthäus Olbers (1758–1840) was a German physician, mathematician and astronomer. He is now most famous for his work on the discovery of asteroids and for establishing a method to calculate the orbit of comets.

p. 347, l. 17: '*Asteroids*': literally 'star shapes'; the name given to Ceres and Pallas and other tiny planetary bodies revolving around the sun, caught between the orbits of Mars and Jupiter.

p. 347, ll. 29–30: 'Captain Trevitheck's Dragons': almost certainly a reference to Richard Trevithick (1771–1833), another Cornishman, and a key inventor of the steam engine.

p. 349, l. 7: 'Teniers and Michael Angelo': the comparison between the Dutch 'realist' and the classical forms of the Italian painter is one between the homely and the sublime.

p. 349, l. 32: 'Mr. Children': J. G. Children, Davy's friend, and co-member with Davy of The Animal Chemistry Club, set up in 1808 to study physiology. Despite the club's name, the members do not appear to have believed that life was explicable purely in chemical terms.

p. 350, ll. 22–3: 'Mr. Brande': William Thomas Brande (1788–1866), the son of George III's apothecary, was the author of a standard manual on chemistry, as well as numerous other works.

p. 350, l. 25: 'Berzelius': Jöns Jacob Berzelius (1779–1848) was a Swedish chemist, who, among numerous other achievements, simplified chemical symbols.

Whewell: On the Connexion of the Physical Sciences

p. 356, l. 7: 'Laputa': the flying island in which the inhabitants are endlessly preoccupied with impractical knowledge in Jonathan Swift's (1667–1745) *Gulliver's Travels* (London, 1726).

p. 357, l. 13: 'Sir Samuel Romilly': Sir Samuel Romilly (1757–1818), the law reformer.

p. 357, l. 17: 'Halley': Edmund Halley (1656–1742), the notable mathematician and enthusiastic astronomer.

p. 357, l. 26: 'Clairaut': Alexis-Claude Clairaut (1713–1765) was a Parisian with expertise in mathematics, optics and celestial mechanics.

p. 357, ll. 33–4: 'Damoiseau and Pontécoulant': Baron Marie Charles Théodore de Damoiseau de Monfort, member of the Bureau des Longitudes; Philippe Gustave Le Doulcet, Comte de Pontécoulant (1795–1874), mathematician and astronomer.

p. 357, l. 43: 'Mr. Lubbock': although by profession John William Lubbock (1803–65) was a banker, he was also a notable English astronomer.

p. 357, l. 46: '"Nautical Almanac"': *The Nautical Almanac and Astronomical Ephemeris for the Year 1835* (London, Board of Admiralty, 1834).

p. 357, l. 23: 'Encke's comet': Johann Franz Encke (1791–1865) was a German astronomer. His star charts aided the discovery of Neptune in 1846. Encke's comet had been reported by Jean-Louis Pons (1761–1831), the French astronomer, who noted three small comets in 1818. Pons declared that one of these comets had first been spotted by Encke in the Berlin Observatory in 1805. From this clue, Encke set to work and calculated that the comet had an elliptical orbit of a period of 1208 days. He successfully predicted the return of the comet in 1822, and it was duly spotted in Australia in that year – only the second time that the return of an identified comet had been successfully predicted.

p. 358, l. 30: 'M. Biela': Wilhelm von Biela (1782–1856) was an astronomer, descended from a Bohemian noble family. His astronomical interests properly began in 1809 as he attended lectures in Prague while recovering from a wound sustained in the Napoleonic Wars.

p. 358, l. 31: 'M. Gambart': I have only been able to discover that J. F. A. Gambart was an astronomer active in the discovery of comets in the early nineteenth century.

p. 358, l. 39: 'M. Olbers': Heinrich Wilhelm Matthäus Olbers (1758–1840) was a German physician, mathematician and astronomer.

p. 358, l. 45: 'M. Arago': Dominique François Arago (1786–1853), French physicist and astronomer.

p. 359, l. 15: 'the stranger in the red-plush inexpressibles': inexpressibles are a knowingly ridiculous euphemistic term for trousers or breeches. This is a reference to Slawkenbergius's Tale in Volume IV of Laurence Sterne's *The Life and Opinions of Tristram Shandy, Gentleman* (London, R. and J. Dodsley, 1761). The stranger wears 'crimson-sattin breeches, with a silver-fringed-(appendage to them, which I dare not translate)' (15).

p. 359, l. 26: 'Mr. Campbell': Thomas Campbell (1777–1844), Scottish poet, from *The Pleasures of Hope* (1799), Part II, line 286, from a passage describing comets.

p. 359, l. 30: '*Annuaire du Bureau des Longitudes*': the periodical publication, *Annuaire … par le Bureau de Longitude* (Paris, 1797–1850).

p. 360, l. 3: 'Scaligers and Vossiuses': Julius Caesar Scaliger (1484–1558) was a physician, literary critic, and botanist. Gerhard John Vossius (1577–1649) and his son, Isaac Vossius (1618–89), were both eminent Dutch scholars.

p. 360, l. 7: 'Hobbes':Thomas Hobbes (1588–1679) was an English philosopher and political theorist.

p. 360, l. 8: 'Goethe': Johann Wolfgang von Goethe (1749–1832) was a poet, novelist, playwright, man of letters, and natural philosopher.

p. 360, l. 35: 'Mr. Coleridge': Samuel Taylor Coleridge (1772–1834) was a poet, critic and philosopher.

p. 361, l. 38: 'Dr. Young': probably Thomas Young (1773–1829) who worked on optics and physiology.

p. 362, l. 19: 'Mr. Faraday': Michael Faraday (1791–1867) was a chemist, most notable for the discovery of magneto-electricity. His career was launched by Sir Humphry Davy.

p. 363, l. 41: 'Biot and Gay-Lussac': Jean Baptiste Biot (1774–1862), pioneer of polarimetry, and Joseph Louis Gay-Laussac (1778–1850), chemist, made in 1804 a daring balloon ascent to a height of 23, 000 feet above sea-level in order to bring down samples of air.

p. 364, l. 15: 'M. Melloni': Macedonio Melloni (1798–1854) was an Italian physicist, whose studies concentrated on the properties of radiant heat.

p. 364, l. 27: 'the produce of Golconda': a place of fabulous wealth, referring to the ancient kingdom of India, west of Hyderabad.

p. 364, l. 33: 'M. Becquerel': Antoine-César Becquerel (1788–1878) was a French electrochemist who worked on the voltaic cell, discovering that electricity was generated by the contact of dissimilar bodies when they react together chemically, differ in temperature or are rubbed together. Using voltaic cells, Becquerel went on to experiment with the synthesis of mineral substances.

p. 365, l. 8: 'Sir Edward Parry': Sir William Edward Parry (1790–1855) was an Arctic explorer.

p. 365, l. 10: 'Captain Lyon': George Francis Lyon (1795–1832) accompanied Parry on his voyages of discovery, and was the author of *The Private Journal of Captain G. F. Lyon … during the recent voyage of discovery under Captain Parry* (London, 1824).

p. 365, l. 17: 'M. Hansteen': Christopher Hansteen (1784–1873) was a Norwegian-born astronomer and physicist.

p. 365, l. 20: 'Captain Ross': James Clark Ross (1800–62) was an Arctic explorer and a student of geomagnetism. He sailed with Sir William Edward Parry several times, in the attempt to find a Northwest Passage.

p. 365, l. 33: 'Mr. Barlow's Memoir': Peter Barlow (1776–1862), the mathematician and physicist, who published an *Essay on Magnetic Attractions* (London, J. Mawman and J. Taylor, 1820).

p. 365, ll. 15–17: 'In regions mild … men call earth': from the song of the attendant spirit in John Milton, *A Maske Performed Before the Præsident of Wales at Ludlow, 1634*, l. 4-6.

p. 366, l. 40: 'Goshen': a place of light and plenty, derived from the fertile land where the Israelites lived among the Egyptians, that remained bright during the plague of darkness.

p. 367, l. 12: 'Hypatia and Agnesi': Hypatia of Alexandria (370?–415) is the earliest recorded woman scientist. Maria Gaëtana Agnesi (1718–99) is one of the greatest Italian natural philosophers of the eighteenth century.

p. 367, l. 14: '"Principia" of Newton': that is, *Philosophiæ naturalis principia Mathematica* (Mathematical Principles of Natural Philosophy) (London, 1687).

p. 367, l. 15: 'a French lady': that is, Gabrielle-Émilie Le Tonnelier de Breteuil, the Marquise du Châtelet (1706–49). Whewell's dismissal probably derives its force from the implicit condemnation of her extra-marital love affair with Voltaire.

p. 367, ll. 16–17: '"Mécanique Céleste" of Laplace': Pierre Simon Laplace, *Traité de Mécanique Céleste*, 5 vols (Paris, 1798–1827), a work that brought together everything done in celestial mechanics since Sir Isaac Newton's death.

p. 367, l. 17: 'a lady of this country': that is, Mary Somerville herself, whose first book, *The Mechanism of the Heavens* (London, John Murray, 1831) explained and added to Laplace's ideas.

p. 367, l. 36: 'Gibbon': Edward Gibbon (1737–94) was an historian, the author of *The Decline and Fall of the Roman Empire* (1776–88).

p. 369, ll. 31–2: '*nugæ academicæ*': academic trifles.